Race, Labor, and Civil Rights

MAKING THE MODERN SOUTH
David Goldfield, Series Editor

RACE
LABOR &
CIVIL
RIGHTS

Griggs versus Duke Power and the
Struggle for Equal Employment Opportunity

ROBERT SAMUEL SMITH

Louisiana State University Press)|(Baton Rouge

Published by Louisiana State University Press
Copyright © 2008 by Louisiana State University Press
All rights reserved
Manufactured in the United States of America
First printing

Designer: Michelle A. Neustrom
Typefaces: Whitman, Swiss 721 BT
Printer and binder: Thomson-Shore, Inc.

Library of Congress Cataloging-in-Publication Data

Smith, Robert Samuel, 1969–
    Race, labor, and civil rights : Griggs versus Duke Power and the struggle for equal employment opportunity / Robert Samuel Smith.
        p. cm. — (Making the Modern South)
    Includes bibliographical references and index.
    ISBN 978-0-8071-3363-7 (cloth : alk. paper) 1. Discrimination in employment—Law and legislation—United States. 2. African Americans—Civil rights—United States. I. Title
    KF3464.S59 2008
    344.7301'133—dc22

                                                                            2008034093

The relationship of the Negro to the worker cannot be summed up, nor even greatly illuminated, by saying that their aims are one. It is true only insofar as they both desire better working conditions and useful only insofar as they unite their strength as workers to achieve these ends. Further that this we cannot honestly go.

JAMES BALDWIN

Contents

VI

FAITHFUL TO CONGRESSIONAL INTENT
Griggs on Appeal   144

VII

THIS THING ISN'T ALL THAT REAL   176

Acknowledgments

Throughout the 1990s, amid the swirling discourse regarding affirmative action, I was a regular audience member at the guest-lecturer-of-the-month talk on the history of equal employment opportunity programs. During most of these talks, lecturers began with some general comments regarding African American employment realities prior to 1965, the role of Title 7 of the Civil Rights Act of 1964 in responding to these realities, and the role the courts and the EEOC both played in mobilizing the employment law. Almost without failure, the Supreme Court decision each lecturer referred to as the seminal case that stimulated more assertive challenges to continued employment discrimination was *Griggs v. Duke Power* (1971).

In many respects, my first round of acknowledgments goes out to the many lecturers who emphasized *Griggs*'s placement in the affirmative action discourse. However, again almost without failure, these lecturers disregarded *Griggs*'s direct connection to the legal activism of the civil rights era and failed to uncover the personal histories of the plaintiffs and their contributions to the black freedom movement, particularly in the South. Instead, as goes the recorded history of equal employment programs, most lecturers moved directly into the political debate over affirmative action and offered their own interpretations of Title 7 and affirmative action case law, commenting on issues of preferential treatment and reverse-discrimination during the Reagan era. These omissions left the door open for this work on *Griggs*.

As is the case with many "first books" by scholars, such projects often have their genesis as dissertations. Thus, I have to offer a reverent "thank you" to my eternal advisor Donald Nieman, who has been a shining example of what a mentor ought to be. A comparable "thank you" goes out to Rachel Buff, who has always encouraged me to remember the importance of telling history "from the bottom up," giving voice to the true originators of social change. And a "thank you" goes out to "Mama" Lillian Ashcraft-Eason, who has always dared me, as a young legal scholar, to broaden my antennas to consider the ways in which law and public policy have impacted various populations across the African diaspora.

David Goldfield, editor of the *Making the Modern South* series, and the folks at LSU Press deserve a huge "thank you" for providing the intellectual space necessary to complete the book. The reviewers of the book were critical, yet helpful, and while we did not always agree on points, they certainly helped me to hone in on those issues most relevant to my approach to *Griggs*. Much respect goes out to Heather Thompson, Gregory Mixon, and Jeffrey Leak. These colleagues read part or all of the manuscript and provided invaluable comments and critiques. And, the collegial support from my fellow members of the Africana Cultures and Policy Studies Institute continues to fuel my intellectual curiosity; keep up the good work people!

Research support for the book came from the History Department at Bowling Green State University and the College of Arts and Sciences at the University of North Carolina at Charlotte. Equally as useful was the advice and expertise from librarians and archivists at both universities and that from the archivists at the Library of Congress and the National Archives. Carole Singer from BGSU's Jerome Library always helped me locate hard to find research leads and in many cases kept the research ball rolling in its early stages. Bridgette Sanders and her fellow librarians at Atkins Library at UNC-Charlotte are owed comparable praise for their assistance with leads during the latter stages.

This book could not have been completed without the emotional and intellectual support of my wife Dr. Nakia Sherron Gordon. "Nikki" has been a steady source of encouragement and creativity despite having to attend to her own research agenda. While on the research trail, "Nikki" was with me every step of the way. By phone, email and luckily, sometimes in person, Nakia Gordon has in many ways shared this process with me, making it an even more enjoyable and wonderful experience.

Finally, I have to thank Mr. Willie Boyd for taking time out for repeated conversations and phone calls. Mr. Boyd and the many other agitators for social change, who often fly beneath our scholarly radars, are treasures uncovered by oral history projects. Extended explorations into what is being framed as the "long civil rights movement" will undoubtedly continue to emphasize the importance of such individuals well into the post-1965, post–civil rights era. Oh, and a well-deserved "good look" goes out to G.N.N. (Good Neighbor Network) for helping make Charlotte, NC synonymous with home.

Race, Labor, and Civil Rights

Testing Cartoon, cover. Reprinted courtesy *New School Bulletin; A Newsletter of Ideas,*
Vol. 28, No. 6, February 8, 1971

INTRODUCTION

At the seventy-fifth annual convention of the National Association for the Advancement of Colored People (NAACP), Judge Damon Keith of the Sixth Circuit Court stated in his address to the assemblage, "Shortly after the act [Title 7 of the Civil Rights Act of 1964] was passed, it was conclusively decided by the Supreme Court in *Griggs v. Duke Power Co.* (1971)[1] that private employers could not use any tests and other screening devices that were not necessary to select employees if their result was to exclude blacks from employment. That decision, in my opinion even more than *Brown*, has proved most significant in combating racial discrimination."[2] Judge Keith is not alone in his praise for *Griggs*. Legal theorists have hailed the case as doing for employment what *Brown* did for education: breaking down the massive barriers to African Americans' full and equal participation. In fact, Keith accurately notes that *Griggs* is an even more seminal decision due to the case's role in delivering blacks and other marginalized groups economic justice.

While countless law review articles have explored the significance of *Griggs* in employment circles, directing the bulk of their attention to the influence of the disparate impact doctrine[3] on subsequent Title 7 cases and the maturation of race-based affirmative action—the merits of which will not be debated here[4]—only a few articles and to date no full-length monograph has delivered an extended analysis of the case's sociolegal history. As a result, very little is known about how the case emerged, who the plaintiffs were, the plaintiffs' struggles on the job, the legal arguments advance by the plaintiffs' lawyers, how the courts addressed questions of employment discrimination associated with the case, what role federal agencies played in this landmark decision, or how the defendant responded to the plaintiffs' claims. Put simply, there is a dearth of information regarding the history of a case of such significance to the civil rights era. This work seeks to fill many of these voids.

Further, only a few scholars have focused on courtroom battles over equal employment opportunity during the latter stages of the civil rights era. Civil rights era legal activism has primarily been linked to litigation over school desegregation and challenges to resecure political participation for blacks across the South. Thus, limited attention has been directed to the legal campaign orchestrated by the NAACP Legal Defense and Education Fund (NAACP-LDF), which was designed to harvest workplace equality. By exploring the virtually untold story of *Griggs*, this book connects the case and the campaign for equal employment opportunity to the broader civil rights movement and in doing so reveals the civil rights community's continued spirit of legal activism well into the 1970s.

This examination of *Griggs* and the employment campaign challenges longstanding assumptions that the reverberations of black power dominated the black freedom movement during the post-1965 era. I assert that alongside the more boisterous expressions of black radicalism in the late sixties, foot soldiers and local leaders of the civil rights community, many of whom were working-class black southerners, mustered continued legal activism in an effort to extract meaningful edicts from the courts regarding Title 7, the employment provision of the Civil Rights Acts of 1964. Indeed, during the first decade of the law's existence, much of the early, policy-shaping courtroom battles emerged from southern industry and a still-vibrant civil rights community.

African Americans battling the vestiges of Jim Crow in employment institutions desired working conditions that included the following: the removal of racially designated jobs offering no advancement, nonbiased union membership and union representation, fairer wage scales, and nonarbitrary placement and promotions procedures. Race and racism had categorically shaped the socioeconomic landscape to distinctly set apart those obstacles limiting blacks in industry, despite white and black workers sharing some grievances with management. Moreover, it is an uncontested fact that African Americans suffered far more deeply in the employment arena as organized labor, white managers, and white workers denied them basic job opportunities in countless ways.

It is important here to emphasize that a fundamental driving force behind the civil rights movement was the push to remove these barriers to equitable labor opportunities and therefore increased economic prosperity. African Americans' efforts to garner full equality in the United States would have amounted to very little substantive change if concerns over job opportunities were not included as part of the broader civil rights platform. The push for civil rights and the complimentary struggles for fair labor opportunities were not mutually exclusive demands but uniquely braided phenomena targeting African American inequality across the nation. The marriage of these two phenomena is highlighted here through the agitation that spawned the *Griggs* litigation.

To effectively underscore this important connection between civil rights era legal activism and civil rights era labor activism, this study focuses on the leader of the *Griggs* plaintiffs, Willie Rufus Boyd, and explores his life as one example of the southern civil rights struggle for equal employment opportunities. In writing a bio-criticism that seeks to stand as one template of the black, southern voices of resistance, this work demanded a grassroots approach. It helps, of course, that Boyd's efforts ultimately wound into a climatic legal decision representing an amalgam of the efforts and attitudes of presidents, Congress, the Supreme Court and lower court judges, federal agencies, civil rights organizations, civil rights activists and attorneys, white southerners, and southern industry. There were, however, scores of other labor activists whose storied lives stood to have as momentous an outcome as did Boyd's. And although these other individual struggles did not result in as much fanfare, notoriety, and national impact, they certainly involved as much risk, investment, and historical significance. By presenting Willie Boyd's account and the record of *Griggs v. Duke Power*, this book provides a glimpse into the history of civil rights activists who served double duty as labor radicals committed to igniting Title 7, men and women who used the courts to challenge racial politics in their communities and their places of employment.[5]

This approach to *Griggs* stems from one basic philosophy: "It is often forgotten in academe that the law is made by the will of clients. Lawyers help to pave the way to affect the will of the people. Black people of this era understood that protest and rebellion, even in the face of death, was a moral duty. Too few scholars concentrate on the real leaders of social and legal change. Lawyers facilitate change. Clients are the originators of change."[6] The histories of clients, lawyers, and the cases they filed have provided some of the most fascinating moments from the civil rights era. Of course, the most gripping accounts have hinged on battles over school desegregation. In crafting case studies of such import, scholars regularly address the sociopolitical antecedents that gave rise to the case, the judicial and political institutions that impacted the decision, the case's progression through the courts, the distinctive roles played by lawyers and clients, and, ultimately, the case's impact on the social and political structures under question. The same will hold true in this work, as suggested by the following premises upon which it rests.

First, this work pivots on the resolute notion that "real social change came from the bottom up. . . . The civil rights movement . . . involved mobilization of an entire community, not just a few leaders and organizations."[7] Grassroots activists not only carried the burden of civil rights agitation locally in indigenous movements that sustained the larger national agenda but also maintained important legal activism, I assert, well into the 1970s. Initiated by the NAACP and effectuated by Charles Houston and Thurgood Marshall of the LDF, the highly heralded victories in housing, voting, and education leading up to the civil rights era often overshadow courtroom battles of the 1960s and 1970s. Yet those who witnessed the judicial abating of Jim Crow understood that persistence in the courtroom, particularly after passage of the Civil Rights Acts of 1964 and 1965, might ultimately destroy the residue left from decades of state-imposed segregation and its outgrowths. In fact, it was this very legal activism on the part of the civil rights community, particularly from working-class laborers, that molded Title 7 into meaningful law. Put plainly, a steady stream of client-activists challenged workplace injustices while confronting comparable patterns of injustice in their respective locales.

Second, this work offers a discussion of the claims posited by black North Carolinians regarding Jim Crow throughout the middle decades of the twentieth century in order to reveal the sociopolitical milieu that shaped Boyd's activism. Maturing in a state with a robust civil rights agenda and an earthquaking eruption of radical resistance helped cultivate the militancy of Boyd and other similarly situated civil rights workers across the Carolinas. Likewise, Boyd's membership in the NAACP provided a platform that encouraged and informed his decision to challenge segregation in his hometown and challenge the employment systems of his employer. However, Boyd's awareness of oppositional forces to Jim Crow in North Carolina and his membership in the NAACP were not simply personally transformative relationships. Boyd's activism dramatically altered the racial politics of his workplace and had an impact on places of employment across the nation.

Third, I direct some attention to the attorneys who crafted arguments that swayed judges to affirm Title 7's goal of including black people in the employment mainstreams of American society. The first generation of LDF lawyers cleared a path of courtroom activism and advocacy for the second generation of civil rights lawyers. And as suggested by the legal jockeying over Title 7, the second generation not only carried the torch in the tradition started by Houston and Marshall but also advanced that agenda by encouraging the courts to consider broader interpretations of discrimination relying on the civil rights legislation of the mid-1960s.

During the post-1965 era, this second generation of civil rights attorneys, led by Julius LaVonne Chambers and James Ferguson out of Charlotte, North Carolina, engineered the legal campaign that helped energize the antiemployment discrimination legislation. The law firm of Chambers, Ferguson, Stein and Lanning stood at the core of a finely tuned, statewide civil rights matrix, buttressing the Title 7 campaign that gave rise to cases such as *Griggs*. In little time, Chambers, Ferguson, Stein and Lanning surfaced as one of the more prominent civil rights institutions of the post–civil rights era.[8]

Finally, without losing Boyd as the centerpiece, this book highlights one of the more significant post-*Brown* legal campaigns engineered by the civil rights community. The NAACP and LDF waged courtroom contests in the immediate aftermath of the protest era in an effort to resecure suffrage rights, desegregate public education, and usher in job equality. Recent scholarship highlights the NAACP's nearly century-long legal battle to regain and protect African American voting rights and political participation.[9] The history of *Brown v. Board of Education* is widely documented, as are post-*Brown* efforts to usher in meaningful school desegregation.[10] This work adds to the body of civil rights scholarship by detailing how NAACP members and lawyers used Title 7 and comparable legal activism to make fair employment a reality alongside voting rights and school desegregation. The Title 7 campaign was designed to remove Jim Crow's vestiges, which were still plaguing employment institutions, and in the process give life and meaning to the employment law. In 1971, *Griggs* became the Title 7 case to unlock opportunities for blacks, women, and other groups protected under the act. In fact, *Griggs* was merely one of thousands of complaints filed by civil rights activists with the hopes of attaining true improvements in their occupational status.

This book positions itself into several niches while urging a reconsideration of the life force of the civil rights community's program of legal activism. First, it explores a lesser-known version of civil rights history, and as mentioned above, it seeks to add to that body of scholarship. Second, this work will obviously add to the growing literature on North Carolina and the state's civil rights struggles. Although hostilities and protests in the Deep South have garnered a deserved amount of attention, racial politics in North Carolina offer interesting parallels and contrasts. Finally, this book doubles as a social and legal history of the landmark employment decision. As such, it strikes a balance between George Lipsitz's work on local St. Louis, Missouri, activist Ivory Perry and Davison Douglas's work on the *Swann v. Charlotte-Mecklenburg* (1971) school busing decision.[11] Lipsitz's *Life in the Struggle: Ivory Perry and the Culture of Opposition* tells of Perry's role in challenging the power structure in St. Louis throughout the civil rights era and beyond and is "a story of continuous commitment at the grassroots level."[12] Lipsitz offers an intriguing bio-criticism of a rank-and-file leader during the 1960s, 1970s, and 1980s, decades after the civil rights movement reportedly lost its social momentum. Shaping the discourse around which one can effectively appreciate the efforts of grassroots activists and the historical significance of their lives of resistance and protest, Lipsitz writes, "People like Ivory Perry rarely appear in history books, but they often make history. Without them, leaders have no followers and ordinary citizens have no means of translating their wishes and desires into coherent political contestations. . . . Gramsci called such people 'organic intellectuals,' and his term helps to identify what is representative and significant in the life of Ivory Perry."[13]

Willie Boyd and countless other blacks fit properly into Gramsci's class of "organic intellectuals." As such, these agents of social change "learn about the world by trying to change it, and they change the world by learning about it from the perspective of the needs and aspirations of their social group."[14] Grassroots organizers were extremely well versed in the sociopolitical terrain that stipulated their militancy, and they mobilized their communities to combat local expressions of white supremacy. While often lacking advanced degrees from prestigious institution of higher learning, organic intellectuals nonetheless exercised a high level of "critical, creative and contemplative intellectual inquiries" designed to challenge dominant social power structures and ultimately affect society. As labor radical James Boggs once wrote, "I am a factory worker, but I know more than just factory work."[15]

Thus it should come as no surprise that when quoted here, Willie Boyd's astute observations are not spoken with academic eloquence. Instead, they are brilliant yet realistic practical assessments of the world shaped by his lifelong encounters with and against white hegemony in rural North Carolina. Informing his wisdom are these very "critical, creative and contemplative intellectual inquiries," which emerge out of an assortment of real-life experiences while coming of age in the Jim Crow South, meshed with politically savvy lessons learned as an active member of his local NAACP branch.

Whereas Lipsitz's work serves as the ideological basis from which to examine grassroots, organic intellectuals, Davison Douglas's book, *Reading, Writing and Race; The Desegregation of the Charlotte Schools,* serves as an insightful case study of another key decision of the post-*Brown* era. And despite Douglas's work pertaining specifically to the *Swann* case, he presents an effective roadmap by which to examine legal activism springing from the civil rights community in North Carolina. My examination of *Griggs,* however, holds steadfast to the argument that grassroots legal activism compelled political officials and judges to offer expanded interpretations of Title 7 and to recognize the Equal Employment Opportunity Commission (EEOC) as a legitimate federal agency. As a result, blacks, other ethnic minorities, and women earned increased employment opportunities years after the civil rights movement's apex. As much as this work is about Boyd's role as an organic intellectual, it is also a case study of the legal decision that many scholars claim was to employment what *Brown* was to education.

I

RACE, LABOR, AND CIVIL RIGHTS

Title 7's journey toward becoming law, and its maturation through the courts during the latter stages of the civil rights movement, was an important development in the history of the era. In fact, the heart of this book and the nucleus of post–civil rights era employment gains rest in the legal victories stemming from Title 7 case law of the late 1960s and early 1970s. This era is most often associated with the reverberations of black power and leftist radicalism, but the work of the civil rights legal community persisted into those years, tackling the residue of Jim Crow in employment institutions. *Griggs v. Duke Power Co.* (1971) is important because of its overwhelming impact on workplace cultures and practices and because it reminds one of the tireless efforts on the part of the civil rights community in using litigation to fight racial injustice. Most of the early Title 7 cases sprang from the South, in fact, because of the civil rights community's concerted legal activism across the region. A compilation of local NAACP client-activists who were often though not always the plaintiffs in Title 7 cases, civil rights lawyers, and other legal advocates, engineered victories that opened the employment arena to black workers and to a wide spectrum of laborers from marginalized populations. To place this book in context, it is useful to understand how developments around race and racism, labor, and civil rights converged during the civil rights era and propelled the movement into its latter stages.

RACE/RACISM

As late as 1968 the EEOC reported, "Discrimination in employment is widespread and takes many forms; it can be found in almost every occupation group, and industry; and it has a crushing impact. In short, it is a profound condition, national in scope, and it constitutes a continuing violation of the American ideal of fair play in the private enterprise system."[1] The EEOC's appraisal substantiates that discrimination remained rampant well after the enactment of Title 7. Although black workers had moved in large numbers from agricultural labor and menial service positions into industrial occupations, workplace discrimination prevailed due to the economic mobility these jobs promised.

The relocation of African Americans into the industrial sector occurred in large part as a result of the mass, steady out-migration of blacks from the rural South to northern, urban industrial centers and the mushrooming industries on the West Coast. And blacks remaining in the South could escape the drudges of agricultural labor due to substantial industrialization across that entire region. The expansion of textile mills—the South's major industrial employer, mechanization in the tobacco industry, and even steam-powered energy plants surfaced during the twentieth century as viable employment options in various parts of the rural South. By the middle decades of the twentieth century, blacks could choose between toiling arduously in the tobacco and cotton fields, work made all the more frustrating given the deceitful practices of land owners, or working in an industrial setting, in somewhat better yet still unsafe working conditions, getting paid a steady wage and maybe even earning a pension.

Much of the economic growth across the South was a direct result of industrial spikes caused by World War II. Prior to the war, the South was the poorest region in the nation, yet by war's end the South was dramatically transformed by four years of unparalleled industrial expansion.[2] However, this expansion and accompanying federal and state antidiscrimination policies did little to positively affect the upward mobility of black laborers.

The standard employment narrative for black industrial workers during the age of Jim Crow, regardless of region or occupation, has been well documented. The race-based occupational system in the North and South forced many blacks to work in a variety of unskilled positions: domestics, waiters and waitresses, bellhops, janitors, caddies, delivery boys, washerwomen, and so on. If able to find work in industrial occupations, black laborers were relegated to performing the toughest and dirtiest jobs in coal mines, iron and steel factories, foundries, tobacco processing plants, and fertilizer plants, to offer only a few examples.[3] In the South especially, African American laborers were routinely consigned to segregated departments, immediately arresting any chances for promotion or substantive pay increases. In fact, the senior ranking black laborer typically earned less than the lowest paid, lowest ranking white worker. In the vast majority of workplaces, a white employee had more seniority after his first day on the job than did a black worker with decades of service.

Making matter worse, African American laborers were consistently denied union membership. When and if they were allowed to participate within organized labor, their union affiliation was often meted out through auxiliary or segregated branches, where they experienced truncated representation and protection. According to labor historian Timothy Minchin, black laborers gained automatic representation and valuable experience within these segregated unions, but if they pushed for more inclusion their claims were routinely rejected by the more numerous and powerful white workers and managers. Whites-only unions further hampered black occupational mobility by negotiating contracts that afforded African American workers a restricted number of segregated jobs though separate lines of progression.[4]

The lack of union representation was particularly problematic for a class of workers forced to perform the most dangerous, lowest paying jobs. For example, blacks were exposed to a horde of job-related hazards such as those requiring them to clean or unclog giant machines that could easily remove digits and appendages. Years of exposure to noisy industrial equipment, dust-filled air, and chemical fumes plagued black workers and whites alike—in ways not fully understood at the time. Yet these hazardous jobs probably took their toll on black laborers first.[5]

Willie Boyd and the "janitors" who worked alongside him at the Duke Power Company's Dan River Station came to know these employment procedures and workplace environments all too well. Racially bifurcated industrial workplaces such as Duke Power's steam-powered plants were not sustained merely by the bigotry of individual white workers determined to preserve their occupational privileges. These workplaces were the products of systemic discrimination perpetuated through workplace cultures that had grown out of longstanding racialized public policy and state code. Indeed, white managers, often in cahoots with white employees, erected racially biased employment structures to preserve their elevated economic status and to minimize the economic opportunities of black workers.[6] However, such employment abuses could never have thrived without the sociolegal support extending from Jim Crow segregation and its corresponding ideologies of black mental inferiority. These racist ideologies reaffirmed the supremacy of whites over blacks in economic institutions, adding credence to the system of labor apartheid. Such employment cultures were so much the norm that prior to judicial interpretations of Title 7, most companies failed to acknowledge that their practices were indeed unfair. Of course, the black laborers of the Dan River Station's Jim Crow department had no union to turn to for help given North Carolina as a state was emblematic of the South's inabilities to effectively mobilize organized labor (notwithstanding a rippling of unionization within the tobacco industry.)[7]

In fact, by today's standards, most workplaces clearly discriminated against blacks. As a result, various approaches geared toward garnering equal employment opportunities emerged across the nation. Although this book focuses on the battles of a particular group of southern industrial workers and their distinctive role in fighting workplace discrimination, it is an important and well-documented fact that resistance to employment prejudice surfaced in widespread movements across the nation, after the Great Depression and into the 1980s.[8] Likewise, black workers staged "daily, unorganized, evasive, seemingly spontaneous" acts of resistance in opposition to the indignities imposed by workplaces saddled with Jim Crowism.[9] In rural North Carolina, with other parts of the South probably responding in similar fashion, attempts at class-based interracial solidarity was undermined by employers who wedged white racial identity solidarity between white and black laborers attempting to unify against elite classes of Tar Heels.[10] Racial identity politics was also effectively used to minimize the reach of organized labor in various locales across the South.[11] White workers were able, therefore, to preserve their privileged positions over blacks by clinging to practices that secured their elevated status.

Scholars tackling topics associated with labor in the United States are routinely faced with the complexities of race and racism on industry culture, particularly prior to the civil rights era. Racially motivated employment mechanisms have ranged from raw, incapacitating barriers hindering blacks to less-obvious though equally as debilitating devices. The illustration below is yet another to add to the ever-sprawling list of clear examples of employment bigotry.

Joey, our protagonist, worked for decades in Detroit's industrial workforce and was in many ways the typical black laborer. He began working in unskilled positions and ultimately secured apprenticeships that opened up employment opportunities in the skilled trades. These jobs allowed him to earn a respectable wage and provide a comfortable life for his family. He took advantage of training programs for higher skilled positions and overtime pay scales that increased his hourly wages as much as three times around holidays, and he enjoyed the camaraderie associated with working alongside men of similar rank. By retirement Joey looked forward to his hard-earned pension, and he could rightfully brag of having provided for his family, which included a wife of thirty years and three children—all of whom attended the more prestigious high schools in the city and, later, the heavily endowed, research-driven colleges and universities across the state. Two of his children earned doctorate degrees, wearing blue tams at graduation signifying the highest level of educational attainment. Joey's story marks the promises of industrial America in one of the most intense labor centers in the nation. Because of his work ethic and his ability to take advantage of skilled, better paying positions, Joey was able to own homes in the city of Detroit and eventually move his family to one of Detroit's most affluent suburbs, Farmington Hills.[12]

Moving to this rather distant suburb was no small feat for a black family, no matter their socioeconomic status. African Americans had been denied access to this and other "white" suburbs for decades. The city's leadership, real estate officials, and white residents endorsed residential segregation, especially with the arrival of black migrants during the world wars. As a result, many blacks were locked into urban Detroit well before the 1970s and 1980s. Black Detroiters, though, moved in impressive numbers to bordering suburbs, spurring even more distant white suburban flight, which greatly extended Detroit's metropolitan geography and geopolitics. But only a spattering of African American families actually made the move to distant, elite areas like Farmington Hills, and even fewer were welcomed.[13]

By the 1980s, however, Detroit had been deeply affected by growing troubles associated with wide-scale industrial decline and the accompanying economic restructuring in a city that was (and still is) an epicenter of industrial exchange. Corporate flight and relocation, the final stages of white and upwardly mobile black suburban flight, and rapidly increasing computer automation in the automotive industry were the major precipitators of transformations in a city that has leant so much to working definitions of "urban." Indeed, cities like Detroit are virtually synonymous with the term. But by the 1980s, Detroit and other major metropolitan areas were regularly described as cities infested with crime, drug-related underworld economies, and urban decay. As such cities began to change or descend, the definition of "urban" too began its change, or its descent.

In the popular imagination of social critics and lay people, by the end of the 1980s Detroit was urban for all the wrong reasons. Most overlooked the blue-collar and professional jobs that remained in the city, many still stemming from the automotive industry, which continued to spawn important cultural outgrowths from Detroit's diverse black middle class. The city, some may have argued, could no longer tout its chic, metropolitan flare, nor could it hype its once brimming labor market, which had once allowed working-class people such as Joey to earn respectable wages. Instead, Detroit was caught in the trappings of rapid deindustrialization and corporate withdrawal, which contributed to overwhelming increases in the city's poverty statistics. Joey made a smart choice and moved his family to where they stood the best chance of continuing to live a good life and progressing in the way all hard-working citizens of the United States had been promised they could.[14] Joey's career reminds one of the economic promises associated with skilled labor that allowed so many working-class families to move into higher tax brackets among the ranks of the middle and upper classes.

Joey's case, though fitting a classic narrative of industrial laborers into the post–civil rights era, is special and important for one other reason. Joey is unequivocally a black man by all legal definitions, cultural practices, and, most important, self-identification. His lifestyle was one typical of a black urbanite of civil rights era Detroit. As a young adult he partied at all the hot spots around town, kept up with the latest fashions (he still does), and tussled with local hoodlums (only when provoked), and he has relatives in nearby cities with smaller yet equally important industrial hubs. Joey was a regular patron and, in fact, was outside the "blind pig" (an illegal after-hours drinking establishment) that was raided by police sparking the 1967 Detroit riot. Joey is, in every capacity, a "brother" from Detroit.[15]

Relying on phenotype alone, however, there is nothing about Joey's appearance, even among those with the most sensitive racial radars, that would allow for the drawing of any other conclusion than he is a white man. The politics of hair would not work on Joey; it was brown (now gray) and bone strait. His complexion, though vibrant, offers no hint of even a light tawny hue. Even his melodic urban drawl is easily dismissed given his physical features.[16]

In the presence of this black man with features similar to those of former NAACP leader Walter White, managers would occasionally, obviously unwittingly, permit him entrance into the exclusive circles of white male occupational privilege. Unlike many black workers who believed they were the victims of discrimination but had little proof or had proof with no place to turn for legal redress, when Joey entered the work force in the 1960s, he witnessed the realities of employment discrimination firsthand. Joey is unsure if he ever suffered occupational racism, admitting that his features shielded him. But on several occasions he witnessed black applicants disqualified for no other reason than their race. He sat in rooms where white men joked condescendingly about black laborers and applicants. He witnessed qualified black friends passed over for apprenticeship opportunities and promotions specifically because of their race. He saw white mangers actually throw the applications of potential black employees in trash cans without ever giving the applicants a fair chance at the job for which they had applied.[17]

Prior to July 1, 1965, the effective date of Title 7, most black workers had little legal recourse against these and various other forms of employment discrimination. All-black departments, limited or no union membership or representation, race-based job assignments, and disgustingly low pay scales were all the norm. And most detrimental, as has been determined about Jim Crow as an institution, such practices were not illegal.

But something changed for Joey and his fellow black workers during the late 1960s and early 1970s. Employment opportunities began to materialize as congressionally supported demands for equality in the workplace gained momentum. The *Griggs* case and ensuing legal victories helped usher in the era of equal employment opportunity, which made less grueling, safer, better paying, and thus more desirable jobs available to increasing numbers of non-whites and women.

Congressional policies and presidential executive orders struggled with eradicating occupational prejudice prior to the civil rights era. By the late 1960s, in an effort to actualize true economic progress, the civil rights community accelerated their longstanding program of legal activism in order to compel the federal courts to reaffirm the congressionally endorsed commitment to equal employment policies and programs, and to give the antidiscrimination legislation practical influence. Legal activism, lobbying Congress, and appealing directly to the executive branch had proved somewhat useful leading to the passage of Title 7, but dismantling the residue of Jim Crow in employment required client-activists and civil rights legal strategists to sustain their agenda.

Indeed, it has been African American resistance to employment prejudice that led to substantial gains in and access to employment institutions across the United States. During the post-*Brown* era, the lingering residue of segregation was still a major obstacle thwarting black progress. Legal activism, encouraged by the Civil Rights Acts of 1964 and 1965, garnered substantial gains in voting, education, and employment on the heels of America's Second Recon-struction. Although these legal campaigns had been born decades earlier, the evolution of comparable resistance strategies peaked in many ways post-1965.

LABOR

Although modern articulations concerning equal employment ideologies and labor fairness for blacks are rooted in the World War II era and the efforts put forth by A. Phillip Randolph, wholesale changes did not materialize until de-cades after the war. It would take some time for the civil rights community and committed labor radicals to force organized labor and employment institutions to share benefits and opportunities with black workers. This was made pos-sible largely by civil rights lawyers and clients working to convince the federal courts of the lingering employment injustices within industry as they molded substantial doctrines from Title 7. Though much of the work by the civil rights community began in the South, northern states too ushered in a level of labor radicalism.

There had been policies in place designed to tackle the problems of job discrimination prior to the 1960s, but some policies and programs springing from federal and state governments were inherently flawed with administra-tive awkwardness, lacking any real enforcement power. Other federal policies, if enforced, could potentially have halted bigoted practices in employment decades earlier. The Fair Employment Practices Commission (FEPC) and its outgrowths, as well as the National Labor Relations Act (NLRA), were either ineffective at battling employment prejudice or failed to use the administrative authority either owned to wage such battles effectively. Both policy efforts, in many respects, bowed to the power organized labor, employers, and white em-ployees wielded in negating employment equality.

A. Phillip Randolph established the March on Washington Movement (MOWM) in early 1941 and found support from key black leaders such as historian Rayford W. Logan, Lester Granger of the Urban League, and Walter White of the NAACP. The MOWM was headquartered in Harlem and touted active regional offices. Randolph and the organization threatened to assemble fifty thousand black workers in Washington in 1941 as a protest to raging dis-crimination in defense industries, surely with some eye on how such dem-onstrations might fight widespread discrimination in other industrial sectors.

Randolph directed the threat to President Franklin D. Roosevelt, seeking the signing of executive orders to ameliorate the problems. Randolph and other black leaders understood that lobbying Congress for fair employment legislation was fruitless since Democrats and some Republicans could block legislative efforts.[18] Randolph's threat to assemble black workers in Washington as part of his relentless efforts to uproot job discrimination before, during, and after World War II marked a significant development in the maturation of protests for fairness in employment. The practice of appealing to the appropriate governmental chamber at carefully calculated moments helped construct the foundation upon which future battles were to be waged.

Realizing the march might actually occur and fearing the impact such a demonstration might have on the United States in the international political arena during the war against fascism in Europe, President Franklin Roosevelt signed Executive Order 8802. The executive order birthed the FEPC, beginning contemporary articulations from the federal government in addressing the problems of employment discrimination, particularly those affecting black workers. Executive Order 8802 declared that the policy of the government would be "to encourage full participation in the national defense program by all citizens of the United States, regardless of race, creed, color, or national origin, in the firm belief that the democratic way of life within the Nation can be defended successfully only with the help and support of all groups within its borders."[19]

African Americans were split over the executive order. Some hailed the first effort since Reconstruction to construct a federal agency to assist blacks. But Randolph, Walter White, and other black leaders believed the order fell short of their ideal law, pointing to its glaring and inherent weaknesses.[20] Randolph sought a federal measure that would have forbidden companies with contractual obligation to the federal government to practice discrimination. He preferred an order that would have demanded the eradication of race-based exclusionary policies in training for defense positions. The policy he championed would have completely abolished segregation in the armed forces, and he desired a policy that would have punished unions for refusing membership and benefits to black workers.[21]

Randolph's understanding of the far-reaching problems of employment discrimination is best highlighted by the following facts. Although the United States emerged from the Great Depression due to the stimulation of the economy from jobs made available during military buildup and mobilization, the percentage of African Americans in industrial occupations was at a thirty-year low. Despite wartime demands and sizable increases in blacks acquiring wartime industrial jobs, "only one in 20 defense workers was black . . . and there was no more than 3 percent Negro participation in the skilled work force in the construction industry." In many respects, when defense programs exploded, African American workers remained on the margins of that growth.[22]

However, instead of a strong, exhaustive policy, the budding civil rights community was given a five-person committee that lacked enforcement power. The FEPC could only receive and investigate complaints, draft policy, hold public hearings, and rely on moral suasion and negotiations to affect job discrimination. The committee could tackle discrimination stemming from federal departments and agencies and organizations engaged in war production, but those companies without such contractual ties were outside the commission's reach. Complicating matters, the committee was designated to perform its duty with a limited staff and virtually no budget. In fact, the initial FEPC had no funding to operate regional offices and fielded a staff of only eight people. The commission as structured was hardly capable of addressing the widespread problems associated with job inequality. Initially, most politicians in Congress ignored the creation of the FEPC as a serious outfit.[23] Subsequent executive order increased budgetary support to the FEPC and swelled its staff to 120 field agents, but its role as an agency that would completely abolish employment discrimination was far from realized.[24]

In the South, the FEPC met resistance from its inception. A leading historian of the region sheds light on this point when he writes, "Federal officials were aware of the persistent discrimination in the South. Those stationed in southern communities, however, felt constrained by indigenous customs," especially since regionally based federal agencies were often staffed by local people.[25] More precisely, most white southerners were averse to working alongside blacks, and unions refused to include blacks under the umbrella of their protection. Despite clear evidence of discrimination, the FEPC had no authority to compel workers, unions, or employers who balked at the committee's directives to treat black workers fairly.

The FEPC succumbed to congressional attack in 1944 only three years after its birth. Conservative Republicans and most southern Democrats finally took notice of the agency and launched what Randolph called a "vicious and destructive attack" on the FEPC. Southern political leadership accused the FEPC of forcing whites to accept African Americans as social equals and warned of pending racial conflict if the committee forced employers to hire blacks.

Spurred by the committee's reorganization and growing influence, Virginia congressman Howard W. Smith instigated an investigation determined to convince Congress that the FEPC needed elimination. Historian Andrew Kersten notes that "the Virginia representative was more than a conservative; he was a 'reactionary,' disturbed by any expansion of the federal government to help certain social groups. In racial matters Smith adhered to a personal code of hatred, especially against African Americans."[26]

Despite the committee's limited authority and quick riddance at the hands of hostile politicians, the impact of the executive's installation of the FEPC is significant on several fronts. First, the FEPC processed roughly eight thousand complaints and conducted thirty public hearings during its brief tenure, highlighting the vastness of wartime employment prejudice. These efforts increased awareness of the various forms of employment prejudice and exposed the collusion between union and management in constructing and maintaining discriminatory structures. Second, African American agency directly impacted the committee's success rate, which was made possible by the alliance of local labor activists and the FEPC, leading to blacks filing more than 90 percent of the committee's complaints.[27] In fact, this alliance with the FEPC aided black communities and organizations in their mobilizations opposite employment prejudice and helped chart future programs of legal activism to enforce the equal employment legislation of the 1960s.[28]

Third, the federal government had committed to addressing racially motivated employment practices with policy inducements. Because African American pleas were answered by Washington, the black community and civil rights leadership would look to the federal government with increased expectations in subsequent decades. Fourth, and closely related, the budding civil rights community had officially become entrenched in contemporary political discourse and jockeying around the various types of racial inequality. In ongoing political contests civil rights leadership and lobbyists would elbow for increased positioning and political space for its constituency. For example, the NAACP has held a lobbying office in Washington, D.C., since 1942. During the civil rights era, the NAACP's Clarence Mitchell was considered one of the most effective lobbyists in Washington.[29]

Finally, the FEPC spawned important outgrowths. From 1945 to 1949, eight state fair employment practices measures emerged specifically in states with heavy concentrations of African Americans, and dozens more followed in subsequent years. Although such developments are significant, the records of these agencies do not reflect entities seriously committed to challenging the practices and customs in industry. State committees approached the eradication of race-based employment discrimination in ways similar to those of their parent federal committee.[30] And because blacks had aggressively pushed for FEPC laws and black agency helped drive the success of the state agencies, political opponents were able to level resistance to both state committees and state fair employment laws by pointing to the potential outgrowth of racial preferences in employment decisions. For instance, racial conservatives opposing New York's FEP law introduced "the specter of quotas" into the discourse over fair employment and equal opportunity as early as 1945, inciting skepticism and some degree of hostility toward the measures.[31]

An important voice in the discussion of African American struggles in industry comes from labor historian Herbert Hill, a longtime labor secretary of the NAACP. On the matter of state FEPC effectiveness, Hill writes that "we must conclude on the basis of the evidence that state FEPC laws have failed." By 1965, the evidence to which Hill alludes included the following: the status of black workers in states with FEPCs had not effectively changed, industries with expanding employment opportunities were rarely covered by fair employment guidelines and antidiscrimination statutes, and many of the committees were directed by "timid political appointees" ill prepared and insensitive to the needs of black workers.[32]

The NLRA potentially could have affected race discrimination in employment as well. An important component to the act was its authority to nullify collective bargaining agreements signed by unions that failed to represent all of its members fairly. However, this provision was rarely used to combat race discrimination. Even as the act matured during the civil rights era to include federal enforcement provisions and cease-and-desist orders, rarely was it called upon to redress racial bigotry in employment. In fact, relying on Hill again, "its history in the area of civil rights has been one of great possibility and little practical effect.[33] But this highlights only part of the problems stemming from organized labor and its failures to protect black workers.

Organized labor virtually had denied blacks union membership and representation en masse, either in their written bylaws or by tacit agreement. Where all-black locals existed, they regularly were forced to the fringes of any real opportunities associated with union affiliation. In many cases, unions created separate lines of seniority and promotional provisions that further hindered black progress. Similarly, unions blocked African American attempts to receive training for skilled, income-elevating positions and often denied blacks access to hiring halls.[34] Some scholars are able to find departures from these traditions on the part of organized labor, but for the most part these tendencies remained in place until the federal courts forced compliance with Title 7.

Labor historian James Jones sums up these customs on the part of organized labor: "It is perhaps naïve to expect organized labor to reflect an attitude substantially different from that of the society which it comes. . . . Efforts to accommodate the interests of blacks and other (nonwhite) workers in organized labor is as painful story as any other historical account of race in America." In fact, A. Phillip Randolph once suggested that the American Federation of Labor (AFL) "was the most wicked machine for the propagation of race prejudice in the United States."[35] The AFL marginalized black workers from its inception and during its rise as the dominant organized labor entity in the nation. Instead of embracing a "single, racially unified labor movement," which early AFL leadership noted would have been in the best interest of all workers, the federation allowed its affiliates to force blacks to the periphery of the employment sector through tacit agreements and formal segregated structures. Employers capitalized on the cheap labor black workers presented while white union members were reaffirmed of their innate superiority and thus deserved occupational position, despite having undercut the potentially awesome power a racially unified front might have presented.[36] In the South, bowing to white identity politics and thus weakening the potential for a broad movement for unionization hurt the region's workers tremendously. Industrial wages across the South were on average 30 to 50 percent lower than in other areas.[37]

The Communist-influenced and left-leaning unions of the Congress of Industrial Organizations (CIO) approached racial egalitarianism in their industrial and agricultural occupations. But the CIO could in no way overcome the vast challenges posed by organized labor's racial politics, nor could it realistically combat the tradition of occupational privileges whites had enjoyed since industrialization peaked in the United States. Once the two groups merged in 1955 to create the AFL-CIO, traditional practices of the AFL affiliates dominated the institution as its locals and members continued excluding black workers from the range of protections provided whites.[38]

Prior to 1965 labor unions used their extensive powers to eliminate or limit black workers as a group. When these practices met congressional challenges from Title 7, which later received judicial confirmations in the courts, they morphed into less obvious techniques that still negatively affected the employment options of black workers. Some of these newer mechanism included written tests and exams designed to measure general aptitude and predict job skills and abilities. These types of tests would become the key issue under review once *Griggs* reached the Supreme Court. The federal courts ultimately found these mechanisms to have a disparate effect on black workers when they failed to accurately measure a worker's ability to perform blue-collar jobs, even if the tests were administered under seemingly fair employment circumstances. *Griggs* marshaled in the legal doctrine that ignores intent to discriminate on the part of employers and instead recognizes the effects of employment practices as fairer interpretations of discrimination.

A strict, literal critique of Title 7 suggests that its language offered no compelling authority that organized labor needed to seriously consider following. *Griggs* became a critically important case because it was a Supreme Court decision that validated the employment law as an instrument for effective change. Although the case involved no complaint in regard to union representation on the part of the plaintiffs, the implications for organized labor would be significant. *Griggs* ultimately had an impact on a wide array of union-related practices, including admittance to apprenticeship programs, full inclusion of all-black locals, and full representation in collective bargaining on the behalf of black workers.[39] After related legal developments, African Americans began entering the channels of organized labor with increased opportunities due to the protections emerging from *Griggs* and its disparate impact doctrine.

CIVIL RIGHTS

The creation and evolution of the disparate impact doctrine was significant for increased employment opportunities for blacks, but theoretical assumptions inherent in the doctrine extended into all other areas of civil rights litigation. The maturation of the doctrine recognized in *Griggs* gave the civil rights community its desired system of analysis in legal battles designed to uproot the institutional vestiges of Jim Crow.

Disparate impact, with its effect standard, minimizes the question of comparable treatment among employees and questions the structural problems associated with discrimination. Disparate impact calls for an appraisal of an entire institution and that institution's relationship to classes of employees, not simply the unitary experiences of individual versus individual. This doctrine showed the most promise in eradicating not only egregious, pattern-centered employment prejudice but also less obvious discrimination that had similar suf-focating corollaries. In every civil rights arena, an effect standard of discrimi-nation was the preferred unit of analysis in the courtroom. Although *Griggs* catapulted the disparate impact theory into employment law discourse in 1971, the civil rights community and its allies had begun the task of convincing the courts to recognize an effect standard that would minimize intent-oriented doctrines even before *Brown*. Along with education and, eventually, employ-ment, the civil rights bar also pushed for an effective standard in voting litiga-tion. One example is the landmark decision *Gomillion v. Lightfoot* (1960).[40]

With the help of the NAACP's Legal Defense Fund, blacks from Macon County, Alabama, challenged state legislation that reshaped voting districts in favor of the maintenance of white political supremacy. Even though African Americans made up a sizable majority in this county, racial gerrymandering had made Tuskegee "an almost wholly white town," preserving white power in the key local positions of the municipal government. By the dawning of the civil rights era, enough black voters had registered to threaten white political control in Macon County. Although no African Americans actually lost the right to vote due to the measure, their electoral influence was diluted to inef-fectual proportions. Regarding Supreme Court arguments in *Gomillion*, histo-rian J. Morgan Kousser writes,

> Robert Carter of the NAACP began his oral argument . . . saying: "Your Honors, our position is simple. This is purely a case of racial discrimina-tion. The *purpose* of this legislation—Alabama Act 140—was discrimina-tory." When Justice William O. Douglas asked Carter whether purpose was "the central aspect of you case," Carter replied, "Purpose and effect—the effect reveals the purpose. . . . " Although the NAACP introduced no direct evidence of intent, no "smoking gun" statements, for instance, the Supreme Court ruled in its favor, declaring that "Acts generally lawful may become unlawful when done to accomplish an unlawful *end*."[41]

In *Gomillion*, discriminatory motive was deduced because of the redistricting plan's effect. In *Griggs*, the Court found that effects and outcomes resulting in discrimination was enough to sustain a violation of Title 7, even absent dis-criminatory intent or motive. This is an important distinction that made *Griggs* such an exceptional ruling.

The Court's recognition of effect-oriented doctrines gave civil rights cli-ents and attorneys their chief weapon in battles against morphing patterns of discrimination. By the late 1960s, scholars, civil rights advocates, and many public officials had become distinctly aware that institutionalized racism had survived as an outgrowth of Jim Crow. Discrimination had matured, becoming more complicated, more structural, and more deeply rooted as a result of decades, even centuries, of racial domination of whites over blacks.[42] Racial bias in government, corporations, and universities was considered inbred and, because of the absence of African Americans in positions of influence, self-perpetuating.[43] The evolution of the disparate impact theory was even more significant to employment battles because Title 7 and the Equal Employment Opportunities Commission left the job of filing cases in the hands and pockets of aggrieved black workers. The theory allowed singular workers and groups of workers in class-action suits to challenge broad institutional practices.

As indication of the overwhelming problems blacks faced in the labor market and those suffered at the hands of organized labor, black unemployment remained nearly double that of whites by 1970.[44] And a great many employed African Americans still lived in poverty given the low wages paid to "Negro" workers. In the aftermath of the civil rights victories of the 1960s, white males who had never attended high school earned more on average than black males with a college degree. A 1966 Department of Labor report found that as both education levels increased, black males' income decreased relative to that of white males. Related research noted that the average black high school graduate earned just over five thousand dollars per year, whereas the average white high school graduate earned just over seven thousand. Likewise, one-third of the difference between black and white occupational rankings was due to lower black education levels, leaving discrimination as a potential factor somewhere in the balance of the other two-thirds.[45] This slow pace of change in the 1960s is attributable to the persistence of discrimination in employment and the shortcomings associated with antiemployment discrimination legislation. The successes witnessed in the 1970s can be attributed to the legal activism of black workers and the civil rights bar and their successful attempts to mold Title 7 into a force that employment institutions need take seriously.

From its inception, Title 7 was designed to achieve two important goals. First, it would bring an immediate end to racial bias in employment, and second, it would hurl blacks swiftly into the economic mainstream. But the "first goal assumed a sort of color blindness and the second a type of racial bookkeeping."[46] This paradox would trouble the discourse and outcomes surrounding equal employment opportunities for decades as debates over racial

preferences stained many of the achievements extending from Title 7 litigation and the EEOC's efforts.[47] Nonetheless, Title 7 was intended to be a serious
response to a major social problem.[48] Soon after "his" civil rights bill became
law, President Johnson spoke these famous words supporting the spirit and intentions of the act: "Freedom is not enough. You do not take a person who has
been hobbled by chains and liberate him, bring him up to the starting line of a
race and then say, 'You are free to compete with all the others,' and still justly
believe you have been completely fair."[49] Johnson emphasized the importance
of addressing the problems of institutionalized racism that stunted black advancement despite the legislative denunciation of segregation. Title 7 and the
EEOC then had clear yet seemingly insurmountable tasks before them. Title 7
was aimed at destroying all aspects of employment discrimination, and the
EEOC was responsible for patrolling, preventing, and eliminating the unlawful
practices defined in the employment law.[50]

Despite race discrimination having thwarted the upward mobility of blacks
almost en masse, passage of the Civil Rights Act of 1964 was no easy task. After
failed attempts from the House and the Senate at passing antiemployment discrimination legislation one year earlier, the House Judiciary Committee "introduced the administration's civil rights bill, H.R. 7152, and opened subcommittee
hearings on June 26," 1963. The committee reported the bill on November 20,
1963, and the assassination of President Kennedy "gave a special urgency to the
enactment of the civil rights legislation."[51] The importance of the antidiscrimination law was amplified in a three-hour speech by Senator Hubert Humphrey
that opened congressional discussion on the bill. Humphrey summarized the
necessity of the bill's broad nature when he stated, "The only way to break the
vicious circle of minority oppression is to break it at every point where injustice, inequality, and denial of opportunity exist. It is for this reason that we
propose enactment of a comprehensive legislation that will touch every major
obstacle to Civil Rights."[52]

House opponents attempted to inflate the act with amendments, hoping
the bill might fail. For example, Representative Howard Smith from Virginia,
chairman of the Rules Committee and no supporter of civil rights, encouraged
the addition of "sex" to the protected classes in Title 7, alongside race, color,
religion, and national origin. Smith's House Rules Committee was considered
the "graveyard" of civil rights legislation. But when he urged the amendment
on the House floor, it led to a standing ovation from the women representatives in the chamber. Smith's motives were suspect, though he had been a sup-

porter of an Equal Rights Amendment for decades. Regardless, the prohibition on sex discrimination was in Title 7 to stay. On February 10, 1964, the House passed a comprehensive civil rights bill by a vote of 290 to 130. The bill was then sent to the Senate, where it faced a fifty-eight-day filibuster, the longest in U.S. history.[53]

Once the bill reached the Senate, Majority Leader Mike Mansfield feared it would never make it out of James O. Eastland's Judiciary Committee and thus Mansfield never referred the bill to committee for review. Senator Wayne Morse, a liberal Republican from Oregon, opposed the move, believing a committee report would be vital to the statute's judicial interpretations.[54] Senator Morse was prophetic to say the least. Much of the legislative history of Title 7 is therefore found in the Senate floor debates.

During Senate debates, questions arose over the vagueness of the concept of discrimination. Previous definitions rested largely on the "subjective intent" of the employer rather than the impact discriminatory practices had on employees. Because it is nearly impossible to determine the employer's state of mind with employment decisions, if such a reading had been injected into the language of the employment law, it "would have emasculated the Act."[55] The lack of consensus over a definition of employment discrimination created some confusion in crafting Title 7's language. Similarly, the lack of congressional discussion on the impacts of past discrimination complicated future legal deliberations aimed at garnering clear and effective interpretations of the employment law. Of course, the absence of these debates and the lack of any agreed-upon definitions gave the civil rights bar room to infuse effect doctrines into the legal discourse because the law did not explicitly oppose such broad definitions of discrimination. However, opponents to an expanded definition could point to the precise language of the law, which failed to recognize any broadened interpretations. Moreover, since the most commonly accepted definition of discrimination rested primarily on differences in treatment, the Senate debates included no discussion of a definition hinging on the impact of past discrimination. Such questions entered Title 7's discourse as soon as the law reached the courts.[56]

Because the bill outlawed overt race discrimination, those institutions still practicing racially motivated disparate treatment would be rare. Many institutions indeed altered their practices, but these newer procedures often resulted in continued discriminatory outcomes while meeting the muster of Title 7's language. Also, much of the opposition to the act was based on a concern that it might "require a regime of employment quotas," compelling employees to hire blacks irrespective of their qualifications. During the 1960s debates increased within black protest communities over whether African Americans were entitled to reparations as a result of the history of economic oppression following slavery, and discussions regarding proportional representation in employment surfaced. These claims, coupled with rising neoconservative rhetoric decrying quotas and prophesying reverse racism, lent support to such concerns.[57]

Three compromises, however, made passage of the employment provision possible and addressed these very issues of defining discrimination and combating beliefs that Title 7 would require companies to develop racial quotas: the Clark-Case memorandum, the Dirksen-Mansfield substitute, and the Tower amendment. In many respects, each of these compromises related back to the then-recent *Myart v. Motorola* (1963) case.[58]

In the case, Leon Myart, a twenty-eight-year-old black man, applied for an assembly-line position with the Motorola Corporation in Chicago inspecting television sets for defects. Myart had failed to complete high school, so he was required to take the company's standard twenty-eight-question, multiple-choice test. Myart's unsatisfactory performance led the company to deny him employment. Myart then registered a complaint with the Illinois Fair Employment Practice Committee. The hearing examiner declared that the test was unfair to "culturally deprived and disadvantaged groups" because it did not consider "inequalities and differences in environment." The examiner ordered Motorola to hire Myart and to "cease and desist" administering the test. As historian Hugh Davis Graham writes, "The hearing examiner's unprecedented cease-and-desist order on testing was attacked and appealed to the full Illinois committee by Motorola, whose outcry was soon joined by the 1400-firm Employers Association in Chicago." The case quickly became a cause célèbre among opponents to Title 7 and its proposed EEOC. Opponents pointed to the Illinois FEPC's actions as a foreshadowing of how the federal agency might approach employment procedures and especially testing mechanisms.[59]

The response by the Employers Association and Motorola may be a clear example of how companies interpreted the role of state FEPCs and how state agencies should not approach conflicts over employment discrimination. The association may have been hostile to the idea of a governmental agency officially advocating for the rights of black workers, but it was certainly opposed to an intrusion on its practices by an outside governmental agency, state or federal. Plus, the fact that hearing commissioner Robert E. Bryant was African American probably helped inflame employer hostility to the cease-and-desist order since whites could target his actions as racially motivated, discrimination in reverse no doubt, and out of bounds with established labor customs.

Yet *Motorola* entailed a few other intricacies many legal theorists have ignored, but deserve attention. First, while Myart initially failed Motorola's test, the company did not immediately release the exam or Myart's score. The exam and score were eventually released to the state agency, and on reexamination in the Illinois FEPC office Myart passed. This chain of events probably raised some suspicion over the company's administration of the exam and the test's reliability. However, at the FEPC's public hearing on the case, Myart miserably failed a verbal examination on the technical aspects of the "analyzer-phaser" position for which he had applied, despite having stated that he had amassed more than 432 hours of related training and education. Next, Myart did have a criminal record and Motorola was reluctant to "hire an applicant about whom there was a question of moral turpitude." Finally, and maybe most interesting, Commissioner Bryant's "order" held no binding authority on actual employment practices at the time of the Senate debates.[60]

In many respects, the stance against *Motorola* amounted to a severe example of reactionary politics. The case was more of an inflated "scarecrow" despite there seeming to be legitimate cause for alarm.[61] The complexities of testing, a rather unclear and undeveloped employment practice in 1963, became all the more complex with the injection of an immature political discourse of such matters into Title 7's legislative framework. The courts would be required to untangle this mess with little legislative clarity beyond scant senatorial direction.

On April 8, 1964, Senate managers of the employment bill, Pennsylvania Democrat Joseph Clark and New Jersey Republican Clifford Case, circulated a detailed memorandum defending the bill against the assertion that the concept of discrimination was vague. The Clark-Case memorandum attempted to add some clarity by providing a definition of discrimination. The memorandum explained, "To discriminate is to make a distinction, to make a difference in treatment or favor . . . based on any five of the forbidden criteria": race, color, sex, religion, and national origin.[62] Similarly, in an attempt to quell opponents concerns over racial quotas, the memo noted that "there is no requirement in Title 7 that an employer maintain a racial balance in his work force. On the contrary, any deliberate attempt to maintain a racial balance . . . would involve a violation of Title 7. . . . It must be emphasized that discrimination is prohibited to any individual."[63]

On May 26, 1964, amid concerns over *Motorola*, Everett Dirksen of Illinois teamed with Senator Mansfield and crafted a compromise that removed the EEOC's power to bring suit in federal court on behalf of the complainants and stripped the EEOC of its power to issue cease-and-desist orders. Instead, the attorney general was granted broad powers to bring antidiscrimination suits "if he had 'reasonable cause to believe that any person or group of persons is engaged in a pattern or practice of resistance to the full employment of any rights secured by this title.'" The Dirksen-Mansfield substitute also added a specific provision denying Title 7 any authority to grant preferential treatment to individuals or groups protected under the act. What became Section 703(j) of the Title 7 read,

> Nothing in this title shall be interpreted to require any employer . . . to grant preferential treatment to any individual or to any group because of the race, color, religion, sex, or national origin of such individual or group on account of an imbalance which may exist with respect to the total number or percentage of persons of any race . . . employed by an employer . . . in comparison with the total number or percentage of persons of such race . . . in any community, state, section, or other area, or in the available work force of any community, state, section, or other area.

The substitute added another section reassuring organized labor that Title 7 would not disturb seniority rights.[64]

Of the amendments adopted prior to passage of the employment provision, the Tower amendment, named for Texas senator John Tower, became the most significant concerning *Griggs*. Tower and other conservatives remained concerned by the Illinois Fair Employment Practices Committee's decision in the *Motorola* case, in which the Illinois FEPC ordered the company to discontinue the use of standard ability tests because such tests were deemed culturally biased. Though Clark and Case had addressed these issues in their interpretive document, and the Dirksen-Mansfield compromise and Section 703(j) sought to clearly denounce quotas, opponents of the bill maintained their reservations. The Clark-Case memorandum firmly stated, "There is no requirement in Title 7 that employers abandon bona fide qualification tests where, because of differences in background and education, members of some groups are able to perform better on these tests than members of other groups."[65] Nonetheless, Senator Tower introduced an amendment allowing employers to use professionally developed ability tests if the tests were administered to all applicants regardless of race and if the tests were designed to predict performance for the job under question. Failure to adopt such an amendment, Tower feared, would allow the EEOC to invalidate various tests necessary for employers to determine the professional ability, competence, ability to be trained, and suitability of a person to perform a job.[66]

Senators Case and Humphrey both found the amendment unnecessary and stated its introduction would create more confusion, making the eradication of testing-related discrimination more difficult. According to Senator Case, "If this amendment were enacted . . . it would give an absolute right to an employer to state as a fact that he had given a test to all applicants, whether it was a good test or not, so long as it was professionally developed. Discrimination could actually exist under the guise of compliance with the statute."[67]

The Tower amendment was initially rejected on June 11, but two days later Senate leadership accepted a modified version of it that was added to Section 703(h). The revised language of section 703(h) stated that it was not an unlawful employment practice "for an employer to give and to act upon the results of any professionally developed ability test provided such test, its administration or action upon the results is not designed, intended, or used to discriminate because of race, color, religion, sex or national origin."[68] The final language of the Tower amendment, however, made no mention of tests having any job-related or job-performance requirement. This undocumented change in the language of the amendment left a chasm, the question of the job relatedness of employment tests, that the courts would have to clarify during early Title 7 cases, and particularly in *Griggs.*

The Civil Rights Act of 1964 passed on July 2 but did not take effect until the summer of 1965. The delay was designed to give the EEOC one-year lead time to establish itself and to provide a transition period for businesses and unions to begin voluntary compliance. Southern industries, such as Duke Power, altered their employment practices and procedures, but most of these changes were cosmetic. These newer practices, as the disparate impact theory suggests, seemed neutral and fair on the surface but in fact perpetuated the subordinate positions of black workers. One particularly debilitating mechanism was the widespread institution of standardized aptitude tests to measure a worker's ability to perform blue-collar labor.[69]

Title 7's language as engineered through congressional debates created a structure in the law that potentially preserved existing white employment privilege in labor opposed to defining a policy that could completely destroy industry-wide practices of employment discrimination and black marginalization. Civil rights groups critiqued the legislative design of Title 7, and the EEOC argued the law was unworkable and pushed to have it amended. In an interview with the *Wall Street Journal*, Jack Greenberg, Thurgood Marshall's successor as general counsel of LDF, stated that Title 7's provisions were "weak, cumbersome, probably unworkable. . . . We think the best way to get it amended . . . is to show that it doesn't work."[70]

Fueling such cynicism, President Johnson failed to appoint the five EEOC commissioners until June 1965, wasting almost an entire year of planning and organization. And Johnson chose as the inaugural chairman a weak administrator in Franklin Delano Roosevelt Jr., whose primary interest in the appointed office was to position himself for return to elected office, with his sights set on becoming governor of New York.[71] The five-person, bipartisan commission could not issue cease-and-desist orders to noncompliant employers, nor could it bring suit in federal court. The EEOC was essentially an investigatory agency commissioned to challenge discrimination by using "conciliation, persuasion, and education." It was allowed to assist individual complainants, who could bring suit in federal courts if conciliatory efforts failed,[72] but aggrieved workers would have to shoulder the financial burden of litigation in the event the commission failed to persuade noncompliant employers to discontinue discriminatory practices.

However, the structure outlined by Title 7 encouraged the pattern-centered, industry-wide legal approach upon which civil rights activists had capitalized given the liberal interpretations rendered from the Warren Court.[73] Alfred Blumrosen, former chief of conciliation for the EEOC, argues that the commission's apparent weaknesses in lacking the ability to bring suit or issue cease-and-desist orders may have been a blessing. He suggests that although the civil rights community preferred a strong federal agency to enforce the employment law, the enforcement record of governmental fair employment agencies was unimpressive. Similarly, the President's Committee on Equal Employment Opportunity had witnessed little success in limiting discrimination by those companies under governmental contract. "In contrast," Blumrosen notes, "civil rights supporters had done well in the courts, winning the *Brown* decision and others which branded discrimination illegal. Based on a decade of experience, the civil rights movement should have welcomed court enforcement, while those who wished to minimize the impact of the law should have preferred an administrative agency with seemingly broad powers which could be 'captured' by the interest it set out to regulate."[74]

Although Blumrosen is correct in hindsight, the civil rights community was probably less willing to leave desegregating industry and fighting employment discrimination up to potentially hostile judges, especially in the South. Racial hostilities remained inflamed during the mid-1960s, generating cause to question the potential outcomes of lower court cases, though the Supreme Court appeared agreeable to uprooting the various types of discrimination. Nonetheless, opponents' attempts to undermine the effectiveness of the EEOC by stripping the agency of its enforcement powers required aggrieved black laborers to rely on their legal resources. Congress provided the scaffolding for the elimination of racially motivated employment practices. The EEOC and the courts were given the jobs of determining what specific practices constituted workplace violations of Title 7.[75] Since enforcement was left to frustrated workers, this structure also circumvented timid bureaucrats appointed for short terms who may have been subject to political and budgetary pressures and constraints.[76] The civil rights community had little choice but to continue asserting legal protests with continued direction from the NAACP and LDF.

Structural deficiencies within the EEOC were glaring. The commission was given a budget smaller than that of the Office of Coal Research, and its staff was too undersized to respond to an entire nation riddled with employment inequities. By January 1967 the commission had received almost 15,000 complaints, 6,040 of them earmarked for investigation, but it had completed only 3,319 inquiries. Many of these complaints arrived through the channels of the NAACP and LDF. By the beginning of its second year the EEOC was requiring nearly fifteen months to process a complaint. By the end of 1967 the commission's complaint processing system was exceeding two years.[77] The commission struggled, largely due to a lack of resources and the lack of an identity. Most companies had little respect for the new commission, often referred to as a "paper tiger," especially since previous state and federal agencies had failed to aggressively tackle employment disparities.

In the years immediately after passage of the employment law, the EEOC, along with LDF, concluded that "traditional notions of discrimination rendered [Title 7] as flimsy as a spider web and as easy to brush aside." Civil rights lawyers and leaders welcomed a major shift in direction that would, through

interpretation, broaden the act to provide remedies against employment policies that had a disparate impact on minorities as well as those that embodied
disparate treatment. In the eyes of civil rights advocates, remedies against *unequal treatment* of an individual, as expressed in earlier civil rights strategies,
had to be replaced by remedies for the *unequal results* for a group. A watershed
victory was one way to gain the legal precedent necessary for this shift in civil
rights strategy. *Griggs v. Duke Power* would be the case to provide the civil rights
community with a tool to achieve equality of results for classes of aggrieved
black workers.[78]

Civil rights litigation ultimately extended the reach of Title 7 through the
recognition of the disparate impact doctrine, empowering what might have
been another ineffective and inadequate tool in the battle against employment
discrimination. The civil rights legal community also evoked the support of
sympathetic judges who were well aware of the limited legal options available
to black workers. However, these accomplishments in the courtroom would
never have been possible without the thousands of black workers who, encouraged by the federal law, filed employment discrimination complaints.

As much as indigenous civil rights upsurges combated Jim Crow locally as
part of the larger interdependent movement, similar assessments can be made
regarding challenges to employment prejudice. Because job discrimination
occurred as both individual acts and in systematic patterns designed to keep
black workers a permanently depressed class, African Americans mustered a
comparable oppositional approach. The national headquarters of the NAACP
worked to secure support for the legislation and encouraged organized labor
leadership to punish its constituents for continuing discriminatory practices,
and the LDF developed strategies to prevail in the courts. Meanwhile, local activists challenged their respective workplaces with protests and lawsuits, both
of which were encouraged and supported by the NAACP and LDF. The civil
rights community understood that, while weak, Title 7 and the EEOC provided
the channels by which employment lawsuits could get into the courts.

Though many scholars equate the assassination of Martin Luther King with
the end of the civil rights movement, with even more having cause to believe it
had given way to northern radicalism years earlier, these arguments ignore
that black southerners remained vigilant and returned to the courts to secure
the promises of the civil rights acts and the movement they had engineered
and sustained for over a decade. If indeed the civil rights movement ended
with King's assassination, or lost its momentum, scholars have to answer for

the important employment cases (and other cases in voting and education) springing directly from NAACP activists and lawyers in the late 1960s and extending into the 1970s.

Although the protests and marches that had gained such sympathetic notoriety expired after passage of the civil rights laws, efforts to garner employment equality were indeed a continuation of that same spirit. In fact, the lawyers and activists leading the employment campaign of the post-1965 era equate it to and modeled it after earlier legal campaigns. When black southerners desegregated local industries, such victories rang as loudly as the desegregation of local schools. And it is well documented that King had articulated the move within the civil rights community toward addressing issues of poverty, joblessness, and employment equality. After all, it was these very issues that brought him to Memphis—a city that had already experienced an important history of labor radicalism in connection with civil rights protests communities.[79]

The civil rights community did not relent in its efforts to realize the promises of a fully equal society in the wake of the passage of the civil rights acts. Nor did the community cower in the face of the more boisterous rants of black power advocates. Instead, it stayed committed to the legal activism that had marked so much of its success in previous years. Scholars have been correct to emphasize the role of the civil rights community in the ten-year period prior to passage of the civil rights acts, and even more correct to explore the fascinating explosion of black power radicalism. However, an equally significant and compelling historical development was the sustained legal activism that sought to actualize employment equality.

Though this is a case study of *Griggs*, those who aggressively dashed to the courts, filing lawsuit after lawsuit with the hopes of giving the employment law meaning and substance, deserve recognition. These folks were keenly aware of legal developments. They were not complacent about their standing in society despite some successes from the civil rights era, nor had they lost all their energy after protesting for years and having their leaders snatched from before them. They were not only looking to combat individual acts of bigotry or working to challenge segregation in principle but also attacking the systemic racial bias that lingered in the aftermath of blatant race discrimination.

II

THE ONLY THING YOU HAD WAS THE LABOR

A Sharecropper's Journey through Rural North Carolina

> Every Supreme Court case that involves a claim of individual rights is brought by a
> real person, who has sought legal redress for some kind of oppression. . . . We often
> learn more from the personal stories of these real people than from the impersonal
> pages of Supreme Court decisions.
>
> PETER IRONS, *A People's History of the Supreme Court*

Willie Boyd emerges out of civil rights era history as one of the many face-
less people who worked diligently to alter racial politics in the South. Without
scholars continually questioning the role played by activists such as Boyd, his
life, along with many others, might be discounted as a rather unremarkable
journey through the twentieth century. Yet like many in his cohort of grassroots activists, Boyd's life was far from unremarkable. His activism dramatically
impacted post–civil rights era employment opportunities and played a role in
the landmark Supreme Court decision tackling white employment supremacy.

We should avoid the temptation to overromanticize the contrast between
the simplicity of Boyd's life and the overwhelming importance of his efforts as
a grassroots organizer and key plaintiff in one of the most significant post-1965
civil rights cases. It is also important to acknowledge, however, that in Willie
Boyd, a man from humble origins who embraced the spirit of sacrifice and
commitment necessary to foster dramatic change, we have a prime example of
the power that lay behind the successes of the civil rights movement.

The grassroots campaigners of the civil rights era were groomed for radicalism in climates that presented little chance of them ever enjoying prosperity.
The risks they faced for standing up to racial oppression could have easily resulted in violence, firings, or other attacks intended to discourage oppositional

stances. Given these circumstances, lesser-known activists such as Willie Boyd are as remarkable as the better known civil rights leaders. In many respects they represent the most committed and the most courageous, given what their life's work meant to the movement.

Had grassroots opinion leaders not heeded the word of national spokes-persons and shirked their responsibility at the local level, changes to America's racial order would have been unlikely. Local radicals such as Boyd bore the burden of actualizing the goals and tactics of the civil rights movement with minimal protection from reprisals and general, albeit astute, guidance from afar. Local activists gave structure and direction to plans that would have fallen to the wayside had they not embraced with relentless dedication the move-ment's mission and programmatic philosophies. In many instances, local activ-ists exhibited high levels of creativity and resorted to unconventional tactics to tackle the issues germane to their respective communities. Decades before Willie Boyd convinced his thirteen fellow "janitors" at Duke Power to file an employment discrimination suit with the federal government, he experienced a life common to blacks in the Carolinas, one serving as an illustration of the limitations prescribed upon African Americans under Jim Crow, specifically in the rural South.

Willie Rufus Boyd inherited a world in which African Americans were mar-ginalized economically, politically, and socially. As a result, large numbers of blacks were both poor and poorly educated. When questioned about his date of birth, Boyd responds in a very serious tone, "A long time ago," a sly grin sneak-ing out from under the elusive comment.[1] But that answer is not far from the truth. Boyd was born in Caswell County, North Carolina, in 1922 and raised in neighboring Rockingham County, in the small town of Ruffin. Both coun-ties sit in the north-central part of the state and rest upon the fertile Piedmont plateau. Boyd's parents, Trodry and Idabelle Boyd, were also born and raised in Caswell County and endured lives as sharecroppers in the heart of North Carolina's tobacco belt. Willie was number twelve of seventeen Boyd children, all of whom were birthed by midwives. Boyd keeps their names, dates of birth, and obituaries in the family Bible, which is so old the pages have yellowed and are easily blown away by the gentlest of breezes. Two of Willie's eleven brothers were born on the same day, May 31, fourteen years apart.[2]

Trodry, or "T. W.," was a physically imposing man to the Boyd children, and his larger-than-life presence was punctuated by his stern discipline. Boyd admits that he and his rambunctious siblings received their fair share of whippings from their father. "My Daddy whipped me sometimes so I thought he was mad at me," Boyd shares. But this disciplined childhood came with no dismay. Boyd admits that he and his siblings were filled with their fair share of youthful exuberance and curiosity, both of which required a heavy hand. As Boyd jokes, "If my father had tried to talk some sense into us, he would have died speechless." T. W. made sure his children understood the importance of obedient behavior and how severe punishment might be if his children acted out. Such lessons prepared them for lives under ubiquitous social conditions as the pressure cooker of Jim Crow limited African Americans' social mobility. Yet somewhere in the disciplinarian's method was the lesson of rejecting mistreatment, a rule Trodry's children also obeyed.[3]

The Boyd home was similar to the types of quarters inhabited by most sharecroppers. "It didn't really have a ceiling, just a bunch of boards thrown together," Boyd recalls. The wooden structure housed the large family, but it was hardly suitable for healthy living. No more than fifty yards from the Boyd's home was the unmunicipalized trash dump for the local sharecropper community. As Willie walked by the trash heap every morning around 5:00 a.m. on his way to feed the mules, he saw dozens of rats scavenging through the garbage mound. Worse, the rodents routinely made their way into the Boyd home. They were in such abundance and so aggressive they would "eat through a loaf of bread before (the Boyds) went to town and back." While the Boyds slept, or tried to sleep, the vermin could be heard chewing on the wood planks of the house and would sometimes "cut holes in a piece of wood in the floor over night." The younger Boyd children complained of rats biting their toes at night, but their claims were routinely dismissed by Trodry, Idabelle, and their older siblings. But one morning Willie slid his foot into a shoe, and before realizing that a rat had camped near or inside the shoe the night before, he suffered excruciating pain from a piercing bite.

At one point the rats nearly overran the household, forcing the Boyds to threaten to leave the farm. The landlord, a white woman named Annie Wersham, promised to spare no expense to keep the rats out, doing whatever necessary to keep the large family of farmworkers on her land. Willie first placed sulfur bombs around the house, but the rats would run out and avoid the smoke or simply not enter the house until the air was clear. Sulfur, of course, made breathing unpleasant for the family for days. But one idea finally worked. Willie was advised by a fellow sharecropper to sprinkle cooking grease and lye on bread slices and spread them around the floor. Willie followed the instructions and went back to work in the fields. When the family returned that evening all the bread was gone and so were the rodents. After three more treatments of cooking grease, lye, and bread, the rats never returned.

Rats and other environmental hazards were only part of the health concerns facing farmworkers. Insufficient health care for sharecroppers led to an array of ill-fated outcomes and health complications. For the Boyds, asthma impaired members of the family. Willie and his mother suffered the worst; in fact, Willie struggled with asthma his entire life, plagued with a nagging cough and shortness of breath. As a result, he regularly takes puffs from his "breathing" medicine—a prescription inhaler. One telling fact underscoring the limited health-care options sharecroppers could summon reveals that as late as 1940 in rural North Carolina, "there was one white physician for every 1,127 white persons, but only one black physician for every 6,499 black persons."[4] As a teenager Willie was hospitalized and nearly died from a complex illness consisting of the flu, pneumonia, and viral meningitis. Charlie Worten, the only black physician for miles, who traveled by horse and buggy with his medicine bag, managed the illness. High child mortality rates were common to sharecroppers as well. Indeed, Willie lost four of his male siblings. One brother was stillborn, Idolphus died at birth, Sam Henry died at birth, and Charlie Toman was born disfigured and died of a seizure at age four.[5]

The Depression hit blacks in the South especially hard, and New Deal programs did little to soften the blow. Though recovery programs and agricultural relief measures promised alleviation from some of the economic hardships stirred by the Depression, most New Deal policies ignored jobs typically reserved for blacks, such as farmwork and employment as domestics. In fact, the National Recovery Act (NRA) programs had the most adverse effects on black North Carolinians, hastening their descent into poverty. For example, higher federally regulated wages attracted unemployed whites to many traditional "Negro jobs." Between 1930 and 1940, as a result of New Deal policies, 25 percent of the black workers in North Carolina were displaced from the tobacco industry. Recovery programs severely hampered an already impoverished community, and the programs accelerated black farm owners' descent down the socioeconomic ladder. It is not surprising, then, why black leaders regularly referred to the NRA as the 'Negro Run Around' or the 'Negro Removal Act.'[6]

Tenant wages were meager, ranging from thirty-eight to eighty-seven dollars per person, per year.[7] Most sharecroppers were already trapped in a cycle of perpetual debt that only worsened during the Depression as landowners raised prices for goods advanced to tenants to cover increasing costs and decreased production. Other federal programs, such as the Agricultural Adjustment Administration (AAA) and the Federal Emergency Relief Administration (FERA), which dispensed grants to locales to aid the jobless, added to the unfortunate situation of black sharecroppers and tenants. The AAA's acreage reduction policies displaced thousands of North Carolina tenants as landlords refused to share funds from the AAA with renters and sold crops to exclusively collect the proceeds.[8] The AAA, a Raleigh newspaper editor stated at the time, "seemed to dispossess rather than serve the rural poor."[9] Similarly, FERA paid black workers monthly allotments noticeably less than that which it paid whites. And at the behest of cotton and tobacco farm owners who argued they could not compete with FERA's wages to black laborers, North Carolina Emergency Relief Administration officials suspended efforts in areas where the agency might compete with labor demands.[10]

The Depression forced many black agricultural laborers off farms, and what few black farm owners existed were some of the earliest to lose their land to foreclosure. Black businesses suffered dramatically, too, as their black clientele lost purchasing power. The economic plight was so dire that by 1935 nearly 30 percent of the African American population was welfare dependent. Conditions in the North and South forced the NAACP, the Urban League, and other organizations to reprioritize the cause of the black worker.[11] However, black sharecroppers isolated in rural areas across the South had far fewer resources to marshal in their efforts to combat a rapidly declining economy.

So the Boyds' life's work came with a multitude of hardships common to the highly racialized world of southern agriculture. For Willie and his family, working very hard for very little under tenuous circumstances became their way of life. As Boyd reports, "Tobacco work was hard but you got used to it. That's what you come up with." Hard it was indeed. The Boyds were not lucky enough to own or rent any big machinery. "Working dark to dark," Willie remembers, "we did it all by hand, walking behind a mule." Highlighting the exploitative economic relationship between landlords and farmhands, Boyd explains, "The landlord owned the tools and the land, the only thing you had was the labor." Boyd's observation understates the reality of sharecropping to some degree. Sharecroppers rarely moved ahead financially yet regularly worked long days and nights in unbearable conditions. They were also at the whim of greedy landowners who exploited the hard work of marginally educated and often illiterate farmworkers.

The men of the Boyd family—Trodry, Joe Wallace, John Thomas, Jim Linwood, Willie Rufus, Trodry Jr., Coleman, and Allen Abraham—worked the fields growing tobacco, the "money crop," bringing home between eight and ten dollars each a month. Working alongside his brothers made farmwork tolerable, Willie admits, "but the pay was too bad." At season's end the Boyds would have to shell out nearly half of their profits, sometimes more, paying expenses incurred from renting farm equipment, purchasing seed and fertilizer, and any other extraneous costs determined by the landlord.

The women of the family—Idabelle, Nannie Lou, Mary, Sandy, Jennie, Sarah and Rosa Elizabeth—worked for and often lived with white families during the week as domestics, each earning on average three dollars a week.[12] Well after World War II black women across the South still had few employment options beyond domestic service. Even after industrialization broadened employment choices for white women, black women remained confined to work as maids for white women earning decent pay in mills and other industries.[13] While the Boyd's large family may have alleviated some of the economic burdens and physical hardships associated with tenant farming—surprisingly, the Boyd's did own a car—they were nonetheless among the thousands of sharecroppers working desperately to keep food on the table and a roof over their heads. As was the case with most other sharecropping families, the Boyd children had to "eat what momma put on the table and shut up."[14]

Yet in growing tobacco the Boyds worked in an industry that created its own demand. The tobacco industry actually enjoyed prosperity during the 1930s as cigarette consumption rose steadily during the tough Depression years. Stress and the frustrations associated with an economy spiraling downward probably drove cigarette sales, as did an escalation in marketing by the tobacco industry, signified by the popularization of the "ten-cent" pack. By 1930 two-thirds of all American cigarettes were produced in North Carolina, but "the relative prosperity of the industry had not filtered down to the [tobacco] workers."[15]

Unlike many black southerners, the Boyds resisted the temptation to move North during the Depression and peak years of the Great Migration. As noted in a history of the state, "North Carolina lost 5 percent of its black population during the decade of the First World War, 7.6 percent during the Great Depression, and 14.8 percent during the 1940s." In actual numbers, 57,000 black North Carolinians migrated out of the state between 1910 and 1930, and a staggering 222,000 left between 1930 and 1950.[16] African American migrants sought better economic opportunities in northern factories, encouraged by labor demands, the chance at a decent education, possible participation in electoral politics, and freedom from racial violence.

But the Boyds stayed put. North Carolina was their home, and they were determined to make the best of their situation. As a young man growing up in Depression-ridden, rural North Carolina, Boyd, like other African Americans, learned the patience and buoyancy necessary to live a decent life under Jim Crow. "You got used to it," Boyd recounts, "but you always wished you were having a better day." When younger generations declare their inability and un-willingness to cope with life during the tumultuous era, Boyd maintains that while living under segregation people learned to manage and navigate the system's debilitating social norms. He and other black Carolinians persistently and strategically challenged the status seeking to destroy the institution that mandated and codified their second-class citizenship.[17]

Although segregation was pervasive in North Carolina, the state enjoyed a reputation of cultivating harmonious race relations during the first half of the twentieth century. However, this "etiquette of civility" and "self-styled progressivism" was largely exaggerated.[18] In fact, the process of acting "civil" required some tacit knowledge and awareness of the social conditions. Whites were well aware of their racial privileges, and this "civility" helped maintain racial stratifications. The fierce segregation across North Carolina led to limited economic options afforded to blacks, low standards of living, poor health, undernourishment, delinquency, lower educational achievement, and higher crime rates.[19]

State-sponsored biracial committees and coalitions designed to interrogate the "Negro problem" added to North Carolina's aura of progressive race relations. One committee, the North Carolina Commission on Interracial Cooperation, had nearly a thirty-year tenure beginning in the 1920s. The biracial organization of educators and church leaders questioned an array of racial concerns, but conflict over integration in the 1950s grew too divisive an issue and forced the group to disband. Another, the North Carolina Commission for the Study of Negro Education, began in the mid-1930s and immediately found glaring disparities between black and white teacher's salaries and suggested these inequities be eliminated. Though this was hardly new information, the state's general assembly ignored the commission's suggestions. In 1913, North Carolina created the Division of Negro Education, with a white man, Nathan

Newbold, as its first director. Newbold boldly reported that "the average Negro school house is really a disgrace to an independent civilized society." These conditions in black schools, he continued, were due to "injustice, inhumanity, and neglect on the part of white people."[20]

The efforts of these and other groups may have seriously focused on improving the quality of life within black communities, and probably interrogated the "Negro Problem" in some detail, but they remained futile, in part because these groups sought to ameliorate the plight of blacks while accepting segregation and disfranchisement, which stood as fundamental barriers to genuine progress. This "etiquette of civility" would never bring about an end to Jim Crow and would only provide, at best, pacifying concessions to the black community through conservative black leadership.[21]

But although white liberal leaders and compliant black spokespersons provided the rhetoric to support the illusion of racial progress, the quest for genuine equality was never abandoned by black North Carolinians. Deliberate, premeditated declarations in opposition to racial subordination were often mistaken for acquiescence and complacency on matters of equality. In fact, as much as nonthreatening coalitions supported the state's aura of civility, a healthy dose of black radicalism sustained the appearance of positive race relations. With African Americans articulating aggressive stances in opposition to Jim Crow there was always the appearance that white leaders across the state tolerated such militancy without threatening or harming black agitators. As early as 1907, blacks in North Carolina began openly criticizing Jim Crow railroad cars, mob violence, and election fraud. Such protests expose that whatever semblance of amicable relationships that supposedly existed between the races was mostly propaganda.[22]

In 1912, Clarence H. Poe, editor of the *Raleigh Progressive Farmer* may have described the actual feelings held by many whites of these relations and burgeoning black resistance to segregation. "There has been. . . a tie of affection between the Negroes and the families of their former owners that made strongly for peace between the races—a tie now rapidly weakening," he wrote. The following year Poe launched a two-year crusade to establish rural segregation throughout the South, styling his plan after South African apartheid.[23]

By the 1920s and the decade of the "New Negro," black assailments on American racism and Jim Crow had spread across the nation. The cultural aesthetics of Harlem Renaissance artists, the rhetoric and militancy of Marcus Garvey's United Negro Improvement Association, and the political and legal activism of the NAACP reached black communities far and wide, finding their way to North Carolina as they did elsewhere. In 1920, more than one thousand black North Carolinians belonged to ten NAACP branches, including the three initial state branches in Raleigh, Greensboro, and Durham.[24] Whites across the South, and those in North Carolina were no exception, deplored the NAACP and its outspoken leader W. E. B. Du Bois. By white southern standards the NAACP was a radical organization certain to upset the social order whites had worked to secure since Reconstruction.

The persistence of lynchings and the growth of segregation forced many African Americans in North Carolina to gravitate toward the NAACP and its activist agenda. The first three initial local branches were chartered in 1917 with four more chapters established the following year in Fayetteville, Winston-Salem, Rocky Mount, and Asheville. In 1919, Wilmington, Charlotte, and Lexington were added. The next two decades witnessed an increase in NAACP chapters and membership throughout the state as lynchings and racial hostility grew concurrently. By the mid-1940s more than twenty chapters and youth councils existed throughout the state with approximately four thousand members.[25]

Resistance to oppression was not reserved for organizations such as the NAACP, however. Church leaders, educators, and popular press agents also criticized racial disparities. At Emancipation Day[26] observances in 1923, Reverend D. Ormonde Walker, a minister at St. Paul's African Methodist Episcopal Church in Raleigh, rebuked the Ku Klux Klan, American imperialism in Haiti, Marcus Garvey's "Back to Africa" movement, and the Republican Party "for abandoning its founding principles." Addressing two thousand blacks, Walker warned whites they were dealing with a new generation of African Americans. No longer were they simply former slaves. Instead, they had come to view themselves as Americans entitled to first-class citizenship who need not repatriate but demanded complete equality in the United States.[27]

Professor William S. Turner of historically black Shaw University embraced the new generation of African American scholars tackling issues of race. In 1928, Turner expressed the growing disenchantment brewing within the black community over the recognition of Emancipation Day celebrations. The yearly observance was more a reminder of slavery, Turner and younger blacks argued, which allowed whites to continually justify discrimination and sociopolitical marginalization. Turner "denied Lincoln's humanitarian motives," arguing that "Lincoln issued the proclamation to further the war effort and infuse the Union cause with idealism. Turner even questioned the proclamation's constitutionality." This rhetoric reveals a budding aura of radicalism decades prior to the civil rights movement.[28]

Louis E. Austin, the "blunt-speaking editor" of the Durham-based *Carolina Times*, equated the struggles of blacks in the North and South, arguing that "African Americans in both regions sought equal justice, opportunity, and political rights."[29] Austin's work in Durham and throughout the state proved critical to the black struggle. He remained a harsh critic of Jim Crow during decades that witnessed some of the most brutal attacks on blacks in the state. Austin played a major role in state politics and social resistance from the 1920s through the civil rights era.

The struggle against racism and Jim Crow remained a central issue for African Americans in North Carolina as tensions slowly boiled toward more dynamic protests and oppositions. In the meantime, black North Carolinians were able to manage some important social and economic progress. Indeed, as political rights and participation waned at the turn of the twentieth century, education, business, and industrial progress became areas of focus within black communities. Though blacks remained committed to claiming political rights, this era was marked by increased defensive expressions of self-help, racial solidarity, and economic uplift. Jim Crow was clearly the catalyst for these preservation responses, yet one person can be called the "ideological godfather" of all-black institutions at the turn of the twentieth century: Booker Taliaferro Washington. And no company better represents the pragmatic successes of this ideology than "the world's largest Negro business," North Carolina Mutual Life Insurance Company.[30]

The black press in the early decades of the twentieth century referred to Durham as the "Black Wall Street" or "City of Negro Enterprise," and North Carolina Mutual was the leading financial attraction in this hub of black capitalism. It is tempting to retell the story of the company in great detail, but Walter Weare's *Black Business in the South: A Social History of North Carolina Mutual Life Insurance Company* does so in splendid fashion. It is pertinent, however, to demonstrate North Carolina Mutual's placement in the mix of black/white social, political, and economic relationships during Jim Crow. These accounts, drawing largely on Weare's work, speak directly to the complexities inherent in deciphering the riddles associated with the proximity of whites and blacks along social and economic formations. The two groups were not strangers, as scholars have shown. They crossed paths and interacted in tobacco fields, at barbershops, and maybe even in boardrooms.

The ancestors of North Carolina Mutual were probably all-black institutions such as the Free African Society and the African Methodists Episcopal Church (AME), both of which were founded in the late eighteenth century by Absalom Jones and Richard Allen. These inaugural institutions encouraged self-help and spiritual and moral improvement, and they offered sickness and burial insurance plans. In 1810, Philadelphia blacks formed a similar organization, the African Insurance Company, though it lasted only three years. By the late nineteenth century, however, these causes were largely assumed by secret societies such as the Prince Hall Masons, often considered pioneers of more contemporary "Negro" businesses. In fact, one such group, the Virginia-based Grand United Order of True Reformers, had as an agent John Merrick, who would later initiate the creation of North Carolina Mutual.[31]

The company was created in 1898, in the midst of the vicious white supremacy campaign of the late 1890s that included white newspapers spreading racial hysteria, black newspapers destroyed by fire, race riots in Wilmington, and high numbers of lynchings across the state. Such violence and terrorism was intended to completely eliminate blacks from the political process. Durham was not impervious to this sort of racial hysteria. In the city known to be a haven for positive race relations, "passions became so heated that a black man rumored to have been living with a white woman (allegedly the wife of a Republican) was lynched and his body left hanging along the roadside between Durham and Chapel Hill to serve as a ghastly lesson in white supremacy."[32] In this climate, successful black business leaders would always harbor some fear of violent reprisals. The entrepreneurs pushed forward nonetheless, seeking safety and prosperity by catering to a sizable black clientele.

Six black men joined Merrick on an October evening in 1898 to create the North Carolina Mutual and Provident Association. The collective included Aaron McDuffie Moore, Durham's black physician; Edward Austin Johnson, a historian, attorney, and dean of the Law School at Shaw University in nearby Raleigh; James Edward Shepard, preacher, politician, pharmacist, and founder of Durham's North Carolina College for Negroes; Durham school teacher Pinckney William Dawkins; tinsmith Dock Watson; and William Gaston Pearson, a school teacher and principal. The company received its charter on February 29, 1899, after a hard-fought struggle with the state legislature. Thomas Oscar Fuller, "a black by-product of North Carolina 'fusion politics'" and one of the last remaining black state senators from the Reconstruction era, maneuvered the charter through the state legislature.[33]

There is one related and rather interesting note concerning the folklore behind the company's creation. Weare's work shows without doubt that Booker T. Washington's theories and the keen business mind and experience of the former slave Merrick, who had at one time owned nine barbershops, were instrumental in the development of the company. But white Durham folklore attributes the beginnings of the company to Washington Duke, father of the powerful James and Benjamin Duke of the American Tobacco Company and the Duke Power Company. Merrick was the personal barber to the elder Duke and his occasional traveling companion. Duke also regularly contracted Merrick to dismantle old barns belonging to the American Tobacco Company. Through these endeavors Merrick created a small construction company and real estate firm.[34]

White and black tales suggest that Merrick was encouraged by Duke to create North Carolina Mutual. White accounts anoint Duke as sole originator of the idea, tracing the business to "paternalistic largesse" that probably worked as a defense mechanism to the white psyche. Such black economic prowess, made explicit in one of the largest businesses in the city, needed rationalizing. Blacks, however, argued that Merrick was often interrupted by working-class blacks "passing the hat" in the barber shop as a means of seeking financial assistance for funerals. Duke one day witnessed this and encouraged Merrick to create the company. Blacks associated very successful members of their race as having been assisted with advice and money by wealthy whites. What is probably most accurate, as Weare suggests, is that Merrick, already an astute businessman, probably sharpened his skills while privy to conversations between Duke and his associates. The creation of the company, nonetheless, is directly linked to Merrick's own ingenuity.[35]

The company struggled early on, and original members withdrew, leaving only Merrick, Moore, and the versatile newcomer Charles Clinton Spaulding to manage the company that engendered "a Soul and a Service." The triumvirate possessed complementary skills that when combined moved the company along the path to success. For these "socially conscious black businessmen more was at stake than organizing an enterprise; they saw themselves organizing a people."[36] The company represents black North Carolinians overcoming or outmaneuvering the obstacles presented by Jim Crow in an attempt to provide for the larger African American community. While it began as a means for bettering the lives of blacks locally, it ultimately reached the national African American community during decades that witnessed the most ferocious attacks on black economic development.

Though Willie Boyd had little in common with John Merrick and the middle-class African Americans who organized many of the states' NAACP chapters, he grew restive under the strict limitations established by segregation. Once tightly woven with the American Tobacco Company, Boyd's hometown of Reidsville is small and rural, so rural, in fact, that the Southern Railroad still passes through the middle of the town. When Willie first arrived to Reidsville in 1947, the town was "a one track road . . . with nothing but rats and snakes"—in the black neighborhood anyway. And although Willie and his family could brag of building their first home, which was not dissimilar from their former share-cropper quarters in Ruffin, one thing was glaringly different, as Willie remembers with some pride: "It was ours!"[37]

As was the case in most other southern towns, nearly every institution in Reidsville was segregated, including the libraries, movie theaters, lunch counters, ballparks, swimming pools, hospitals, schools, and the courthouse.[38] One story that typifies black life in Reidsville involves a local restaurant, Short Sugar, which openly discriminated against blacks. On any given evening, Boyd and friends might develop a craving for some of Short Sugar's prize-winning barbecue, "some of the best barbecue around." As Boyd recalls,

> Back in the 50s and on back, we'd be sitting around here around nine on a Saturday night, any night. We'd like to have a sandwich, so we'd go get some barbecue. Now, we knew how we were going to have to get that barbecue. Pull around to the back, little wood door. . . . It could be sleeting, raining, it could be sunshine. Wouldn't make no difference what kind of weather, that's where you had to get your barbecue. You'd pull close as you could, get out in the rain, knock on that door and when *they* got ready and got time and wasn't working out in the front they would run and take your order. Then you had to wait 30 or 40 minutes, depending on clients they had inside, for them to come back there and bring your barbecue. And I'll tell you, it was good! It was good too man. [Laughing.] Wouldn't be good now, 'cause I can go in front. My son said I wouldn't have done that. I said well you could have got by then . . . if you didn't want no barbecue.

Over the years, Willie and his cohort of local organizers worked through their local NAACP chapter to eradicate segregation throughout the city. But it would be a struggle. As Boyd puts it, "That NAACP is a Man in communities where they are really active."[39] A strong local NAACP chapter, buttressed by North Carolina's powerful, statewide organization, provided its members with the support and organization necessary to effectively battle local segregation. "It was a powerful source," Boyd insists. "It was the only thing [black] people had." For decades, the NAACP in North Carolina was the backbone of black protests throughout the state. And despite the frustrations associated with Jim Crow, Boyd's efforts in fighting segregation would eventually pay off for him and most other blacks. Reminiscing, he said, "My time did get here. I'm thankful of that. I lived long enough to see some of my dreams come true."[40] The growth and impact of NAACP chapters across the state are detailed in the following chapter.

Boyd dropped out of high school in the eleventh grade after his father became ill to help the family meet the landowner's quota of tobacco production.[41] For a black teenager from a sharecropping family to nearly graduate from high school was an impressive feat. Boyd's large family allowed him and his siblings a bit more flexibility than most sharecropping youth, and Willie was a good student who cherished his time spent in school. Yet before his twenties, he had become head of the huge Boyd household. He continued farming until he "made his last crop" in 1948. Boyd, like millions of southerners, escaped the drudges of farmwork due to the World War II economic boon, which stimulated the South's industrial economy. Wartime needs pushed textile production to full capacity as mills across the South churned out high volumes of uniforms, tents and other military essentials. For white and black workers alike, industrial occupations often doubled their income.[42]

Unlike his brother Trodry Jr., Willie did not go off to war. Trodry Jr. became a Worlds War II veteran and returned with many other black veterans to small towns like Ruffin and Reidsville, acutely aware of the discrimination they faced. As Boyd remembers jokingly, "White folks wanted us to go to war 'cause we might get killed there." Willie also recalls that unlike other cities and towns that erupted in violence with an increasing presence of black men in uniforms demanding rights they had fought for overseas, little violence occurred in areas in and around Reidsville.[43]

Reidsville, North Carolina, is forty miles north of Greensboro and rests in the plateau region of the Piedmont. This region is not only ripe for tobacco and agricultural production but also, because of its natural resources, an environment highly conducive to industrialization. Duke Power began providing hydroelectric power to North and South Carolina soon after World War I and opened the Dan River Station in the early 1950s.

When the Dan River Station opened alongside its namesake near Boyd's home, the demand for blue-collar labor accompanied it, and Boyd took full advantage of the opportunity. Companies such as Duke Power knew it had at its disposal plenty of unskilled laborers who would jump at the chance to escape farmwork. Plus, people who had labored on farms most of their lives were reputed to be good workers who appreciated a lighter workload than that promised in sharecropping, though industrial work could be equally as brutal in some instances. Boyd began working on the construction of the plant in 1948 and was hired at Dan River when the steam station opened in 1952. His job at the plant would be hard, but no harder than chopping tobacco. Most important, it provided a weekly paycheck, freeing Boyd from the cycle of credit and debt that had characterized his sharecropping. Soon, he would have enough money to pay his bills and even buy a few items on credit.[44]

Boyd's new employer was the brainchild of entrepreneur James Buchanan Duke. Led in large part by brothers James Buchanan and Benjamin Newton, the Duke family rose from yeomen farmers, forced to rebuild their operations after major losses during the Civil War, to become leading entrepreneurs in North Carolina and the New South. Earning most of their wealth from the tobacco industry, the Dukes used their fortunes to move the Southeast, most notably North and South Carolina, into the modern age of hydroelectric and steam-powered industry. The Dukes quickly became North Carolina's premier family. Their affluence and influence was made apparent in 1924, when James "Buck" Duke bequeathed nearly $60 million to Trinity College in Durham. He also donated $4 million for the creation of a medical school to be given to Trinity upon his death, which occurred only one year later. On December 30, 1924, at the behest of the school's board of trustees, Trinity College formally became Duke University.[45]

James Duke was born in 1856 to Washington and Artelia Duke outside Durham. Washington Duke was raised under the influence of the temperance movement and the spreading of educational reform during the middle decades of the nineteenth century. He was also a devout Methodist due to "the impassioned evangelical movement that swept through American Protestantism in the early decades of the nineteenth century." In fact, Washington Duke may have never owned slaves and is reported to have been opposed to the institution of human bondage. However, he became a member of the Confederate navy late in the Civil War, though he appears to have been a "Union man" who never "became a professional 'Wearer of the Gray.'"[46]

Near the war's end, Washington was captured and imprisoned by Union troops, and after gaining parole he was shipped to New Bern, North Carolina.

The muscular man of six feet tall allegedly walked from the coastal city to Durham to be reunited with his wife and children, Brodie, Mary, Ben, and James. Once home, he found the family's farm in severe decline, except for an abundant amount of dried leaf tobacco. Legend has it that "Wash" Duke loaded up a wagon with all of the tobacco, some flour, and a "victuals box" for basic cooking and headed back to the eastern part of the state, a hub of economic exchange, to peddle and barter his product.[47]

This business venture had both risks and advantages. The Virginia and Carolina region was naturally endowed with an abundant supply of the gold leaf tobacco, along with an encouraging demand. But a number of more established companies were already manufacturing tobacco and reaping major profits. Nonetheless, the Dukes prospered, albeit modestly. In roughly ten years, "Wash" had traveled many miles selling the family's various tobacco products. Company records show names of tobacconists from Maine to California with whom the Dukes shared commerce. All the while, brothers "Buck" and Ben were learning the particulars of the trade. In 1873, W. Duke, Sons and Company purchased a small, two-story building in Durham that became their offices, factory, and home. Despite having powerful competitors the likes of Bull Durham tobacco, owned and manufactured by W. T. Blackwell and Company, the Dukes sharpened their business skills and worked their way up the tobacco industry hierarchy.[48]

The Dukes had little choice in their family business venture. Post-Reconstruction agricultural production in North Carolina relied heavily on cash crops such as cotton and tobacco. Small farmers such as the Dukes were drawn into the production of cash crops, however many suffered drastically as cotton and tobacco prices plummeted in the latter decades of the nineteenth century. Cotton, for example, fell from twenty-five cents a pound in 1868 to seven cents a pound in the early 1890s. Although prices plunged significantly, production boomed for cotton and tobacco alike. Small farmers' debt increased forcing them to gamble even more heavily on cash crops and pushing them more into tenancy. Indeed, the number of tenant farmers nearly doubled from 1880 to 1900.[49]

One key move engineered by Buck was the addition of cigarettes to the chewing and smoking tobacco already in production. They also hired energetic salesmen to complement the hard-working Buck. By 1882, W. Duke, Sons and Company had introduced their products in Europe, South Africa, India, the East Indies, Australia, and New Zealand. The family business quickly became a force to reckon with in the tobacco industry. Buck Duke, the emergent family leader, expanded the business further when he headed to New York to compete with the "big dogs."[50] Buck not only competed, he excelled. In less than a decade the company had cornered 8 percent of the nation's cigarette sales.[51]

The second half of the nineteenth century was highlighted by rapid industrialization across the nation. The 1860s and 1870s witnessed the growth of future giants in industry and finance. John D. Rockefeller founded Standard Oil Company after striking oil in Pennsylvania. Andrew Carnegie formed United States Steel, eventually turning it into a conglomerate. William Henry Vanderbilt transformed his father's $100 million inheritance into the New York Central and Michigan Central railroads. And John Pierpont Morgan, "with an eye on owning almost everything," created the investment-banking firm J. P. Morgan and Company, which by 1905 had offices in Paris and London. America had entered the industrial age.[52]

To compliment the growth of these industrial empires, ingenious scientists introduced society-transforming ideas and inventions to the world. George Westinghouse and Thomas Edison revolutionized electricity with their respective strides in alternating current and direct current energy. Elijah McCoy's patented lubricating mechanism, aptly called the "real McCoy," gave engines the oil needed to run for hours nonstop. George Washington Carver developed hundreds of inventions with the peanut and hundreds more with the sweet potato while researching feverishly at Tuskegee Institute. Louis Latimer improved the filament that made Edison's success in developing incandescent light possible. And Garrett Morgan created the gas mask and soon after the three-way traffic light with great timing as Henry Ford's production schemes and sales of automobiles accelerated.

This was the America in which young Buck Duke emerged as a giant in the tobacco business. The family company expanded to New York, where by the late 1880s, Buck's energy and crafty business acumen had forced the other "Big Four" tobacco companies to take notice. W. Duke Sons and Company produced an "Honest Long Cut" of tobacco that doubled as a smoking and chewing product. Duke also introduced his machine-made cigarettes to a reluctant public that remained true to the hand-rolled smoke. One year, spending more than $800,000 on advertising, Duke hired the largest sign-painting company in the nation to paint ads on barns, roadside signs, and any other object that could display the company's products. Duke also introduced coupons for redemption that included images of stage personalities and sports figures on the cover of the packages.[53] One Harlem merchant recalled, "Soon collecting pictures [of celebrities in Duke's cigarette packages] became a craze and we had to order the cigarettes in quantity. As I look back now, I think that one stunt, more than any other, really put the cigarette over with the public."[54]

Duke's creativity confused his four competitors, W. S. Kimball and Company, Goodwin and Company, the Kenney Brothers, and Allen and Ginter. They were sure he would go broke sooner than later. When Duke's energy and success proved unyielding, the Big Four initiated talks of buying out their young competitor. A man of few words, like his dad, Buck replied, "We are accustomed to ask, not to give, hostages."[55]

Duke, feeling disrespected, became even more aggressive in his attempts to coerce the Big Four into a merger. Economic retardation across the nation and the fierce competition within the tobacco business were driving all of the companies to potential ruin. Duke's plan would save them all, but would of course privilege and profit Duke the most. In one exchange Les Ginter demanded, "Listen Duke, you couldn't buy us out to save your neck. You haven't enough money and you couldn't borrow enough." Buck answered firmly, " I make $400,000 out of my business every year. I'll spend every cent of it on advertising my goods as long as it is necessary. But I'll bring you into line."[56]

True to his word, Buck Duke navigated the five companies into a merger. In 1890, the American Tobacco Company was chartered and James B. Duke was unanimously elected its president. Ironically, Congress passed the Sherman Anti-Trust Act the same year. Although little used in the immediate years after its adoption, in part because of restrictive interpretations by the Supreme Court, the act would return to haunt the company seventeen years later.[57] With Duke as president, the American Tobacco Company controlled 90 percent of the cigarette, chewing, and smoking tobacco business in the United States. The young pigeon-toed farmer, rising from abject poverty through a family business, had engineered a financial empire.[58]

In 1906, the Justice Department took notice and sued the company as a prohibited monopoly under the Sherman Anti-Trust Act. When the Supreme Court ultimately dissolved the company into fourteen separate firms, "Duke was called upon to unscramble his own omelet."[59] Five years later John Rockefeller's Standard Oil Company was dissolved under the act.[60] The Duke family and its economic empire were truly among the nation's financial elite. "Washington Duke's son Buck made no idle boast when he pledged 'to do for tobacco what . . . Rockefeller did for oil.'"[61]

During the 1890s, among his many economic ventures, James B. Duke stumbled upon an interest in hydroelectric power. In 1904, Duke pursued developing the waterpower of the southern Piedmont and by 1905 had formed the Southern Power Company, operating two full-fledged electric plants in South Carolina. With the help of his brother Benjamin and business associates William States Lee and W. Gill Wylie, the team of entrepreneurs led the industrialization of the Piedmont and could brag of developmental projects extending as far north as Quebec, Canada.[62]

Long before the Southern Power Company was established, Buck and Ben were interested in providing power to the burgeoning textile industries of the late-nineteenth-century Piedmont. The Duke Brothers had dreams of increasing the production capacities of the mills so the mills would mature into industrial giants. These investments in textile mills were financed with the surplus capital from tobacco manufacturing. After helping the family build a tobacco powerhouse, brother Brodie Duke founded the Pearl Cotton Mill in 1893. The same year Ben and James established the Erwin Cotton Manufacturing Company, which was named for the newly hired superintendent, William A. Erwin.[63]

From 1885 to 1900, the Piedmont counties of Alamance, Cabarrus, Gaston, Guilford, Randolph, and Mecklenburg witnessed the birth of seventy new mills. The Dukes and their team were priming the family business and region for the future of Carolina manufacturing.[64] Slowly, "through salesmanship . . . and most of all, the promise of financial backing from the Dukes, the textile industry started to glow with the power pouring out of the lazy, muddy Catawba River." The introduction of hydroelectric power gave mills a much less expensive, more flexible, yet reliable power source. In 1893, the South Carolina–based Columbia Mills Company became the first mill in the nation to run purely from electricity, drawing energy from the Congaree River. By 1905 the Southern Power Company, which later became Duke Power, was leading the way for Piedmont mills while extracting power from the Catawba River. Even mills in urban areas such as Charlotte were turning toward electricity for power.[65]

Ben and Buck were determined to electrify the entire region. The Dukes made huge investments in mills throughout the Piedmont to further stimulate the mill-based economy. In anticipation of these endeavors, the duo had already purchased a textile plant in Greenville, South Carolina, prior to the formation of the Southern Power Company.[66] An even more fitting business idea led Buck Duke to organize the Mill Power Supply Company "for the purpose of selling the mills the switches, motors, machinery and equipment necessary to convert to that new energy marvel, electricity."[67] Industrialization had finally arrived to the South, just in time for World War I.

The Duke Power Company, as the firm was known by the mid-1920s, supplied electricity to textile factories and individual residences. After the death of W. Gill Wylie in 1923 and James Duke in 1925, William S. Lee began installing steam plants to its existing electrical plants. At the outset of this project, the company owned and operated fifteen hydroelectric and six steam-power plants, which supplied all the light and power used by three hundred cotton mills and more than one hundred cities and towns in central North Carolina and western South Carolina. Although most companies suffered during the Depression years, the 1929 crash forced Duke Power to rely more heavily on its residential sales of electricity. American homes had recently purchased appliances that required electrical power. The company originally had no plans of supplying electricity to residences, nor had it originally planned to sell electrical appliances. But one could not exist without the other, and both quickly became domestic essentials.[68]

Duke Power regained its earlier rapid pace of expansion thanks to World War II–era industrial spikes. With the first generation of leaders deceased, William S. Lee, grandson of the company's cofounder, took over the helm. In the years after World War II, Duke Power spent $200 million revamping its system of plants and developing a number of highly efficient steam facilities. The company established plants throughout the Piedmont, naming many of the power stations after family members, company founders, and executives. The largest of these new facilities were the Dan River Station and Plant Lee, both put into service in 1952.[69]

For laborers like Willie Boyd, the Dan River Station in Draper, North Carolina, was a typical blue-collar industrial workplace with its fair share of machines that seemed to grind and hiss nonstop.[70] Like other industrial employers in the Jim Crow South, the Dan River plant openly discriminated against blacks in its hiring and placement procedures. Boyd and other black workers were relegated to the lowest jobs, positions that offered virtually no opportunity for advancement, whereas whites were most often in jobs that guaranteed higher starting wages, future promotions, and pay increases. The plant's facilities also reflected the region's culture of segregation. Dan River "provided separate lavatories, locker rooms and drinking facilities for Negro and white persons. . . . The locker rooms and drinking facilities were marked 'Colored' and 'White.'"[71]

The plant was organized into five operating departments: Labor, Coal Handling, Operations, Maintenance, and Laboratory and Test. The Laboratory and Test Department used technicians to analyze and test the water to determine its fitness for use in the boilers, and they conducted analyses of the coal samples to determine the coal's fitness for fueling the power station. The Maintenance Department maintained all of the plant's electrical and mechanical equipment. The Operations Department was responsible for the station's boilers, turbines, electrical substation, and the plant's power system. These three departments were located "inside" the plant, where white men "monitored the shiny dials and gauges."[72]

Labor and Coal Handling, however, were "outside" departments. The Coal Handling Department required workers to operate diesel and electrical equipment, bulldozers, conveyor belts, and crushers in order to unload, weigh, sample, crush, and transport coal received from Appalachian mines.[73] The least desirable positions were in the all-black Labor Department, where "the highest paying jobs paid less than the lowest paying jobs in the other four operating departments in which only whites were employed."[74] Laborers performed janitorial work throughout the entire plant. They mixed mortar, collected garbage, built miscellaneous structures, shoveled coal, and performed other assorted tasks.[75] Shoveling coal by hand, as the black men were forced to do when inbound coal trains screeched to a halt, was made all the more difficult by the elements on cold winter days, rainy spring mornings, and, especially, hot, humid summer afternoons.

Though the black men at Dan River were referred to and classified as semiskilled labor, or simply "laborers," by management, they called themselves "janitors." As Willie Boyd puts it rather frankly, "We called ourselves janitors, 'cause that's what we did, we cleaned up."[76] Blacks in the labor department not only performed the back-breaking task of shoveling coal but also cleaned the plant's restrooms and they cleaned large and very hazardous machinery.[77] The "janitors" were denied raises and could expect to do the same jobs for all of their working days at Duke Power.

An example of the Dan River Station's labor culture is best detailed by the following anecdote found in one of the few newspaper articles about the *Griggs* case:

> Trains would haul in huge loads of Appalachian coal, rolling along the tracks beside the slow, brown-green waters of the Dan. White workers would mechanically transfer the freight, adding it to the plant' coal pile

that rose higher than any building in this part of the Carolina uplands. . . . Sometimes dust and grime would clog the claws as they scooped up the lumpy fuel. The janitors were then summoned to help with the filthy work of unclogging the machinery. Only whites, however, were allowed the job title of "coal hauler" and only they earned the extra pay.[78]

Whites held the coal handling jobs in the outside department, but white "coal haulers" operated the machines that moved massive amounts of coal. This job was far more desirable than the work blacks performed in the Labor Department.[79] Keeping with the racial hierarchy required under Jim Crow, the "maximum wage ever earned by a black worker . . . is $1.645 per hour. This maximum is less than the minimum ($1.875) paid to any white in the plant. It is drastically less than the wages paid to whites . . . in the other departments where tops jobs pay $3.18 or more per hour."[80] Duke Power, though, was no different than other industrial employers across the state and region. In many respects, textile mills, the leading industrial employer in the state, led the way in informing such employment cultures. For example, well after the effective date of Title 7, "black male employees at Dan River Mills, one of the South's largest textile companies, earned only $1.89 an hour, while their white counterparts made $2.35 an hour."[81] Duke Power's Dan River Station was merely a reflection of a larger industrial culture germane to the state and region.

Despite such invidious discrimination, the Labor Department jobs offered livelihoods far superior to those Boyd and his co-workers had known as sharecroppers. However, as years passed, white men with no more education than they had were promoted through the ranks and became managers and supervisors. By the 1960s, of the eighty-six men at the Dan River plant, only fourteen were black. Of the seventy-two white men, only sixteen had high school diplomas and some of them had never received any formal education.[82] Yet some of these workers were promoted to positions that included comfortable offices with bathrooms nearby, the same bathrooms Boyd and the other janitors had to clean but were forbidden to use. The janitors of course had to use the "Colored" bathroom and a shower located outside, across four railroad tracks and behind the coal pile. As Boyd jokingly remembers, somewhat softening the blow from working for decades under Jim Crow, "Even if you had taken some Castor Oil you better not use the bathroom in the plant."[83]

Boyd however did not sit by idly while the white workers moved through the ranks. He would sometimes challenge management on why black workers were denied opportunities for promotion to the better jobs. Management replied over and over that he and the other janitors had no chance at promotion given the company's policies.[84] Yet Boyd and the janitors often did the same jobs as whites working in the other departments whenever they were called to fill in at various intervals. Boyd's earlier pleas, while legitimate given the unfair practices, received little attention. Racialized practices and attitudes were deeply entrenched in employment institutions because whites felt compelled to protect their economic mobility. So while Boyd and his peers were disturbed by Duke's practices, they had no way of channeling their discontent.

In an effort to upgrade the quality of its workforce, Duke Power began requiring a high school education in 1955 for new employees in all of the departments except Labor. According to Duke Power representatives, the "company realized that its business was becoming more complex and that it had employees who were unable to grasp situations, to read, to reason, and in general did not have an intelligence level high enough to enable them to progress in the Operations, Maintenance and Coal Handling Departments."[85] The high school diploma, or its equivalent, was also required for incumbent employees to transfer from the Labor Department or the watchman position[86] into the three higher-paying departments on the inside. This same requirement applied to employees in Coal Handling attempting to transfer to the inside departments.[87]

The supposed effect of the policy was that no new employees, except those in the Labor Department, would be hired without a high school education, and no current employees could transfer to a department other than Labor without a degree.[88] However, white employees hired to the "inside" Operations, Maintenance, and Laboratory and Test Departments, areas that required a degree, were essentially exempt from this policy. They were still promoted and continued to perform satisfactorily.[89] Laborers and coal handlers, as well as the watchman, needed high school diplomas for promotion, but watchmen and coal handlers earned decent wages already. With the institution of a policy that further hindered black workers' advancement opportunities, and it being a policy few whites were compelled to follow, Duke Power's purpose for the implementation of the high school requirement is worth questioning.

Duke Power may have indeed wanted to "upgrade the quality of [its] workforce" by instituting the high school requirement. However, white fears over integration in the wake of the *Brown v. Board of Education* decision probably prompted concern among managers about their ability to maintain a racially bifurcated work force. Heightened albeit ridiculous tensions over miscegenation and "race mixing" in the post-*Brown* South were probably followed by more practical fears of black economic mobility, especially in blue-collar work where African Americans could effectively compete if not hampered by race prejudice. For companies such as Duke Power, one way to maintain company-wide white supremacy would be to implement a policy that, though it appeared fair on its surface, had a detrimental affect on blacks because of the long history of separate and unequal education across the South. By installing such policies, hiring and promotion procedures would continue to shield the racial hierarchy to which whites had grown accustomed. As late as 1960, only 12 percent of black males in North Carolina had earned a high school diploma. Not outstanding but much better, 34 percent of white males were high school graduates.[90]

Civil rights legislation emanating from Washington in the mid-1960s resulted in further changes to Duke Power's personnel policies. After Title 7 took effect in the summer of 1965, Duke Power's headquarters handed down an edict desegregating its operating departments. Meanwhile, at the Dan River Station on July 2, 1965, the day after Title 7 became effective, the plant again altered its employment requirements. For initial employment into the Labor Department the only requirement was a satisfactory score on a very basic examination, the Revised Beta Test.[91] New employees in all other departments were required to have a high school diploma *and* achieve acceptable scores on two tests: the E. F. Wonderlic Personnel Test and the Bennett Mechanical Comprehension Test, Form AA.[92] All other promotion policies remained the same, with a high school diploma still required for departmental transfer, though no black workers had been promoted out of the Labor Department despite some having high school diplomas.[93]

Both the Bennett and Wonderlic tests were widely used in industry. Yet they were questionable tools for assessing an employee's ability to perform industrial labor. The Wonderlic Personnel Test is "a very general test with questions on arithmetic, vocabulary and verbal reasoning which appear to be highly related to formal education," and the Bennett test "questions understanding of basic physical principles such as leverage and centrifugal force by using illustrated questions." Both of these tests were developed before World War II. The copy of the Wonderlic used by most employers of the 1960s had a copyright date as early as 1939, and the Bennett a copyright of 1940.[94]

Although the reliability and validity of the tests became debatable in the court proceedings, their discriminatory impact on blacks was clear. Because the tests, the Wonderlic especially, measured concepts and skills learned through formal education, whites typically outperformed blacks. Results from a 1966 case involving the EEOC revealed that 58 percent of whites and only 6 percent of blacks performed adequately on the Wonderlic.[95] Whereas the exams offered some practicability for choosing a range of better equipped employees, their usefulness for shoveling coal was questionable.

Some white workers found the department transfer requirement of having a high school diploma too steep as only a small minority of them had earned high school diplomas by 1965. The fact that a few black workers hired into the Labor Department had earned high school diplomas and may have been open to transfers, especially after Title 7 became law, may have prompted some coal handlers to petition for an alternate means of promotion. In September 1965, Dan River management, at the behest of the coal handlers, instituted a policy allowing employees in the Labor and Coal Handling Departments and in the watchman classification to become eligible for transfer into the inside departments after attaining satisfactory scores on the Bennett and Wonderlic tests. Because white coal handlers could not meet the diploma requirement, the company bowed to their requests while maintaining barriers to the advancement of its back laborers.[96] Despite these changes in hiring and promotion, whites already in the inside operating departments were not required to have the high school diploma or take the exams to continue their upward moves.[97] And it would still be a year before a black worker would be promoted out of the Labor Department. That is, after Willie Boyd and his fellow frustrated black workers filed a complaint with the EEOC in the spring of 1966.

Willie Boyd had seen many changes since his birth in 1922. Yet even by the mid-1960s the segregation that had shaped so much of Boyd's life persisted, despite the upheavals of the civil rights movement.

While Boyd's activism was still in its infancy, he was privy to a burgeoning civil rights community and civil rights agenda that further shaped his awareness of how to effectively combat Jim Crow. The 1955 Montgomery Bus Boycott informed a wide range of local NAACP branches and members of what was possible through collective action. Similarly, Boyd and many other grassroots activists were deeply impacted by the early successes of NAACP legal campaigns attacking segregation in education and housing, as well as legal efforts to resecure voting rights. As these civil rights remonstrations matured nationally and statewide, Boyd's own organic intellectualism ripened alongside them. Ultimately, Boyd was especially shaped by his involvement in the local Reidsville NAACP chapter, which provided him an important connection to North Carolina's most potent civil rights organization. His frustration with Jim Crow and the segregated Labor Department energized his activism, and his involvement in the NAACP provided the complimentary training and support necessary to propel his radicalism.

III

SO WE JUST STARTED PUSHING
Civil Rights in North Carolina

Civil rights activism in North Carolina serves as a microcosm of national civil rights struggles. As opposition to state-mandated segregation swelled, African Americans, black North Carolinians being no exception, viewed the courts as the forum in which they were most likely to achieve some success. Denied access to the legislature due to pervasive disfranchisement, black activists sought refuge in the federal courts, where constitutional arguments might trump local political power. In North Carolina, protests targeting segregated public education shaped the legal activism of the state's civil rights community.

An investigation of the growth of civil rights activism across North Carolina underscores the sociopolitical landscape that shaped Willie Boyd's activism decades before he initiated a lawsuit against the Duke Power Company. As Boyd remembers with some defiance, "I didn't have nothing when I come here so if they run me away then I'll leave with nothing. . . . So we just started pushing." Inherent in Boyd's observation is his astute awareness of the potential for unfortunate repercussions for challenging the racial hierarchy of his day, as is his belief in the potential for successful legal activism and an awareness of how to use the law in his and his fellow workers' favor. Equally apparent in his words are his resilience and moral responsibility, both of which were main ingredients in the larger struggle for black equality.

When Willie Boyd initiated a lawsuit against Duke Power, charging that its hiring and promotion policies discriminated against African Americans, he did not react in a vacuum. His bold action grew out of a long tradition of socio-legal activism against Jim Crow by North Carolina blacks. Indeed, Boyd would become a constituent in the state's most powerful civil rights organization, the National Association for the Advancement of Colored People. His involvement in the NAACP afforded him knowledge of the shifting political and legal landscape, a sense that change was indeed possible, and some understanding of how change might be affected. By the 1960s, when Boyd filed the lawsuit, the NAACP-LDF had used the law to effect social change, and did so by working closely with client-activists and cooperating attorneys. Willie Boyd became a part of this tradition and in the process struck a severe blow against the institutional vestiges of Jim Crow in employment.

Boyd's decision to challenge one of America's most powerful corporations was rooted in three decades of civil rights activism in North Carolina. In fact, the modern civil rights era of protest in the state was ignited much the same way the national movement began—with legal challenges to segregation. In fact, Tar Heel activists provided the litmus test for legal challenges to segregated education. *Hocutt v. Wilson* (1933) laid the early foundation for legal remedies targeting segregated education and shaped the future of the LDF's cooperating attorney program.

Thomas Raymond Hocutt, and two young, local African American lawyers, Conrad Pearson and Cecil McCoy, initiated the first legal challenge to segregated graduate education.[1] The twenty-four-year-old Hocutt was headwaiter for the Washington Duke Hotel in Durham when he was encouraged to apply for admission to the University of North Carolina's school of pharmacy by the young lawyers. Pearson, McCoy, and newspaper editor Louis Austin, president of the Durham NAACP chapter, accompanied Hocutt to Chapel Hill on March 13, 1933, seeking to enroll him into the School of Pharmacy and acquire for Hocutt assignment to a dormitory room.[2]

The University of North Carolina (UNC) was the "pearl" of the state's public education system. Although it was considered one of the most progressive systems in the South, by 1933 not one black student had enrolled during its 144 years of existence.[3] This stands as yet another smudge on the veneer of progressive race relations touted by the state. Accordingly, Pearson insisted that North Carolina's image of being a very liberal state was largely undeserved and the university had "never been liberal, in reality." The University of North Carolina at Chapel Hill, Pearson suggested, used the judiciary to resist integration well into the civil rights era, and any concessions the university made toward integration it was forced to concede.[4]

Nonetheless, Hocutt's groundbreaking action proved central to the evolution of civil rights protests across the state and, indeed, the nation. *Hocutt,* some twenty-one years before *Brown,* "awakened people to the idea that state schools should be open to everybody" and that the separate but equal doctrine should be challenged in court.[5]

Raymond Hocutt attended the North Carolina College for Negroes in Durham, where he was a B student, but the school did not offer a program in pharmacy. The University of North Carolina immediately rejected Hocutt's application and advised him that black residents could pursue their studies at one of the five state institutions earmarked for their exclusive use, notwithstanding the fact that none of these schools offered a program in pharmacy. In response, the two young attorneys filed a mandamus action on behalf of Hocutt in Durham County Superior Court.[6] Conrad Pearson and Cecil McCoy were recent graduates of the newly revitalized Howard Law School and took to heart the tutelage they received there under mentor Dean Charles Hamilton Houston. After graduating from Howard Law, Pearson and McCoy "wasted little time in getting into the fight against racial injustice in a fashion urged by Houston."[7]

Though NAACP headquarters in New York was not directly responsible for bringing the case forward, it sent William Hastie, Charles Houston's cousin, to Durham to oversee the legal proceedings. Hastie was more experienced than Pearson and McCoy and was therefore better suited to guide the litigation.[8] Houston, general counsel of the NAACP by 1933, believed in his young protégé's abilities but did not want to risk losing the very first battle against segregated education. In this case, Houston could initiate the idea of attacking school segregation and the doctrine of "separate but equal" at the graduate and professional school level, where it seemed most vulnerable. North Carolina would either have to admit Hocutt or supply the state's black population with a school of pharmacy equal to that of Chapel Hill's program.[9] The state chose the latter course with much help from conservative black leadership, who saw this as an opportunity to expand black institutions.

This challenge by Hocutt, Pearson, McCoy, and Austin placed the foursome squarely at odds with North Carolina's most prestigious black leaders, who believed Hocutt was unqualified for this pioneering effort and promised to identify a more suitable student, though that better-qualified candidate never materialized.[10] Older, more prominent black leaders were certainly not opposed to racial progress, but they held personal and political agendas that conflicted with the efforts of the young legal activists. C. C. Spaulding, for example, was as "a very cautious man, a kind man, a gentle man [who] was really interested in advancing his race," yet by 1933 he had become president of North Carolina Mutual and Provident Association and had some vested interest in how such actions might upset the political and economic relationships between whites and blacks across the state, particularly in the Durham area. During a heated meeting Spaulding tried to discourage the Hocutt action for fear of retaliation from resistant whites. Lingering memories of the Wilmington race riot of 1898, which was spurred by white hostilities to economic and political progress in the black community, reinforced notions of what might occur if African Americans pushed too aggressively against the social hierarchy.[11] Tactically directed mob violence in the Wilmington riots, though it had taken place decades earlier, was still an effective deterrent to aggressive challenges to white supremacy in the minds of Spaulding and other blacks who had lived through the turn-of-the-century massacre.

The particulars of intraracial differences toward agitating for equality were further complicated by the public and private stances taken by leaders in the black community. For example, although he did not openly support the case, Spaulding did encourage Pearson and McCoy to seek the expertise of the NAACP headquarters. Spaulding also attempted to orchestrate a compromise with state officials hoping to obtain out-of-state tuition grants for black students seeking graduate and professional education. Attempts to desegregate educational institutions, he figured, might encourage state officials to provide such opportunities given the absence of programs at the state's black colleges.[12] During the trial, the state's attorney general offered Pearson a deal. If the lawyers and Hocutt dropped the suit, blacks would receive tuition waivers to schools outside the state. Immediately following the offer, Pearson consulted the crowd of African Americans who had gathered to hear the proceedings, forced to witness them in the "Negro" section, which was in the hallway of the courthouse. When Pearson asked the supporters if Hocutt and blacks across the state should they take the deal, the crowd emphatically retorted, "Don't give in, don't give in."[13] Community mobilization in support of legal challenges to white supremacy would prove critical for future success.

The most prominent black educator in the state directly undermined the entire case. James E. Shepard, founder and then president of North Carolina College for Negroes, generally opposed legal and political activism as a means of improving blacks' positions. Shepard was especially concerned that Hocutt's action could potentially subvert his plans of securing graduate programs for his college, chiefly a school of pharmacy.[14]

Shepard was a shrewd and cunning politician with contacts in the state legislature. He was such the "ultraconservative" that he even opposed organizing agricultural laborers into unions during the most suffocating period of economic subjugation faced by sharecroppers like Willie Boyd's family. Nevertheless, Shepard was so well connected and politically savvy that Pearson believed he could have been governor of the state if he had been a white man.[15] It is important, however, to highlight that this generation of leadership as identified by the likes of Shepard and Spaulding were holdovers from Washingtonian era of black politics. Leaders such as Spaulding and Shepard were genuinely committed to racial progress but approached sociopolitical activism with cautious, nonthreatening moves typical of their ideology and representative of the options available to them throughout their maturation into sociopolitical leadership during the onset of Jim Crow.

They clearly were more conservative than Pearson, McCoy, Austin, and the small but growing numbers of NAACP members who favored legal protests and socioeconomic boycotts designed to rid the South of segregation, but as predecessors to more radical stances, their politics were important displays of resistance deserving some appreciation. Less overt challenges to Jim Crow, avoiding challenges that might be deemed radical, staying committed to gradual advances for blacks, and maintaining a strong commitment to peaceful coalition earmark the leadership styles of the more conservative blacks of the period. Pearson harbored no resentment toward Shepard, who was a close friend of Pearson's uncle. Pearson even admitted that Shepard, a highly educated Republican and a former Reconstruction era elected official, "did more good than harm."[16]

So although Shepard opposed Raymond Hocutt's candidacy to Chapel Hill and the legal challenge Pearson orchestrated, his ultimate goal was the establishment of better educational facilities for those black Carolinians who might not ever be allowed into white institutions. Shepard's opposition appears to have been less a matter of acquiescence to southern racial politics and more a function of his ideology regarding the betterment of education for African Americans in the state and some selfishness to make sure his college would be the recipient of those resources. When the *Hocutt* proceedings concluded, Shepard's North Carolina College for Negroes received additional funding to build a law school and the state passed a statute allowing the college to build a school of pharmacy (which never materialized).[17]

For Hocutt, the rules for admission to the state's most prominent university stipulated that applicants who had attended other universities supply recommendations and transcripts from the last school attended. Shepard refused to recommend Hocutt or supply his transcripts to UNC.[18] Shepard also promised to respect the confidentiality of the lawyer's plans, but he leaked details of the lawsuit to a Greensboro newspaper. To counter the disclosure, Pearson and McCoy offered to tell a white editor in Durham their side of the case. The tactless editor, however, refused the invitation and countered with a trite, racially derogatory response. "As far as I'm concerned," he growled, "all of you can go back to Africa. It'd be better off for the country."[19]

Hocutt's high school grades were unimpressive, and despite having attended college, he appeared to be marginally literate when testifying. On the witness stand, he was asked to read his high school transcript but had trouble with pronunciation. The state lawyers used Hocutt's poor performance as proof that he was unqualified for the rigors of Chapel Hill and even suggested he was the pawn of agitators who had devised an elaborate scheme to promote intermarriage and social equality. Even the expertise of the skilled Hastie could not overcome Shepard's opposition and Hocutt's poor performance in court.[20]

The case conjured a racially charged atmosphere and quickly became a highly publicized event across North Carolina. State courts recessed to allow lawyers to attend and law school professors came to view the hearing, drawn by an interest in the case and Hastie's reputation.[21] Judge M. V. Barnhill sustained many of Hastie's objections but regularly tried to derail the brilliant attorney, which he failed to do. Later, the local press and Judge Barnhill praised the work of the NAACP co-counsel.[22]

But the obstacles faced by Hocutt and his lawyers had little impact on the court's actual decision. The only requirement for admittance into the school of pharmacy at Chapel Hill was a high school diploma, which Hocutt had earned. The primary obstacle was bringing the case to state court. This was a "cardinal mistake," Pearson recalls. State courts were of course "committed to the status quo, and Jesus Christ couldn't have won the case."[23] Most other challenges to segregated graduate and professional programs were thereafter tried in federal court, under the Fourteenth Amendment.[24]

With local black leadership failing to support the legal maneuver, NAACP headquarters declined appeal. In a letter to Walter White at the NAACP's headquarters, McCoy wrote, "Those upon whom we counted on for our staunchest moral support has been found leading the attack against us and a few loyal supporters."[25] Thurgood Marshall would later admit that this lack of community support by leaders such as Shepard presented a major obstacle to more extensive legal challenges to segregated education in the South.[26]

Despite the failed effort, *Hocutt* provided insight into managing desegregation cases and the importance of local control over litigation. The NAACP and its legal staff became fully aware that success in future legal battles would require the support of local attorneys, local leaders, and local residents. In Durham, Walter White capitalized on the *Hocutt* case by establishing several new branches of the NAACP with help from McCoy and Pearson.[27] Thurgood Marshall summarized the importance of *Hocutt* by suggesting that although the legal team from North Carolina lost the pioneering case, they ultimately laid the groundwork for *Brown v. Board of Education* more than twenty years later.[28] Challenges to segregated education were thereafter taken out of state courts and filed in federal courts, where federal law might outweigh state authority. Likewise, legal protests would be accompanied by supporting NAACP chapters and community leadership.

Hocutt also underlines how intergenerational conflicts over appropriate levels of radicalism effected civil rights campaigns. Shepard and more senior black leadership arguably saw Pearson and these new legal activists as young and somewhat misguided, but with hearts and minds aimed in the right direction. Similarly, civil rights lawyers, a brand new title for a brand new field with many young disciples of Charles Houston, including their accompanying plaintiffs, probably viewed their elders as people whose strategies were once effective but by the 1930s had become antiquated. Over the next several decades the impact of legal protests peaked with successes in federal court. Client-activists such as Willie Boyd stayed true to the tactics that had jumpstarted the movement. But despite decades of successful challenges and the removal of legally sanctioned segregation, younger generations of the 1960s would ultimately question the radicalism displayed by Boyd's contemporaries.

In fact, black youth jolted early contestations against Jim Crow, ultimately forcing the hand of more senior activists and the federal government. At the NAACP's twenty-fifth annual conference in St. Louis in 1935, youth members presented a resolution asking for the opportunity to "become a more integral part of and to have a more vital share in the functioning of the organization."[29] The NAACP Board of Directors later agreed with the energetic youth and moved to organize junior divisions and stimulate others already in existence.

The task of bringing the youth councils together under one umbrella ran adjacent to efforts to better coordinate intrastate organizations. Youth councils and college chapters worked in conjunction with the goals and objectives of the national office and state chapters to combat segregated education, employment discrimination, racial violence. and disfranchisement.

An impressive list of young adults who, in succeeding decades, would take charge of the civil rights agenda were members of the NAACP. In the 1930s and 1940s, young NAACP leaders included J. St. Clair Drake of Dillard University, Gloster B. Current of the Detroit youth branch, and Clarence Mitchell of North Carolina. An often overlooked component to the sustained achievements of the NAACP from the 1930s to the 1970s was the association's ability to mold and mentor up-and-coming leaders and keep them committed to the NAACP's program of political and legal activism. Over the next several decades, young and old would mesh efforts and build an effective coalition aimed at dismantling segregation. Rifts in the relationships developed over the level of militancy necessary for effectiveness, but ironically, these rifts proved vital for continued victories.

Central to this discussion of Willie Boyd and the *Griggs* case is the overwhelming significance of clients throughout the history of civil rights litigation. Raymond Hocutt's stance further emphasizes the role clients played in the materialization of a strong program of legal activism. Attorney Pearson admitted that Hocutt was the only plaintiff his legal team could find to stand firm in opposition to North Carolina's racial customs and codes. In fact, James Shepard and his colleagues "did all they could to get Hocutt to withdraw, but he wouldn't." Hocutt was resilient in his belief that segregated education should be challenged. And although he never attended graduate school, ultimately moving to New York and working as a subway supervisor, he remained proud of the role he played in laying the groundwork for the eradication of segregation in public education.[30]

Further, if Hocutt's claims were to have any legal standing he needed his lawyers to embrace a similar spirit. Pearson was, in his own words, "born to be a rebel." With tutelage from Houston and peers the likes of Thurgood Marshall and his local comrade Cecil McCoy, Pearson embodied the evolving course of legal activism in opposition to segregation. Before attending Howard Law School, Pearson graduated from Wilberforce College in Ohio, a school whose curriculum decried the ills of segregation. As a young adult he assisted his uncle in forming black lodges for the Royal Knights of King David. That experience exposed him to the gross inequities of southern society and the wide array of harsh realities predicated on the racial subordination of blacks. These realities were probably far more grotesque than those he experienced growing up in Durham, home of the Black Wall Street.[31]

After the loss in *Hocutt*, protests and rallies targeting lynching and legal battles aimed at securing the suffrage accelerated across the state. Although these protests may not have been direct outgrowths of the *Hocutt* affair, they do suggest that black North Carolinians were orchestrating interdependent protests well before the 1950s and 1960s. In October 1933, the Raleigh NAACP branch sponsored a rally "to voice their protest against the rising tide of white oppression, violence, and discrimination." Nearly three thousand blacks participated in the demonstration, with over a thousand from outside of Raleigh, from over three hundred towns. In 1935, black leadership in Durham created the Durham Committee of Negro Affairs and encouraged more black political participation. Further, as a result of a victory in *U.S. v. Cashion*, in which black North Carolinians challenged laws denying them suffrage, a registrar from Wilkesboro was fined and given three years probation for failing to register fourteen blacks voters. One year later several Northampton County blacks were permitted to vote after filing complaints with the U.S. Department of Justice. Moreover, North Carolina NAACP branches paralleled the work of chapters from neighboring states in opposition to lynching. Tar Heel chapters produced "Stop Lynching" buttons, sent telegrams to the governor, and sent petitions to the legislature in support of antilynching legislation. The chapters also raised money to support the Scottsboro case, in which nine young blacks were falsely accused of rape, received insufficient counsel, but were jailed nonetheless. "Hence," notes historian Raymond Gavins, "well before the early 1940s and by a trial and error method, determined NAACP constituencies had developed a working civil rights agenda."[32]

Pearson and McCoy were particularly encouraged by the support they earned from rank-and-file members of the black community and some liberal whites during *Hocutt*. The two remained diligent in their efforts to bring about social change through the law, staying true to their Howard training. And because of their resourcefulness and courage, more legal battles followed as blacks witnessed the growth and success of antisegregation cases. Over the next several decades, with Pearson serving as the state NAACP legal director, African Americans instigated a number of desegregation suits, including successful challenges to the law school and undergraduate program at the University of North Carolina.[33] Many of these petitions emerged directly from local NAACP members with Pearson, McCoy and future civil rights attorneys directing the cases. Subsequently, by the time Willie Boyd brought his case forward some thirty years later, the NAACP, LDF, and other client-activists had developed finely tuned relationships coupled with finely tuned strategies and tactics.

Five years after the *Hocutt* case, the University of North Carolina's policies of segregated education were tested yet again. This time, however, the applicant made upholding segregated education much tougher for the school and state. In 1938, Pauli Murray, a North Carolina native and graduate of prestigious Hunter College in New York City, applied for admission to the Chapel Hill graduate school. University President Frank Porter Graham, who had remained virtually silent during the *Hocutt* proceedings, "became personally involved in Murray's case, beseeching her to be patient and allow North Carolina the appropriate time to make segregated educational facilities across the state truly equal."[34]

In 1936, the LDF won a key victory when the University of Maryland was ordered to admit black applicant Donald Murray to its law school.[35] Two years later the NAACP legal staff won an even more significant decision in *Missouri ex rel. Gaines v. Canada*, in which the Supreme Court ruled that states must honor the "separate but equal" doctrine in full or admit qualified black applicants.[36] The Court found that the promise of creating future schools or even the policy of providing out-of-state subsidies for blacks when the state failed to provide graduate and professional educational facilities violated the equal protection rights of African Americans.[37] Southern institutions were feeling the pressures of defending the "separate but equal" doctrine before the Fourteenth Amendment. The lack of graduate and professional programs in North Carolina available for African Americans made the state vulnerable.

Pauli Murray was born in Baltimore, Maryland, and raised in Durham, where as a youth she was a classmate of Raymond Hocutt at Hillside High School and worked a paper route for Louis Austin's *Carolina Times*. Murray was therefore exposed to radical ideas in opposition to white supremacy at an early age. In fact, during Murray's entire UNC contest, Austin was her "greatest supporter." Because of her upbringing, experiences with segregation, and evolution of her radical spirit in adulthood, Murray opposed the second-class treatment blacks received. Murray was astutely aware that "it was not the fact of separation that hurt so much; it was, as everybody knew, the fact that the overriding purpose of segregation was to humiliate and degrade colored people."[38]

Murray ultimately led an amazing legal career, championing causes ranging from antilabor exploitation to challenges to racial and gender oppression.

When Murray applied for graduate study in sociology, her academic qualifications were beyond reproach, virtually impeccable. She also had become a "young Socialist radical" and through correspondence had established a long-distance friendship with first lady Eleanor Roosevelt. Despite her "café au lait" complexion and "Caucasian features" she was still too dark for "the finely calibrated Southern color detector," making her ineligible for admission under North Carolina's Jim Crow laws. Her application was "quickly and routinely rejected" until, with much valor, she appealed directly to President Graham. Murray was keenly aware of the recent NAACP victory in *Gaines*,[39] and she knew that southern institutions were obligated to meet the equal protection standards of the Fourteenth Amendment. Despite an opinion poll in which graduate students favored Murray's acceptance by two to one, North Carolina state law mandated segregated educational facilities and President Graham's final decision was in line with southern law and custom. Graham wrote to Murray that now was not the appropriate time for a "popular referendum" on race segregation. He promised to begin searching for the "next possible solution" but in the meantime asked that Murray remain patient.[40]

Even Murray's influential and progressive pen pal Eleanor Roosevelt was not keen on forcing desegregation. The first lady cautioned Murray in one letter, stating, "The South is changing, but don't press too hard."[41] Pauli Murray's case reached far beyond basic questions of constitutional rights and privileges for blacks. According to a white journalist writing for the *Crisis* in April 1939, "When Miss Murray submitted her application to the graduate school she was not merely submitting it to President Graham and a few university officials. In reality she was submitting it to the South and especially to the State of North Carolina."[42]

Murray decided not to pursue litigation and ultimately graduated from Howard Law School in 1944, president of her class (of which she was the only woman). It would still be another twelve years before the University of North Carolina would admit a black student. But in 1939, the North Carolina College for Negroes and the North Carolina Agricultural and Technical College in Greensboro received their first graduate and professional programs. The limits of North Carolina's racial "civility" were made clear as Governor Clyde Hoey remarked in 1939, "North Carolina does not believe in social equality between the races, and will not tolerate mixed schools for the races, but we do believe in equality of opportunity in their respective fields."[43] Nevertheless, developments during the 1930s made it clear that blacks had stepped up the legal assault against Jim Crow.

Other important remonstrations occurred in more conservative circles that also shaped civil rights ideology and practice in North Carolina and across the South. On October 20, 1942, fifty-nine southern black leaders convened in Durham for the Southern Conference on Race Relations. Two months later the brilliant collective, led by Charles S. Johnson of Fisk University, issued a document titled "A Basis for Interracial Cooperation and Development in the South: A Statement by Southern Negroes," also known as the Durham Manifesto.[44]

The Southern Conference on Race Relations convened at James E. Shepard's North Carolina College for Negroes and included members of the black economic and intellectual elite. Charles S. Johnson, Benjamin Mays, Rufus Clement, C. C. Spaulding, and Gordon B. Hancock, among others, were in attendance.[45] Black leaders from the North and South viewed this gathering as excessively conservative given its membership. Editor Louis Austin questioned the conference's credibility because the meeting did not include Walter White of the NAACP or A. Phillip Randolph of the Brotherhood of the Sleeping Car Porters. In the *Carolina Times* he editorialized, "Negro masses . . . are suspicious of all Negroes who are so smart they never ruffle the feathers of the oppressor."[46] W. E. B. Du Bois was the only bona fide radical invited to the gathering. Du Bois, however, declined the invitation, further damaging the credibility of the conference and its attendees as a cadre seriously committed to racial progress.[47]

But the Durham Manifesto was a "brave departure" from the conservative politics typical of its sponsors. Even Louis Austin was forced to concede the declaration did not have the "Uncle Tom flavor" he expected. However, Austin misjudged the potential impact of the statement when he argued that it would do neither harm nor good. The manifesto ultimately provided much of the philosophical foundation upon which future protests were shaped across the South. It avowed, "We are fundamentally opposed to the principle and practice of compulsory segregation in our American society, whether of races or classes or creeds." The manifesto's list of demands also included a call for the "abolition of the white primary," federal antilynching legislation, and increases in the overall skill development of black workers.[48]

The Durham Manifesto emphasized the call for a victory at home over racial fascism, as trumpeted through the Double V Campaign. The manuscript acknowledged that World War II had generated elevated racial tensions, aggressions, and fears at home, stemming from rising claims for black equality, which were ignited by the international conflict to secure democracy. The manifesto reemphasized questions over the continued existence of racial segregation and discrimination and the denial of basic human rights and democratic freedoms within the United States as the nation fought a war against fascism abroad.[49]

Prior to the Durham conference, complimenting such philosophical arguments in opposition to segregation, Ella J. Baker persuaded North Carolina NAACP branch presidents Louis Austin of Durham, T. V. Mangum of Statesville, and Kelly M. Alexander of Charlotte to organize state chapters to develop an orchestrated plan for combating Jim Crow. On September 24, 1943, state branch leaders caucused in Charlotte at Friendship Missionary Baptist Church and created the North Carolina State Conference of NAACP Branches. Baker stood as the unofficial architect for the origin of the organization and with Charlotte funeral director Kelly M. Alexander presiding, the conference elected T. V. Mangum president and Alexander vice president.[50]

The North Carolina state NAACP sought to develop a strong statewide body by stabilizing existing branches and organizing new ones. The group created North Carolina's most important and vocal instrument of protest as chapters worked interdependently in challenging discrimination by city, county, and state officials. Likewise, they added vision to a burgeoning civil rights platform. NAACP headquarters was so thoroughly impressed with the work of North Carolina activists that President Roy Wilkins returned from a wartime visit to North Carolina convinced that "Negroes are organizing all over the state to secure their rights. They are not frightened."[51] The structured protests orchestrated by the state executive staff served as the foundation for the important efforts of local branches throughout the civil rights era.

Thus, as early as the 1930s and definitely by 1943, activists in North Carolina were directly tied to the battle against racial segregation and discrimination and were encouraged to take dynamic roles in the push for equality. With direction from NAACP headquarters and the maturation of a powerful state organization leading the way, grassroots activists in North Carolina could rely on a network of strategists and fellow organizers for support and development of tactics. The loose organizational structure of the NAACP emphasized local resistance and legal activism. And because local concerns varied to some degree, grassroots organizers used their own ingenuity and sheer guts to advance their community's specific agenda.

Asheville's Leila Michael, state organizer of branches, further synchronized the work of local chapters, aiding the spike in NAACP militancy and membership. By 1945 the state could brag of having fifty affiliates and a total membership of 9,799. Rural areas accounted for more than half of the chapters and 42 percent of the membership. Anson County in the lower Piedmont, infamous for its lynching and racist vigilantism, posted a chapter with 51 members. Urban membership, though, led the way, with the oldest chapters reporting the highest numbers. Chapters in Raleigh (595 members), Greensboro (575 members), Charlotte (677 members), and Winston-Salem (1,088) were the backbone of the state's association. Though the possibility of reprisals was ever present, particularly in rural areas, African Americans remained unshaken, especially as now many felt a sense of belonging to an organization and program that could boast of key victories in the battle against white supremacy. The decade immediately following World War II saw major boosts in the number of branches and the scope of their location. By the 1950s, rural membership and the percentage of rural chapter affiliates surpassed their urban counterparts.[52]

Mangum led the state NAACP with "cool headedness and vision" until 1948, when he was succeeded by Kelly M. Alexander, who had already become the organization's chief spokesmen. "More outgoing than Mangum," notes Raymond Gavins, "he used his economic independence as a funeral director and his ideals on racial service to develop an outspoken style of leadership."[53] Alexander led the state chapters for the next thirty-six years, through the tumultuous 1950s and 1960s. Alongside his brother Fred, the Kelly Alexander worked tirelessly for the rights of blacks. The Alexanders were openly critical of black leaders and their complacency in agitating for civil rights. Kelly, nicknamed "Big Daddy" by Boyd and other constituents, led under the belief that until the black community used the courts to challenge white political power, little progress would occur. The North Carolina state chapter under Alexander became one of the most aggressive in the South. During the 1950s it filed more school desegregation lawsuits than any other state chapter.[54] Ultimately, however, this leadership style and approach toward black equality would be called into question by up-and-coming radicals.

By the 1950s civil rights protests had primed the pump for the ultimate showdown against Jim Crow. NAACP legal challenges to segregated education infused a strong spirit of protest within the black community nationwide. And more important, African Americans began to sense that Jim Crow was beatable. Thurgood Marshall and the LDF had won significant victories in cases involving graduate and professional schools, as well as victories in voting, residential segregation, and teacher salaries. The emergence of other organizations, namely, the Congress of Racial Equality (CORE), along with swelling numbers of NAACP local chapters, helped advance social agitation to complement legal efforts.

At the 1949 state NAACP meeting, Kelly Alexander called for a "county by county campaign" to fight segregated education. "This fight," Alexander explained, "should include court action on the elementary, secondary and university level. The goal is an integrated school system."[55] In North Carolina, the desegregation of graduate and professional schools occurred in 1951, when Edward O. Diggs gained admittance into the University of North Carolina School of Medicine and Floyd B. McKissick (along with three other African American males) was admitted into the university's law school. Only two years prior, black pianist Hazel Scott had refused to play for an audience on the Chapel Hill campus because black people were confined to the balcony. The ever-radical Louis Austin, who also served as the NAACP chairman of public relations, wrote a stinging commentary attacking UNC. He questioned if the university was a "bulwark of Democracy in our Southland" or if the campus was merely a "reactionary pig pen in which white youths will be taught to wallow in all the murk, ire and filth of segregation and race hatred." He demanded an end to UNC's "moronic practices" and challenged the university to instead "adopt a policy of not inviting Negroes any longer." A related editorial witnessed Austin demanding the school to admit black students because their presence would be welcomed by white students. In closing, Austin took one more parting shot at "the little men at U.N.C." who, he deemed, were "slaves of a dying past."[56]

A dying past it was, but not one that would pass quietly. The first black undergraduates to UNC did not arrive until 1955, one year after the *Brown* decision. John L. Brandon, Ralph Frazier, and Leroy Frazier (Ralph's brother) were also graduates of Durham's Hillside High School, the same school Raymond Hocutt and Pauli Murray had attended, and they too were initially denied admission to the University of North Carolina at Chapel Hill. Pearson and McCoy persuaded a three-judge federal tribunal to force the school to process their applications without regard to race. The legal team out of Durham finally won the victory it had started in 1933. Desegregation had made its way to North Carolina, but not before the federal courts forced compliance. The NAACP, however, sensed the opportunities that lay ahead to further dismantle the legal underpinnings of segregation. The 1950s witnessed lawsuits challenging unequal support for black schools in the towns of Wilson, High Point, Old Fort, and Lumberton and in the counties of New Hanover, Pamlico, Washington, and Gaston Counties.[57]

The state, however, embarked on its own efforts to desegregate secondary and primary education. North Carolina had to live up to its self-proclaimed progressivism and amicable race relations, especially while much of the South erupted violently in resistance to desegregation. In 1951 a North Carolina court found that black children had been discriminated against on the basis of race in educational facilities. White schools were bigger, less crowded, had more supervision, better laboratories and equipment, better recreational facilities, nicer buildings, and lighter teaching loads. Also in 1951, Fort Bragg military base outside Fayetteville, North Carolina, quietly desegregated its elementary school with little fanfare.[58]

Despite these minor advances, North Carolina continued to miss the mark of its self-proclaimed mantra. The Supreme Court interpretation of school desegregation in the second *Brown* decision in 1955 did little to move North Carolina forward in the lower schools. Willie Boyd admitted that after 1954 schools were slow to desegregate in Reidsville, and when new schools for blacks were built in the wake of *Brown*, the allocation of resources remained grossly lopsided. As Boyd noted, "Yeah, we had nice new buildings, but there were barely any books in there."[59]

In August 1954, Governor William Umstead appointed a nineteen-person committee that included three African Americans to study potential desegregation plans. Most white politicians across the state were opposed to desegregation, staying true to their constituent's demands, and were shocked by the *Brown* decision earlier that year. The committee, chaired by Speaker of the House Thomas J. Pearsall, finished its work on December 30, 1954. In the aftermath of *Brown*, southern states closed or altered their school systems to avoid desegregation. Pearsall's primary objective, therefore, was to preserve public schools and thus preserve North Carolina's image. Umstead resisted pressure from segregationists who promised to defy the Supreme Court's ruling. He carefully ignored petitions and avoided any "racial demagoguery that could harm the state" and its reputation.[60]

Because Umstead died on November 7, 1954, the Governor's Special Advisory Committee submitted its final report to his successor, Governor Luther Hodges. The committee concluded that race mixing in public schools was unachievable and should be avoided because it "would alienate public support of the schools to such an extent that they could not be operated successfully."[61]

The report called for legislation allowing local school boards full control over enrollment and assignment of children in schools and on buses. Earlier in the fall of 1954, North Carolina's attorney general had submitted a brief to the Supreme Court addressing remedy in the *Brown* case. That brief also argued that desegregation was not possible across the state.[62]

The three black members of the Pearsall committee, as the group was known, were prominent figures. Ferdinand Douglas Bluford was president of North Carolina A&T College, J. W. Seabrook was president of Fayetteville State Teacher's College, and Hazel Parker was a home agent in Edgecombe County. But the trio selected for such an important endeavor raised concerns within the black community. All three were state employees, and two of the three benefited from segregated education as leaders of black colleges. Kelly Alexander and the NAACP issued a statement claiming the three did not represent the majority opinion of blacks across the state and the trio had not been allowed to express their own opinions. Complicating matters in the black community, not all African Americans were in favor of school desegregation. Some were concerned over their children's safety and the potential loss of employment associated with school closings and mergers of school staffs to meet desegregation orders.[63]

The state assembly enacted legislation the following March that vested local school boards with authority over pupil assignment, but "the statute expressly directed local school boards not to consider race as an assignment criteria." Though this legislation appeared racially neutral, all school boards continued assigning pupils based on their race well into the 1960s.[64]

One year later the North Carolina General Assembly created another Pearsall committee, with the same chairperson but this time minus any African American members. Governor Hodges believed that groups such as the NAACP exerted too much pressure on African Americans to push for immediate desegregation. This new committee looked to further reduce threats of desegregation, concluding its work with a clear desire to maintain segregated schools. The committee argued for a new school system built not upon a foundation of legally imposed racial segregation but according to natural racial preferences and administrative determinations based on the children's welfare. The committee's report declared that education in North Carolina was built on the foundation of segregated education and the Supreme Court had destroyed the system that best served southern realities and customs.[65]

Governor Hodges publicly supported the new Pearsall plan, and the bill was adopted as a constitutional amendment in July 1956 by a four-to-one margin in a statewide referendum.[66] But the bill did not mandate school closings, urge outright defiance of the *Brown* decision, or attack the NAACP, as other southern legislatures had after the *Brown* ruling. In fact, no school ever closed in North Carolina. If a citizen's group petitioned for a school closing after token integration in a given district, the local school board simply denied the request. As legal scholar Davidson Douglas argues, "Desegregation would inevitably come to North Carolina, but the Pearsall Plan gave the state's political leaders an opportunity to appease segregationist sentiment without undermining public education. This was moderation, North Carolina style."[67]

While the "safety valve" approach to managing desegregation orders in the wake of *Brown* may have been necessary according to the state's political leadership, ingrained customs and attitudes throughout North Carolina must not go understated. For example, Greensboro, argued by some to be the South's most progressive city failed to comply with federal desegregation orders until 1971. This striking paradox in a state that bragged of harmonious race relations is accentuated by the fact that the case which ultimately led to court-ordered busing would arise out of nearby Charlotte.[68] In fact, "it took more than three decades of court-ordered desegregation to deinstitutionalize the racial policies that had been in effect in the state since before the *Brown* decision in 1954."[69]

Brown changed the legal environment in major ways, but it did little to affect attitudes among southern whites. The decision sparked a massive backlash and increased racial hostilities toward African Americans. The second *Brown* decision did little to help matters. By remanding lawsuits to the courts from which they originated and ordering them to desegregate "with all deliberate speed," the Supreme Court, in effect, issued what became an open invitation to delay even token integration.

The backlash resonated from Congress down to the common white southerner, who probably had little interest in education but was enraged at the thought of Negroes attending school with white children, especially black boys going to school with white girls. On March 12, 1956, all but three southern congressmen signed what became known as the Southern Manifesto, a segregationist denunciation of *Brown*. Nineteen southern senators and eighty-two members of the House of Representatives spoke with force as they offered their perspective on the Court's rulings. The southern bloc declared, "We regard the decision of the Supreme Court in the school cases as a clear abuse of judicial power. . . . It climaxes a trend in the Federal judiciary undertaking to legislate, in derogation of the authority of Congress, and to encroach upon the reserved rights of the States and the people." The congressmen offered direct support to forces in southern society that refused to abide by the Supreme Court ruling. In concluding their statement, they wrote, "We pledge ourselves to use all lawful means to bring about a reversal of this decision which is contrary to the Constitution and to prevent the use of force in its implementation."[70] Southern political leadership gave a blanket endorsement for their constituents to ignore and outmaneuver the Supreme Court ruling, even if that meant to the physical detriment of African Americans daring to expand the tightly calibrated prism of white hegemony.

The months immediately following the *Brown* decision witnessed a resurgence of Ku Klux Klan activity, which included an upsurge in racial violence and cross burnings. In 1955 whites in Mississippi organized the Citizen's Council to maintain racial separation. Other southern states soon followed Mississippi's lead. That same year, three prominent black leaders were murdered in Mississippi, including Lemar Smith, who was "shot to death in broad daylight on the grounds of Pike County Courthouse." In 1956, mobs of white students prevented black students from enrolling in the University of Alabama. The same tactics were repeated at public schools in Texas and Tennessee. One of the most horrendous attacks on blacks, Emmit Till not withstanding, occurred when African Americans attempted desegregation efforts in Birmingham, Alabama, in 1957. There, a "black man was savagely beaten and castrated by a group of whites who told him, 'This is what will happen if Negroes try to integrate the schools.'"[71] The most widely known conflict occurred in Little Rock, Arkansas, in 1957, when nine students desegregated Central High School only after President Eisenhower was forced to send in the National Guard to counter Governor Orval Faubus's efforts to block desegregation.

The South was in an uproar, but the standoff in Arkansas was a clear statement that, despite all the violent reprisals, African Americans would not stray from the course and the federal government might intercede on behalf of desegregation, albeit at a snail's pace and with lingering deference to states' rights. With *Brown* and legal victories against segregation in other public facilities, including parks, buses, golf courses, and beaches, federal law nonetheless mandated dismantling Jim Crow.[72] Blacks knew this and stepped up their efforts, ushering in the era of nonviolent direct-action protests.

When Rosa Parks defiantly remained in her seat, yet again, on the segregated municipal bus in Montgomery in 1955, the civil rights era of nonviolent protest found its ideological "queen mother." And one reality became distinctly clear: If blacks rallied protests during this moment in America's history, federal courts would support their claims, albeit slowly. However, African American youths were one element of the civil rights community uninterested in waiting for the courts to force whites to honor black rights.

Ezell Blair Jr. roomed with the studious physics major Joseph McNeil, and David Richmond and Franklin McCain shared a room at North Carolina A&T in Greensboro, only a thirty-minute drive from Reidsville. As freshmen in 1959–60 they "ate together, studied together and spent long evenings in their dorms resolving the world's problems, armed only with unlimited idealism and several cans of cold beer. . . . Inevitably, though, their conversations returned to a single, gnawing question: when would blacks do something about the racial barriers that mocked their ambition and self-esteem." Then, on February 1, 1960, the four young students entered the Woolworth store in downtown Greensboro and sat down, setting in motion the most effective social confrontation against segregation to date when they were supported by successive waves of protestors. The sit-ins had begun, and they spread like wildfires across the South. Nashville, Atlanta, and other cities hosting black colleges witnessed the insurgence of young black and white protestors.[73]

In little over a month, Shaw University in Raleigh was the meeting place of hundreds of young radicals ready to share their protest experiences and coordinate protest strategies. Ella Baker, again serving as a behind-the-scenes architect, returned to her alma mater to help provide organization for the energetic youth. Ever the radical, Baker had grown displeased with the cautious approach favored by her older, established male activists. As executive director of the Southern Christian Leadership Conference (SCLC), Baker knew the movement needed a healthy dose of youthful radicalism. At Shaw University in April 1960, the students created the Temporary Student Non-Violent Coordinating Committee. Only one month later they reconvened without their elders and created the Student Non-Violent Coordinating Committee (SNCC). Young and old, despite differences in approaches, would have to work together to tackle Jim Crow. The marriage, though not always blissful, was central to ending segregation. Radical if not reckless, young adults initiated direct, confrontational protests while many of their elders continued less combative approaches such as marches, boycotts and litigation.[74]

Chapel Hill and Durham witnessed student-led protests that included students from the historically black University of North Carolina Central as well as students from Duke University and UNC–Chapel Hill. In Rock Hill, South

Carolina, student protests extended the sit-in movement to an even higher ideological level as "Jail No Bail" practices left the protestors locked up in overcrowded cells. This sort of transformative protest brought southern culture face to face with yet another unyielding, pious method of confronting the evils of Jim Crow. Even Tuskegee Institute, known for its reputation of nonconfrontational politics, caught the mood.[75]

But not all protests in North Carolina were handled through the courts or through nonviolent, direct action. In Monroe, North Carolina, black people were forced to defend themselves with guns to ward off Ku Klux Klan attacks. By 1957 Monroe had a population of about eleven thousand, one-third of them African American. The town, a county seat, rests in Union County, fourteen miles north of the South Carolina border and twenty-five miles southeast of Charlotte. The black community had an NAACP chapter but increased racial hostility after the *Brown* decision nearly forced the chapter out of existence. Robert Williams returned to Monroe in 1956 after completing his duties in the Marine Corps, where the discrimination he experienced fueled his desire to come back home, join the local NAACP chapter, and fight against segregation.[76]

Williams and the only black doctor in town, Albert E. Perry, rejuvenated the Monroe NAACP chapter. But as the chapter began asserting African Americans' rights to basic public services, the Klan's rolls increased, encouraged in large part by a resurgence campaign led by James "Catfish" Cole. The chapter successfully desegregated the town's library in 1957 but met resistance over the local swimming pool. Blacks could not use the public pool, and the town refused to provide a separate "Colored" pool. In the meantime, the Klan claimed three thousand signatures after their first week of advertising in the local papers. Williams, as president of the Monroe NAACP chapter, contacted Governor Luther Hodges as well as NAACP national headquarters regarding the situation in Monroe but received no assistance. He even contacted President Eisenhower and the Department of Justice, but neither responded.[77]

In Monroe, black women had been raped, beaten, and attacked, and young boys under the age of ten had been arrested for assault under circumstances that amounted to routine childlike play with white children.[78] Court proceedings were overtly racist, and Monroe blacks were regularly denied basic rights under law. Once violence became customary, with Klansmen riding through the black community firing willfully and randomly, Williams and his fellow Monroe citizens were left with no choice but to defend themselves. They engaged in shootouts with the Klan and formed all-night patrols of twenty men organized by the former marine Williams. Roy Wilkins and the NAACP headquarters disapproved of the chapter's tactics, seemingly unaware of the day-to-day perils Monroe blacks faced. And yet Wilkins certainly understood the potentially grave circumstances African Americans faced in these and other isolated communities. Monroe blacks were wedged in a remote abyss of staunch, violent racism. And by defending themselves, they ultimately changed their circumstances and renegotiated power relationships in Monroe. When Monroe activists formed sit-ins in the 1960s, they were not attacked as were other protestors. Monroe blacks were indeed "Negroes with Guns," representing a rare departure from the norm in the history of the southern civil rights era. As Robert Williams explained to his frustrated community after a pregnant black woman was beaten and raped and even white eyewitness testimony failed to convict the perpetrator,

> I told them in a civilized society the law is a deterrent against the strong who would take advantage of the weak, but the South is not a civilized society; the South is a social jungle, so in cases like that we had to revert to the law of the jungle; that it had become necessary for us to create our own deterrent. And I said in the future we would defend our women and our children, our homes and ourselves with arms. That we would meet violence with violence.[79]

This was the North Carolina in which Willie Boyd came of age. It was in this sociolegal battleground that he and his fellow workers learned to maneuver. It was in this cauldron of mounting resistance that Boyd learned to embrace the moral responsibility of fighting racism and learned how to wage that battle effectively. As the civil rights movement leapt into full swing, Willie was taking part through his local NAACP chapter in Reidsville. And as a result of the burgeoning sense of equality he shared with fellow NAACP activists, Boyd was becoming increasingly impatient with the discrimination he faced at Duke Power.

In the early 1960s the youth chapter of the Reidsville NAACP ranked Willie Boyd and co-worker Clarence Tucker as two of Reidsville's most influential Negro leaders. This was a rather impressive honor, as by then the sit-in movement was encouraging many youngsters to regard their elders as having "sold out" to the white establishment. This is also an indication that Boyd and some of his peers displayed a level of militancy that impressed the youth council.[80]

Though overshadowed in light of national protests that drew media and therefore national attention, Boyd and other grassroots activists led indigenous civil rights struggles in their very own communities as part of the widespread yet interdependent effort to topple segregation. Boyd recalls that many of the chapters in North Carolina and throughout what was then the Fifth Region— which included North Carolina, South Carolina, Mississippi, Florida, Georgia, and Tennessee—stayed in regular communication through state, regional, and national meetings and correspondence. These chapters maintained a clear awareness of the struggles of their peer branches across the Southeast and produced distinct yet mutually dependent strategies that would result into some successes. Occasional lectures by state president Kelly Alexander and the rare visit by national president Roy Wilkins to Reidsville chapter functions added to the connectedness of Boyd's branch.[81] NAACP headquarters meanwhile provided much-needed information, tactical advice, and select resources that further glued state chapters to the national office. Local communities were tied to the national movement through numerous channels while pressing forward with their own specific operations.

In Reidsville, Boyd and his fellow NAACP colleagues initiated an impressive array of protests targeting the municipal government and surrounding political institutions. Reverend A. D. Owens organized the Reidsville Chapter in 1947, three years after the establishment of the North Carolina State Committee. During the 1950s, Reverend Owens initiated a school desegregation campaign in Reidsville with the help of a local family, the Browns, as plaintiffs (they had been run out of town for agitating for school equality). Owens and the Reidsville branch of the NAACP also worked to secure positions for African Americans on the local police force, seeking to install blacks in power-wielding positions.[82] During these earlier years, Boyd was participating, watching, and learning. Thus he witnessed firsthand the initial wave of intense civil rights protests and activism in his community.

By the early 1960s, Boyd and his fellow Rockingham County members had "caught the mood," leading sit-ins against local establishments still clinging to Jim Crow. Ultimately, four groups led the charge out of Reidsville: the Reidsville NAACP, the NAACP's youth group, the Rockingham County Improvement League, and the Youth and Young Adult Association. After the effective date of the Civil Rights Act of 1964, nearly five years after the sit-ins started, Boyd and his cohort led statutorily supported protests demanding black representation in the Rockingham County Tax Office, the Clerk of Courts Office, the Register of Deeds, the Auditor's Office, and the Sheriff's Department—which Willie was asked to join. Boyd and his fellow protestors were fed up with the segregation and discrimination that had shaped so much of their lives, and they were fully aware of the legislative authority from Congress outlawing such practices. By challenging segregation within governmental units, they called for the redistribution of economic and political power in local communities across the South. Such stances were not dissimilar from Stokely Carmichael's claim that "black power will mean that if a Negro is elected sheriff, he can end police brutality. If a black man is elected tax assessor, he can collect and channel funds for the building of better road and schools serving black people—thus advancing the move from political power into the economic arena."[83]

Although much of the civil rights agenda focused largely on segregated education in previous decades, and as boycotts, marches, and sit-ins challenged segregated public spaces, concerns over discriminatory employment practices steadily absorbed more attention as the civil rights community recognized that equality meant little without substantial progress on the job. Similarly, demands for economic equality marked an evolution in the civil rights agenda, an evolution of which grassroots activists were acutely aware as many of them faced glaring inequities at work. Helping to shape this evolution in North Carolina, the state NAACP had worked with the CIO to organize tobacco workers immediately after World War II in Winston-Salem, not far from Boyd's hometown.[84]

Boyd was not alone in his efforts to combat Jim Crow in Reidsville and the surrounding areas. Both Boyd and his NAACP comrade James Arthur (Jay) Griggs were very dynamic in Reidsville due to their affiliation and roles in the Reidsville NAACP chapter. Griggs followed Reverend Owens as president of the Reidsville branch of the NAACP, presiding from 1958 to 1972, after which Boyd succeeded him and led the chapter for another ten years. Boyd's involvement in the struggle for equal opportunity would ultimately span nearly four decades, from the 1950s well into the 1990s.

Combating segregation through local NAACP chapters culminated in well-organized movements. However, it is important to note that the impetus for specific stances often did not necessarily stem directly from the institutionalized structures within the NAACP, though they certainly informed such decisions. The moments upon which African Americans decided to advance their claims against Jim Crow were especially personal and sometimes random. Awareness of a powerful organization backing such claims, along with the knowledge of potential success and the legal justification supporting these claims, certainly added to the growing awareness of injustice compelling many African Americans to action.

In this respect, Willie Boyd and the evolution of *Griggs v. Duke Power* is no more exceptional than the legal claims advanced by his fellow NAACP comrades across the South, who also took their fights to the courtroom during the post-*Brown* era, particularly after the passage of the civil rights acts. In fact, Jay Griggs had listened to Boyd complain again and again about the discrimination he and his co-workers faced at Duke Power. Griggs would impatiently urge his friend to file a complaint against his employer, but Boyd hesitated and continued to complain.

The dedication James Arthur Griggs gave his community earned him praise from a local black newspaper, the *Reidsville Review*, which noted that there had been no other servant in Rockingham County who had worked and sacrificed as much of his time for the advancement of black people through legal and peaceful means.[85] While Jay Griggs (as Boyd and others called him) never graduated from high school, Boyd remembers, "nobody knew as much about civil rights laws as him. . . . When he got up to talk, people listened because they knew he knew what he was talking about."[86]

At some point during 1966, Jay Griggs grew tired of Willie's incessant whining. As any good friend would do, Griggs gave Boyd clear and exacting advice, advice of which Boyd was already well aware but apparently needed some reminding. Wagging his index finger in Boyd's direction and speaking in an earnest tone, Griggs advised and somewhat scolded his NAACP companion, "Now Mr. Boyd, I'm going to tell you something. I have gotten tired of hearing you complain. What I want y'all to do is start your complaint right. Get you a suit against them. First thing to do is sit down and write a letter. Lay that on the managers desk. He won't do nothing with it, he knows better. He's going to call you up to the office and talk with you and try to discourage you."[87] The guidance was correct and filled with experience. Griggs was entirely cognizant of the new law and its provisions, and he was embroiled in a similar case against his employer, the American Tobacco Company.

Both Boyd and Griggs knew that Congress had passed the Civil Rights Act of 1964 and that it had become effective in 1965. They knew the act contained a provision, termed Title 7, guaranteeing equal employment opportunities for African Americans. And they knew there was a federal agency charged with monitoring compliance with Title 7 named the Equal Employment Opportunities Commission. Boyd's and Griggs's knowledge of policy developments was fortified during yearly state and national conventions and by various informational supplements mailed directly to association members from LDF and NAACP headquarters.[88] Plus, they were informed of the equal employment law by the tactical efforts of a promising legal campaign targeting unfair employment practices (highlighted in the following chapter).

Finally fed up with the racial politics of the Dan River Station, aware of his options under Title 7, taking his friend's advice, and doing his part to uproot segregation, Boyd, with Griggs's help, drafted a short letter at the home of fellow employee Clarence Jackson detailing their grievances with Duke Power. Then, on March 1, 1966, Boyd took the letter to work and sat it on a bench in the "Colored" locker room. Boyd signed it first, then turned to the other thirteen black workers and commanded, "Now I want all of you to sign this." Lewis Hairston read the letter, turned to Boyd, and said, "I want to know one thing—do we have a complaint?" Boyd's voice rose in disbelief. "Do we have a complaint?" he said. "I've had one since we been here, I don't know about you." Moments later, in a little known and unheralded act of resistance, all fourteen of the black workers in the Labor Department signed the letter. The letter read:

> We the following undersigned employees of the Duke Power Steam Plant, Draper North Carolina, who have given a number of years, of satisfactory service with the company. We the employees under the Civil Right Law of 1964 feel justified in requesting the company for promotion when vacancies occur, in the following job classifications, coal handling, shop, storekeeper, and general plan operation.

By 8 a.m., the letter was given, along with specific instructions, to the janitor who cleaned the offices. He was told to place the letter on the plant manager's desk and not to give it to anyone else or the plant manager may never see it. Plant Superintendent J. Donald Knight encountered the signed statement from the janitors when he arrived at his office about 9:00 a.m.[89]

At 10:00 a.m., an announcement aired across the plant intercom requesting "all of the semi-skilled laborers to be in the office at 10:30 a.m."[90] At exactly 10:30, the fourteen janitors were in Knight's office. "What is this all about?" Knight asked them. All of the men made a statement. Lewis Hairston, the elected spokesperson of the group, was fearless. He boldly told his boss, "We're seeking opportunity. We want a crack at some of the better jobs." Hairston recalls,

"The most a black could make was $1.65 an hour. The whites started at $1.81."[91]

Knight said nothing to the men that they had not heard before.[92] He reacted courteously but firmly. "Company policy," Knight reminded the men, "was that no one gets those jobs without a high school diploma. Certainly you men can see the importance of education. Duke Power," he continued, "was moving into the atomic age. The company was buying computers and automating every which-way. Black or white," he concluded, "all workers needed an education to advance." Then after a pause, he added, "Or you can take a test."[93]

The men knew nothing about this test, and to them, requiring that they take it was no fairer than requiring they possess a high school diploma, a rarity for blacks (and whites) in rural North Carolina. The men understood that tests had little relation to their jobs and were nothing more than another obstacle to block their advancement out of the Labor Department. Most of the jobs at the plant demanded physical, blue-collar-styled labor, and in the entire plant of nearly one hundred workers only sixteen whites had diplomas. "Yet no one had demanded that they take a test but they all had jobs on top of us," Hairston recalled.[94] By 1966 Boyd and some of the black workers, who were also members of the NAACP, were aware that Duke Power was in violation of the new employment law, and to combat the morphing discrimination, which continued to undercut their employment advancements, they would need to go to court and battle Duke Power with the weight of a federal law and agency behind them.[95]

The following morning Duke Power headquarters in Charlotte sent a representative to the Dan River Station to meet with the aggrieved workers, recognizing some legitimacy behind the laborers claims. But the official only recounted the same information the "janitors" had discussed with Knight. The men were hardly impressed with the rhetoric they had heard only one day before. Boyd recalls, "We made up our minds before we went up there that we were going to hold our ground. He started going on about 'we were doing good and this was the best we could do and that we had to have a high school diploma before we could get promoted.'... That's what he brought us. We let him know good, not no arguing, but from our perception of it, he wasn't saying nothing about that high school diploma."[96]

Boyd and Hairston eventually decided to take the test given by the company. The Wonderlic test included fifty questions to be completed in twelve minutes. To rate their ability for hauling coal—the promotion they were seeking—they were asked questions such as this:

In printing an article of 24,000 words, a printer decides to use two sizes of type. Using the larger type, a printed page contains 900 words. Using the smaller type, a page contains 1200 words. The article is allotted 21 full pages in a magazine. How many pages must be in the smaller type?

Neither man passed the test.[97]

Four days after meeting with the Duke Power executive, Boyd mailed off the worker's complaint to the EEOC. By the end of April, the fourteen black workers were meeting with two EEOC investigators from Atlanta late at night, being as discreet as possible.[98] Fear of being fired, harassed, driven from town, or worse were all possibilities in the rural Carolinas. The late-night meetings allowed the EEOC officials to improve and clarify the affidavit filed by the workers. The summary of the charge of discrimination found:

a) All Negro employees are restricted to two classifications—semiskilled and laborers
b) Upgrading requirements for Negro employees are not and were not required for white employees
c) Locker rooms, showers, water fountains and toilets are segregated.[99]

After the final meeting between the workers and the EEOC officials, the investigators visited the Dan River facilities as a part of their conciliatory efforts. Interestingly, one of the EEOC investigators was white and the other black. Working and watching the following morning, Boyd noticed the two men approaching. "What looked good to me," he chuckled, sensing change in the air, "was the white man was toting the luggage."[100]

But the Dan River officials did not greet the EEOC officials with open arms. Knight initially refused to cooperate with the investigators until he called company executives in Charlotte. Duke Power considered itself a progressive company, and when the Dan River Station's managers refused to share their files with the EEOC, Duke Power executives in Charlotte forced them to comply. Apparently, the threat of federal intervention had some impact on the company. After Knight finished his phone call, the plant's files flew open. For the rest of their two-day visit, Knight went as far as he could to show the EEOC representatives the Dan River plant was above racial antipathy. While escorting the men through the plant, Knight took the opportunity to drink from the "Colored" water fountain, for probably the first and only time.[101]

The rules of racial segregation and the norms of southern culture were confusing if not complex. The easiest version to tell would suggest the overarching realities were such that all whites and blacks avoided, distrusted, and disliked one another. Scholars have provided countless examples of why such a narrow interpretation of southern culture would be grossly unfair and inaccurate. However, the workplace culture of the Dan River plant did mirror regional industry practices and the larger socioeconomic culture from which the workforce sprang. While Jim Crow codified a certain social distance between the races, they worked and lived in relatively close proximity. In fact, the economic subordination of blacks into menial, subservient jobs almost guaranteed the races interact far more frequently than the law and white attitudes would have found appropriate.

Similarly, even though the Dan River Station was a segregated workplace, Boyd and the other laborers maintained amicable relationships with some of the white workers and even befriended a few. In fact, when Boyd made mistakes, plant managers typically treated him fairly when resolving the problems. So although he was clearly discriminated against with regard to pay and promotion, and although he worked with some men who were openly racist, Boyd remembers that "things weren't that bad working at Duke Power." In fact, two white workers, Hugh Meadows, a storekeeper, and Ralph Martin, a control operator, agreed to testify at the district court in Greensboro on behalf of the janitors.[102] Boyd admits that none of the white workers reacted with any overt physical hostility to the janitor's suit. Elements of North Carolina's racial civility had apparently found their way to Duke Power's Dan River plant.

Boyd's job was significantly better than sharecropping, and after working at Dan River for nearly two decades, Boyd and his fellow laborers had mastered "planning their work and working their plan." When told to do landscaping, the men did this work in the morning to avoid the sun's afternoon heat. They knew when they heard the rumble of train cars they would have to shovel coal. And although they shoveled coal regularly, it was hardly the only assignment they were given, and it was thus temporary. They knew that gigantic, noisy industrial machines required precision when cleaning to avoid serious injury. Even though they rarely were given easy jobs like monitoring gauges, they knew how to if and when called upon to do so. The laborers figured out how to manage a day's work at the plant, making sure to minimize excessive workloads and avoid white workers known to embrace more fierce racial attitudes. But working for decades with virtually no promotional opportunities and minimal raises equates to the sort of injustice that could make the most amicable of workplaces seem brutally hostile.[103]

The efforts of workers such as Boyd and his fellow laborers, coupled with aggressive lawyers and a federal agency attending to issues of employment discrimination, made North Carolina again a hotbed of protest. But instead of sit-ins, the protests were directed at using Title 7 to escape unfair employment practices. By 1966 more than four hundred charges of discrimination had been investigated by EEOC field representatives in North Carolina alone.[104] Rather fitting, the first Title 7 case ever filed sprang from the Tar Heel State.[105]

Perceived weaknesses of the EEOC by the civil rights community proved to be potential problems in the *Griggs* case. The agency could not bring suit nor issue cease-and-desist orders against Duke Power. It could only investigate complaints and offer conciliation efforts aimed at eradicating discriminatory practices. Aggrieved workers were therefore forced to absorb the costs and hassles of finding legal representation against powerful employers. Other governmental agencies charged with patrolling workplace inequality had not offered the aggressiveness necessary to achieve valiant strides in eradicating workplace discrimination, making the EEOC's work tougher. But there had been major gains arising from the private bar through the efforts of LDF. So all was not lost because Boyd and his fellow workers would ultimately turn to their fellow NAACP legal activists for assistance. Legal Defense Fund lawyers were already at the forefront of the campaign to energize Title 7 and provide relief for the thousands of black workers languishing in racially restrictive employment conditions.

The EEOC attempted conciliatory efforts with the company but "due to the heavy workload of the commission" was unable to log any more hours trying to convince Duke Power to alter or eradicate its practices.[106] Duke Power, however, responded with a half-hearted effort of its own. They issued an order to desegregate the locker rooms, drinking fountains, and toilets. Once the showers were integrated, many white men refused to use them. And even though Jesse C. Martin, the first black man promoted from the Labor Department, was moved up to the Coal Handling Department in August 1966,[107] it is clear that the Dan River officials were far from altering the ingrained patterns of its work environment.[108] The company was not nearly as progressive as it envisioned itself. Duke Power snubbed the EEOC's suggestions and refused to budge on its job practices.

As a result of Duke Power clinging to its longstanding practices, Boyd and his fellow co-workers enlisted the assistance of the LDF, willingly absorbing the long delays of litigation. On September 9, 1966, the *Griggs* case began its five-year journey through the courts to Washington, D.C.[109] Willie Griggs (no relation to Jay Griggs), the youngest man among the complainants, was the first plaintiff listed by residual prudence—meaning that because he was youngest, he would stand to benefit the most. The others also figured that because he was not married, he stood to lose the least in the event of firings.[110] Courageous but patient, the men assumed their actions would not change the world in which they lived overnight. Their experiences in North Carolina and in the South in general had taught them quite a bit about changing attitudes and practices associated with segregation. But they stoically hoped their actions might pay off for them down the road and clear a path for future generations of workers.[111]

In three decades, African Americans in North Carolina organized a systematic, statewide movement designed to battle Jim Crow. Although the course faced various hurdles, setbacks, and its share of related complications associated with a resistant status quo, many in the civil rights community believed that Jim Crow had suffered fatal blows and was weak enough to be crushed. In some respects, civil rights activists were correct. But as Boyd and his cohort of radicals facing labor discrimination learned, the reach of white supremacy was elongated, remained suffocating, and had chameleon-like properties. Boyd recognized that although some gains toward equality had been achieved, this by no means called for a respite from their sociolegal activism.

Jim Crow politics in the South were as tricky as they were incapacitating. Boyd bore witness to the morphing qualities of the system, and like many other rebels, he redirected his strategies to challenge the residue Jim Crow left behind. This residue came in the form of sustained economic subjugation preserved by highly suspect employment tests Boyd and others were forced to take when it became illegal to blatantly deny them equal employment opportunities purely based on race. Similar examples of this residue included piecemeal school desegregation, lingering disfranchisement, and simmering hostility that could erupt into violence aimed at blacks and civil rights sympathizers at a moment's notice.

The Civil Rights Acts of 1964 and 1965 outlawed the various mechanisms that codified race segregation and discrimination, but the laws would also need to counter the remnants and residue of the old system. Title 7 was the instrument civil right agitators used to battle Jim Crow's progeny in the workplace.

IV

PHASE TWO; NAMELY, ECONOMIC FREEDOM
The Title 7 Campaign

Civil rights cannot belong to the legal community, it belongs to the community. We have law degrees and understand the law so we are to bring to that struggle that knowledge and those skills. The legal community worked well with the entire community in the past because a part of the struggle of the community is vindication and justification of rights through the courts.

GERALDINE SUMTER, 2005

In his history of the NAACP's Legal Defense and Educational Fund, former LDF director counsel Jack Greenberg writes, "Before lawyers can win cases there have to be clients willing to stand up for their rights."[1] Clients have played a vital role in the course of civil rights litigation. Although the LDF has enjoyed a rich history as the chief institution working to secure equality for African Americans via the law, its attorneys are quick to recognize the importance of clients in channeling cases into the courtroom, an attitude that has been invaluable in encouraging client-activists to bring a range of cases to the lawyers.

Attorneys with the LDF provided astute counsel for grassroots clients who were often connected to local NAACP chapters and shouldered the burden of bringing cases forward, positive their lawyers would complete the journey through the courts. Together, these two entities managed to extend the civil rights agenda and actualize the promises of civil rights legislation of the mid-1960s. One law firm based in Charlotte, North Carolina, benchmarked the enduring tradition of the civil rights bar into the post-*Brown* era. Chambers, Ferguson, Stein and Lanning were among the second generation of civil rights litigators who provided endless support throughout the state to clients such as Willie Boyd. Julius Chambers and partners anchored the state NAACP's platform of legal activism, and by the mid-1960s the firm was the centerpiece of the civil rights matrix in North Carolina as client-activists began filing suits. This generation of civil rights attorneys and their fellow public interest lawyers earned significant victories designed to advance the gains from previous campaigns.

Chambers and staff were not alone in their efforts, as a growing number of civil rights firms surfaced across the nation. Local civil rights attorneys, many of whom took part in the LDF cooperating attorney program or were tangentially connected to LDF, were deeply and often directly connected to adjoining grassroots movements. The lawyers learned from client-activists of the obstacles still limiting their lives and in turn helped clients realize their options under the law. Civil rights lawyers provided judicial solutions to the lingering needs of African Americans, doing so through established channels within protests communities.

LDF headquarters at 20 West Fortieth Street in New York City was small, housing only a handful of lawyers.[2] Most civil rights attorneys working with the LDF did so by litigating in their respective communities. The LDF took full advantage of local attorneys' physical location and position of influence by using them to carry the initial casework in those areas. It formalized this practice and created a fund to help upstart cooperating attorneys become established and assist more directly with civil rights litigation.[3] This national netting of litigators could, as instructed and assisted by LDF headquarters, more effectively impact legal campaigns by directing cases in their important initial stages which required local insights and connections. These networks proved vital as the NAACP, LDF, and their clients-activists looked to the civil rights acts of the era to complete the quest for equality.

Willie Boyd and Jay Griggs would often take the ninety-minute ride to Charlotte from Reidsville with little planning, almost impromptu. In fact, as Boyd remembers, "We would go see Chambers just like we were going to the store."[4] Regularly arriving unannounced, Boyd and others felt entitled to see "their lawyers"[5] any time and just about any day. For example, when asked by a staff member if he had an appointment to see Julius Chambers, one client barked back, "Mr. Chambers don't make me have no appointments." The client's frustrated response was correct and highlights the personal approach encouraged by like-minded attorneys. As the firm's longtime office manager notes, "It was their law firm and they were our people." Clients regularly received services that reminded them they were at home, they were safe to air their frustrations, and everyone was in struggle together.[6]

This informality also helped negate potential reprisals more formal channels might have extracted from whites hostile to such formalized resistance. These and other strategies were learned during earlier movements, when violent attacks were commonplace. Plus, to a population of southern, rural, nonformally educated folks, informality was a way of life. Lawyers like Chambers and his partner, fellow North Carolinian James Ferguson, were as much southerners as they were practitioners of the law. They understood and appreciated social customs, they recognized the risk and importance of their client-activists bringing them cases, and they ultimately meshed this wisdom with their legal training to provide clients with relief, all the while doing their part in the struggle for equality. But they also understood white southerners, their racial antipathies and their racial attitudes—wisdom they would employ in the courts.

Protest networks also provided essential reinforcement to the psyche of blacks resisting racial indignities. For many rural activists, access to elite lawyers confirmed their importance to the movement's success. It was a validation and reaffirmation of their individual belonging and importance, attitudes and beliefs Jim Crow had attempted to destroy but to which blacks clung fervently. Chambers and staff graciously welcomed their comrades with every intention of providing relief to their troubles where possible. Respectful relationships enhanced the potential for continued successes and in the meantime kept the collective encouraged that their work would meet a useful outcome.

Willie Boyd approached Chambers's firm in 1966 after the cessation of the more notable developments from the protest era. However, by initiating *Griggs* and related Title 7 cases, local activists and lawyers commenced the final phases of the civil rights era's program of legal activism. With Jim Crow back peddling, though not whipped, the civil rights community turned its focus on the residue left from decades of segregation. Battling this new foe required as much diligence, ingenuity, and bravery as did outright segregation. In fact, by the mid-1960s blatant discrimination had hardly lost its muscle and was still a serious impediment to black employment equality. Legal activism proved a valuable mechanism to supplant the various types of employment prejudice with the equal opportunity guaranteed in the employment law. There was little choice left for the civil rights community as Title 7 was a policy that required judicial molding, interpretation and enforcement.

Complimenting the urban uprisings and black power radicalism of the late 1960s was this continued legal activism, which was seen in challenges to continued discrimination in the southern workplace. Client-activists and attorneys filed an increasing number of class-action lawsuits that forced industrial employers to honor Title 7's demands, ultimately leading to a modicum of equal employment opportunities.[7] These challenges surfaced as courtroom radicalism targeting structural problems associated with employment prejudice.

Employment and economic concerns reached the top of the list for the NAACP and LDF as early as 1961. At the organization's annual meeting in 1961, meetings Willie Boyd admits he never missed, Congressmen Adam Clayton Powell addressed the collective and urged "an immediate acceleration of Phase Two; namely, economic freedom." Powell explained that the Freedom Riders and "sit-inners" merely represented the first phase of the struggle for full citizenship. He concluded, "For the right to sit in a restaurant is meaningless unless one has the means to purchase a meal."[8] Two years later at the national meeting, Boyd heard Columbia University professor of economics Eli Ginzberg address NAACP leaders on the ten major problems facing "Negro" unemployment. He detailed the low educational achievements of African Americans, the lack of jobs throughout the United States, the growth of a "white collar economy" while "Negroes" remained trapped in blue-collar jobs, and the demand for government intervention to remediate the problems.[9] Ginzberg forecasted a deindustrialization that would greatly impact black employment options in succeeding decades.

During 1963, the same year debates in Congress swirled over the passage of the 1964 act and the same year as the famed March on Washington, which was initially intended to target poverty, the national office of the NAACP sent an informative pamphlet to all chapters titled *Some Questions and Answers on the Civil Rights Bill.* The pamphlet explained the key provisions of the bill and encouraged the "millions of Americans to join, through their civic, labor and religious organizations, in unprecedented support of the bill." After the legislation passed the House of Representatives later that same year, NAACP headquarters mailed another brochure to its chapters further detailing the restructuring of the bill.[10] These communications informed even the most remote NAACP branches of civil rights policy developments, meanwhile reminding and encouraging association members to personally muster the reserves to go forward with future complaints.

Boyd admits confidently, "Yeah, we knew the laws were there." He and other local leaders knew the importance of the legislation because they had participated in protests emphasizing the law's necessity, and they were kept abreast by NAACP and LDF headquarters of the civil rights legislative landscape, which demanded their sustained militancy. Boyd and his fellow association members were also well aware of their obligation to finish the movement they had helped start decades earlier. This new law, though noticeably weak, included areas that presented hope for the civil rights community and some hope for workers still victims of job discrimination.

The campaign for equal employment was a major operation. It not only intended to provide employment justice for blacks, but it did so in direct consultation and coordination with the federal commission designed to police employment discrimination. Such political ties saw the civil rights community help sculpt the law into meaningful policy. In 1967, Samuel Jackson, an early EEOC commissioner, gave a lecture on the civil rights acts at the twenty-fourth annual convention of the North Carolina NAACP branches. During his speech, Jackson clarified the role of the maturing EEOC and detailed the role of the employment provision in garnering equal opportunities for African Americans.[11] But more so, he detailed the expansive approach the EEOC sought for its influence as a federal agency. Jackson explained to Boyd and the entire assemblage that "the EEOC has taken its interpretation of Title VII a step further than other agencies have taken their statutes. . . . This approach would seem to disregard intent, then, as crucial to the finding of an unlawful employment practice."[12]

Jackson and the EEOC sought to harvest legal protection against intentional acts of discrimination, as well as biases not stemming from blatant racial animus. Denying a black person employment or a promotion purely because of race was explicitly illegal under Title 7. However, cleverly concealed devices and employment practices that appeared fair and neutral but had the same effect reinforced those barriers to black progress erected under Jim Crow. These were the practices Jackson and the EEOC knew had to be uprooted.

NAACP members were therefore trained to recognize more complex forms of discrimination and to understand the legal doctrines associated with the newer discriminatory tactics they faced on the job. Similarly, Jackson's presence at the meeting and his careful articulation of the EEOC's approach affirms that laborers, activists, and attorneys across the state were in the belly of the campaign to end employment prejudice. As Jackson spoke, the case involving fourteen black workers from Duke Power, initiated by Willie Boyd of the Rockingham County chapter of the NAACP, was making its way through the federal courts, advancing the very agenda Jackson articulated. And in charge of the case and the Title 7 campaign was a team of LDF-cooperating attorneys led by Julius Chambers.

Julius LaVonne Chambers was born and raised in Mount Gilead, North Carolina, to William and Matilda Chambers. The middle of four children, all three years apart, Julius was a "rambunctious child who put all of himself into any task he set out to accomplish." Chambers would demonstrate this trait throughout his academic career and efforts as a civil rights attorney. Young Julius regularly traveled throughout North Carolina with his father on weekends and during the hot and humid Carolina summers. Like his predecessor Conrad Pearson, Julius encountered a wide array of black North Carolinians suffering under race prejudice. He also learned ways to massage and maintain personal relationships with a broad spectrum of black southerners. These skills would prove extremely valuable years later once he emerged as the state's leading civil rights attorney.[13]

Julius's older brother Kenneth started a trend among the Chambers siblings of attending Laurinburg Institute, a small, private boarding and day school for black high school students in Laurinburg, North Carolina. But Julius had to attend segregated Peabody High School twelve miles away from his home. Peabody, like most segregated schools, was furnished with inferior facilities that paled in comparison to those of the white high school only blocks from the Chambers' home. A small but solid athlete, playing quarterback and shortstop for Peabody's football and baseball teams, Julius recalls the school's sports teams played on fields ill equipped for athletic competition. Indoor facilities such as the basketball gym were equally as dilapidated.[14]

Julius was unable to attend Laurinburg because his parents could not afford the tuition. A number of white citizens near and in Julius's hometown owed his father money for work performed but simply refused to pay their debts. Unfortunately, William Chambers was unable to find a lawyer to help him sue for the funds. This defining moment in Julius's young life fueled his desire to become a lawyer.[15] Julius had no way of knowing he would become part of and ultimately direct the organization that provided African Americans with legal support in the fight against segregation. Nor could he have imagined he would become the lead attorney on two of the most important cases of the post-*Brown* era. One of those cases was *Swann v. Charlotte Mecklenburg*, in which the Supreme Court ruled for the first time that busing could be used as a remedy to desegregate public schools.[16] The other was *Griggs v. Duke Power*.[17] Both cases reached the nation's highest court in 1971.

Julius attended North Carolina College for Negroes in Durham, which later became North Carolina Central University. Even though he tried out two consecutive years, Julius finally accepted that he was too small to play football for the university. But all was not lost. He devoted himself to his studies and to college politics and was elected president of the student government and president of his fraternity, Alpha Phi Alpha. He was also named the college's most outstanding senior and graduated summa cum laude.[18]

Upon leaving Durham in 1958, Chambers attended the University of Michigan and earned a master's degree in European history. One year later he entered the University of North Carolina Law School. Only eight years earlier the law school at Chapel Hill had admitted its first African American student, Floyd McKissick of North Carolina, after being ordered to do so by a federal court. Chambers received a stellar education at Chapel Hill, both in class and through his extracurricular efforts as a budding young activist. The sit-in movements in Greensboro, Chapel Hill, Durham, and Rock Hill, South Carolina, as well as regional upsurges in civil rights, further radicalized the already deeply committed law student, who provided representation and support at protests whenever and wherever possible. Chambers later recalled the student protests were testaments to the fact that "the only way to change their circumstances was to assert their rights."[19]

Chambers compiled an astonishing record as a law student. He earned top rank in his class and was the first African American to serve as editor-in-chief of the *North Carolina Law Review*. He also became the first African American to win membership in the Order of the Golden Fleece, the university's highest honorary society. These accomplishments did not go unnoticed by black Carolinians tuned into the successes of desegregation efforts at the state's most elite institution.[20] "Yet these academic achievements did not remove the indignities of segregation," notes author Davison Douglas, as "during his time in Chapel Hill Chambers was excluded from a school-sponsored dance because of his race."[21] Once Chambers graduated and returned to North Carolina to practice law, he did so with a contingency of supporters who had tracked his accomplishments through the state's press. Chambers was a homegrown standout returning to continue the fight against segregation.[22]

A dean at UNC–Chapel Hill gave Chambers some friendly counsel, suggesting that Chambers, a southerner born and bread, "go to New York and get some culture."[23] Upon graduation Chambers took the dean's advice and en-rolled in a one-year master's in law program at Columbia Law School. He also joined the U.S. Army Reserves while at Chapel Hill, and his required two years of active duty was reduced to limited active duty once he began the program at Columbia. After completing his law studies in 1963, Chambers joined the NAACP Legal Defense Fund in New York City for a one-year internship, where he learned to research and process race discrimination cases under the mentorship of Constance Baker Motley.[24]

During the internship, Chambers also worked closely with Derrick Bell, Norman Amaker, and Mike Meltzner. On Chamber's first day of the internship he was summoned to Albany, Georgia, along with Motley to assist cooperating attorneys C. B. King and Don Holloway with that city's movement.[25] This was not a rare occurrence. There was always civil rights work to do as direct-action protests reached their zenith, and it was common for Chambers and his LDF colleagues to travel long distances in response to the needs of protestors. Chambers recalls that Motley frequently finished typing briefs and other reports while in the car, a frequent practice among many LDF attorneys.[26]

At the end of his internship, Julius returned to North Carolina ready to advance the fight at home. The LDF had a valuable cooperating attorney who in less than one year "filed thirty-four school desegregation cases, ten public accommodations lawsuits, ten suits challenging discrimination in public hospitals, and several other lawsuits seeking to save the jobs of black teachers faced with dismissal." Chambers produced such results by himself from his Charlotte-based firm. But he discovered a lesson he had probably learned as a child and young adult in North Carolina: Some white North Carolinians despised any challenges to their racial privileges and cultural supremacy. While giving a speech in New Bern, North Carolina, in 1965, a city on the eastern seaboard of the state, Chambers's car was destroyed by a bomb.[27] His "stoicism in the face of these attacks became almost legendary. When his auto was bombed on a public street . . . 'Julius didn't get excited at all,' recalls an attorney who was present at the incident. 'He went and took a look at his car, and went back and finished his speech.'"[28] Chambers was not injured, but this would not be his last brush with violence. His home was bombed soon after the New Bern incident, and in 1971 his Charlotte-based law firm was destroyed by arson. Other civil rights leaders in Charlotte experienced similar attacks.[29] The homes of Kelly Alexander, Fred Alexander,[30] and Reginald Hawkins were bombed and the parties responsible were never arrested.[31] Such incidents further challenge

North Carolina's self-proclaimed civility. These reprisals indicate that efforts to advance equality across the state elicited vicious acts of racial violence even as late as the 1970s.

Chambers's law firm at 405 1/2 East Trade Street in Charlotte worked closely with the North Carolina NAACP. Kelly Alexander Sr., president of the state chapter, provided support as the two filed case after case. A few years after the installation of the firm, two bright young lawyers joined Chambers. James E. Ferguson, II, a black lawyer from Asheville, North Carolina and graduate of Columbia Law School, and Adam Stein, a white lawyer and graduate of George Washington Law School, who had worked with Chambers as an intern during the summer of 1966, joined the firm in the summer of 1967.[32]

James E. Ferguson II was no stranger to the racial politics of Jim Crow North Carolina. Every institution was segregated in his hilly hometown of Asheville. Although he grew up facing "a wall of inferiorization," his parents managed to keep such notions from creeping into the consciousness of their children. One example of Ferguson expressing the values his parents instilled was his participation in ASCORE, the Asheville Student Committee on Racial Equality. Established in 1960, the committee successfully battled segregation in the small western North Carolina town, alongside other student movements across the region. But Asheville had no black college from which to draw radical young adults as was the case in southern cities and towns with high volumes of sit-in protests. What makes Ferguson and his peer's movement special is they began their work as high school students.

Once Ferguson went off to attend North Carolina Central University in 1960, from which Chambers had just recently graduated, he returned home during the summers to help complete the work he and his peers had begun. ASCORE was never forced to lead any sit-ins to be successful however. With effective organization and assistance from adult leadership, this committee of teenagers negotiated the desegregation of Asheville's public facilities. And thanks to the role modeling of two civil rights attorneys in Ruben Daily and Harold Epps, Ferguson was fully aware what his career would be by his senior year of high school.[33]

Ferguson's and Chambers's coming of age in the late 1950s and early 1960s blurs an accepted polarity in the scholarship of the civil rights era. These young activists, who were willing to take part in student-directed movements and even create local protest movements similar to those initiated by SNCC, ultimately went on to brilliant careers of legal activism. Legal challenges have

regularly been dismissed as passive, nonthreatening stances typically not associated with the more boisterous, confrontational protests of those sparked
by younger and seemingly more militant activists. That two leading civil rights
attorneys of the post-*Brown* era were actually molded during the era of spawning black radicalism forces scholars to continually reconsider definitions of
radicalism moving into the black power era. Continued scholarship challenging this polarity may uncover much more synergy between the two camps than
previously accepted.

Chambers and Ferguson found their chosen forms of resistance significant
to the larger struggle for equality even as they recognized that some practices
within the movement had indeed become antiquated and comfortable to both
blacks and whites. The *Griggs* case progressed alongside the expansion of black
power rhetoric and ideologies and was directed by a legal team that undoubtedly was influenced by their more militant peers. Civil rights litigation during
the black power era pressed for broader, more radical interpretations of and
solutions to discrimination in the courts. In many respects, legal campaigns
of this era were affected by the more audacious ideologies of black power
while maturing as extensions of the civil rights movement's programmatic
efforts. As black power advocates demanded inclusion from the U.S. government through more boisterous, theoretical rhetoric, backing this up in some
cases with community programming and campus protests, second-generation
civil rights attorneys were indeed using the judiciary to codify key elements of
that inclusion in employment, education, and voting, as promised in the civil
rights acts. Further, the lawyers regularly provided counsel for their more radical comrades.[34]

The legal campaigns of the 1960s worked to eradicate lingering discriminatory practices in education, public accommodations, employment, and voting. The stances were supported by law because Congress had outlawed such
practices, but the civil rights bar and their clients looked to advance beyond
the limitations inherent in the civil rights acts. Civil rights attorneys used these
measures to go beyond ending the blatant, clearly intentional discrimination
that characterized the Jim Crow era, and civil rights strategists embraced a
shift from equality of opportunity for the individual to one that focused on
equality of results for the entire group of blacks. No longer would it suffice to
have an insignificant presence, if any presence at all, in institutions that once
openly discriminated but were recently denied by law to continue these practices. During the post-1965 era, civil rights lawyers and client-activists ques-

tioned whether opportunity in theory and the end to blatant discrimination were truly enough. They insisted the law provide remedies for centuries of racism and discrimination, which had created institutional cultures that in practice, even as policy reflected the rhetoric of equal opportunity, still denied advancement to African Americans.

While completing his law studies at Columbia University, Ferguson happened to bump into Chambers one day while visiting the LDF headquarters. Ironically, Ferguson was there retrieving information about the fund's cooperating attorney program because he had plans to practice law in his hometown of Asheville. After an unofficial, unscripted business meeting, the partnership was secured over a handshake and an unspoken but mutual commitment to fight discrimination back home. Civil rights work was never specifically tied to one location, and as cooperating attorneys, Ferguson and Chambers would of course litigate statewide. Ferguson would therefore get plenty of casework from Asheville, even though the firm was located in Charlotte. For civil rights attorneys who did not attend Howard University there was little civil rights course work to draw on, if any at all. Thus many attorneys learned on the job and through the ranks of the LDF community. Ferguson would get plenty of practice and receive practical tutelage from his new LDF partners, who were more veteran to civil rights legal battles. Further, after working alone for three years, Chambers had established himself as the lawyer to turn to within the state's civil rights community, allowing Ferguson to step in and get right to work.[35]

Adam Stein's road to civil rights litigation was a bit more circuitous, but that he arrived at the practice of law was not surprising given his influences as a youth. Stein's parents were liberal whites who loathed segregation. Young Adam attended all-white schools in Washington, D.C., and from his position in society witnessed glaring disparities between the resources allocated to black and white educational institutions. In tenth grade Adam enrolled in a boarding school after his father accepted a faculty position in Princeton University's Woodrow Wilson School of Public Policy. Adam's dad and his father's pals were longtime members of the liberal, New Deal establishment of the 1940s. As a result, young Adam was regularly exposed to household discussions regarding matters of public policy, which helped inspire his interest in the law. Similarly, a close friend to Stein's parents enjoyed a celebrated career as a lawyer in Washington.

Joseph Rauh was a principal attorney and lobbyists with the Leadership Conference on Civil Rights and was the primary counsel for African American challenges to the Democratic Party's exclusive policies. In fact, Rauh represented the Mississippi Freedom Democratic Party during its bid for recognition. Rauh also represented Arthur Miller before the House Committee on Un-American Activities (HUAC) and graciously opened his home to Miller and his wife, Marilyn Monroe. Just knowing Monroe was sleeping at a neighbor's home excited young Adam, helping him to view this particular colleague of his father's more favorably. Rauh's work as an attorney etched the profession into Stein's brain at a young age. Stein was particularly moved by that aspect of the profession that encouraged working on the side of oppressed people.[36]

After attending a couple of universities, joining the military, and getting married to his high school sweetheart, and all the while witnessing social upheavals spurred by his generation of liberals, Stein settled in on a career in law. He finally enrolled in law school alongside his brother at George Washington University in 1964, feeling somewhat left out of the movement for racial equality. In the ten years or so after graduating high school and completing his college degree, Stein concluded that he would become a lawyer and practice civil rights law. His wife's close friend was married to Mike Meltzner, who was an established attorney with the Legal Defense Fund. In 1965, Stein interned for Julius Chambers in Charlotte, and the following summer he helped organize the fund's Title 7 campaign. Stein and the campaign were both headquartered in the South, out of Charlotte, North Carolina, in the Chambers law firm.[37]

Chambers, Ferguson, Stein and Lanning[38] received financial backing from the New York office in their role as cooperating attorneys, one of the first firms to be formally introduced under the program. The establishment of the firm "marked the first time in the history of North Carolina and one of the first times in the history of the South that a black and a white lawyer had joined forces."[39] The founding partners, and those that followed, agreed to mold their firm into a microcosm of what American society ought to be. Their firm would become a reflection of the nation's multiracial possibilities as they went about their work in the region that still required massive efforts to uproot the vestiges of inequity.[40]

Though the firm focused its energies on civil rights litigation, it could hardly stay afloat financially without taking a mix of other cases. Nonetheless, the attorneys knew that civil rights demanded the bulk of their time and energy, and required that they not long for lucrative careers. Much civil rights representation was done either pro bono or under the understanding that clients pay what they could afford. Not only did the social conditions demand this

approach, but as lawyers they understood the legal arena necessitated continued, selfless action. As James Ferguson explains,

> We were part of a movement. We weren't practicing law in the abstract.
> We were the legal arm of the civil rights movement in North Carolina, and
> when people wanted a better education for their students . . . they came to
> us and wanted to know what they could do. . . . When people looked a the
> workplace and saw that there were no blacks above the rank of janitor or
> chief clerical worker, they wanted to bring about some change. . . . And we
> felt then that we had a judicial climate that was receptive to the claims we
> were making.[41]

In only a few months following Chambers arrival in Charlotte, Kelly Alexander Sr. and a large group of black parents approached the firm to represent
them in a case against the Charlotte-Mecklenburg school system.[42] Not long
after in 1966, two local NAACP leaders, J. A. Griggs and Willie Boyd from the
Rockingham County chapter, had approached Chambers and his partners to
handle an employment discrimination case involving fourteen men working
at the Duke Power Company plant in Draper, North Carolina.

As with the campaign against segregated education, the LDF brought in a
team of legislative scholars to address how to approach the procedural requirements of Title 7. This new law included areas that presented hope for the civil
rights community, and it was believed that the most should be made of the law
while political momentum seemed in favor of marginalized groups.[43] Congress,
which throughout the twentieth century had been immobilized due to southern resistance; the Supreme Court, which had enough liberal-leaning appointments; and the president were all working under an umbrella of social liberalism
that made success possible. The political moment was ripe for pushing forward
any and all efforts aimed at maximizing and broadening the scope of Title 7.

Jean Fairfax arrived at the LDF in 1964 and created the fund's Division
of Legal Information and Community Services. Fairfax's efforts helped LDF
formalize important links to various black communities. The fund targeted
areas of excessive black unemployment that pointed to patterns of discrimination in semiskilled and skilled blue-collar jobs. Cooperating attorneys identified industries and practices that fit the profile, encouraging the LDF to zero
in on steel, railroads, trucking, shipbuilding, tobacco, and paper industries.
As Ferguson states, "You could choose your target, really. Everybody was discriminating." The South therefore was the region that made the most sense

for the initiation of the campaign, with other regions to follow.[44] As a result, "most of the early charges filed with the EEOC came from southern states, and consequently most of the early Title VII litigation took place in federal courts in the South."[45] Within these industries, the cases focused on segregated locals, seniority systems that locked blacks into low-paying jobs, and discriminatory hiring and promotion practices. Many of these employment scenarios also involved non-job-related testing, high school diploma requirements for blue-collar jobs, and word-of-mouth recruiting. Jack Greenberg and Fairfax met with EEOC officials in 1966 and persuaded the commission to focus its efforts in similar fashion.[46]

During the summer of 1965 the NAACP and LDF went to work educating black communities about their rights under the civil rights act and gathering facts about discrimination. Adam Stein supervised Ruth Abram, a seventeen-year-old Sarah Lawrence College student from Atlanta, who coordinated the Title 7 summer project out of Chambers's office. According to LDF attorney and Title 7 strategist Robert Belton, "The aims of the project . . . were to inform black persons of their Title VII rights, to solicit media publications of the new Act, to assist in the preparation of charges to be filed with the EEOC, to stimulate the interest of local leadership in an ongoing project of a similar nature, and to train local workers in community organizations to participate in the enforcement of the new Act."[47]

The LDF employed law students to help execute the program through the Law Students Civil Rights Research Council, which funded summer internships to assists civil rights attorneys. Law students, under the direction of LDF cooperating attorneys, met with local leaders, worked with civil rights and civic groups, and made presentations at churches, barbershops, businesses, and social groups to establish community-based fair employment committees. Stein also supervised and coordinated the efforts of three other field interns responsible to various regions across the state.[48]

The efforts of the Title 7 campaign were crucial because the EEOC was riddled with shortcomings that curtailed its effectiveness. Plus, Title 7 required judicial clarity about what the law would mean for employment practices. The LDF was directly involved in litigating cases because the EEOC could not bring suit, and it also helped shape important facets of the commission's filing processes. For example, to add structure to the administration of the fund's Title 7 campaign, Stein created the complaint forms the EEOC would ultimately use to document cases. By the end of the summer these efforts had led to more complaints filed out of North Carolina than any other state. In fact, by the end of the third week after the effective date of Title 7, many of the charges then pending before the EEOC were filed through these efforts. Greenberg and the LDF had planned to file one thousand complaints with the EEOC on July 1, 1965, the day Title 7 became effective. Greenberg writes, "We filed 476 complaints with the Equal Employment Opportunities Commission (EEOC) in July 1965, right after the act went into effect, and another 374 soon afterward." LDF target institutions included U.S. Steel, Union Carbon and Carbide, A&P, General Motors, International Paper, and numerous unions and state employment agencies throughout the South.[49] In fact, "many of the 8854 charges received by the EEOC in its first fiscal year were directly attributable to the summer project."[50]

One important outgrowth of the Title 7 project was its impact on litigation stemming from the Carolina-based textile industry, which was funneled through the Textile: Employment and Advancement for Minorities (TEAM) project.[51] Cases arising from TEAM's efforts significantly propelled Title 7 case law, added clarity to the employment law, and helped lend focus to the EEOC's efforts. Black textile workers experienced the same glaring injustices on the job as did most other black industrial workers across the nation, and maybe worse given the textile industry was probably seen by southern laborers as the best quick-ticket to economic prosperity. The histories of black textile workers, as chronicled by historian Timothy Minchin in his book *Hiring the Black Worker*, repeat the familiar conditions African American laborers experienced as white workers and managers erected and maintained segregated work environments.[52]

TEAM held a textile forum in Charlotte, North Carolina, in January 1967, out of which the EEOC promised to make the textile industry a primary target "to win better jobs for Negroes." "In the vast majority of the textile cases, the plaintiffs were represented by . . . Julius Chambers and James E. Ferguson. Their Charlotte law firm was at the forefront of a drive to represent black workers and make Title VII of the Civil Rights Act a reality," and as Ferguson put it, to do away with the "labor apartheid" that plagued the South.[53]

Robert Belton and Gabrielle Kirk, an LDF attorney, were largely responsible for the initial phase of Title 7 cases between 1965 and 1970. Belton and Kirk, along with local lawyers, tried most of the cases at the district courts, though LDF lead attorneys usually managed the appeals. Because Title 7 was unclear about how to process and file cases, the LDF was concerned about narrow interpretations that could undercut the law's utility. To aid the fund, Jack Greenberg enlisted the expertise of Albert Rosenthal, an experienced litigator and scholar and former law clerk under Felix Frankfurter.[54] Rosenthal gathered a group of scholars and practitioners to help orchestrate courtroom approaches.[55]

Rosenthal, Belton, Kirk, Herbert Hill, and the team of strategists determined through the campaign's research efforts that one of the many ways companies continued to discriminate against blacks was through testing mechanisms. According to Belton, "Many employers and unions had begun to cloak exclusionary and discriminatory policies in superficial neutral practices, such as testing and educational devices . . . that appeared facially neutral or color-blind but operated to perpetuate the effects of past discrimination."[56] LDF's theoretical approach to dealing with this testing issue was developed by George Cooper, a Columbia Law School professor and graduate of Harvard Law School; Richard Sobol, a University of Michigan Law School professor and graduate of Columbia Law School; and Richard Barrett, an industrial psychologist. Barrett was the expert in *Griggs,* and he counseled the legal team on similar employment cases. This group of legal theorists maintained that "where a pre-employment test has an unfavorable impact on blacks and does not predict ability to do the job, it violates Title VII." Accordingly, Julius Chambers, with the help of Belton, set out to prove that Duke Power's tests were not professionally developed and did not predict job performance.[57]

Although scholars offer interpretations of historical developments and refashion them into splendid tales, often such depictions overlook the basic, day-to-day grind that truly shapes history. For example, longtime NAACP labor director Herbert Hill, along with one full-time lawyer, researched target institutions, held Title 7 seminars in city after city, and held large meetings with black industrial workers to assist them in the preparation of Title 7 complaints. Hill would periodically stop by EEOC headquarters in Washington, D.C., and dump "a suitcase full of complaints on the desk of the chairman."[58]

On any random day, as part of his work with LDF's portion of the Title 7 campaign, Belton might walk into Hill's office and thumb through Hill's files looking for promising cases to litigate. While together, the two might discuss case strategy or a particularly disturbing employment scenario either may have witnessed, or after a dull morning of case research, the two might go for lunch and not talk shop at all. Nonetheless, case information and the legwork needed to direct cases into court do not make for exciting accounts. But, indeed, "this is how history is made."[59] Similarly, the random drop-ins by clients to law firms add to the unsystematic record of social change. Although strategies and campaigns were certainly well coordinated, the day-to-day particulars were as routine, yet as unpredictable, as with any job.

Most companies had discriminated against black workers for as long as they had employed them. In fact, most companies probably failed to recognize why their practices were now considered illegal, given such longstanding traditions of racial partiality. Companies certainly had no reason to take seriously another employment law or an associated federal commission that lacked enforcement authority. Employment institutions were accustomed to a national employment culture that denied blacks union membership, denied blacks the full benefits of unions when allowed membership, and relegated blacks to menial, lower-paying positions. Duke Power had little reason to assume its practices would ever be met with serious opposition from the federal government, and they certainly had little reason to believe any repercussions would follow its practices.

To complicate matters more, Title 7 prohibited discrimination in employment but failed to define the broader nuances of what might constitute workplace discrimination absent subjective intent and disparate treatment. The EEOC and LDF had to shape a definition in line with Title 7 then persuade the federal courts to accept their interpretation of what constituted comparable forms of employment discrimination.[60] As Alfred Blumrosen, chief of conciliation for the EEOC from 1965 to 1967, stated, "In a way it's a good thing that there hadn't been [a working definition]. Because if there had been one it probably would have been a narrower one." The EEOC, therefore, ultimately adopted the broadest view possible, insisting that racially neutral practices that served to perpetuate past discrimination were discriminatory.[61]

Overt practices of discrimination, such as denying people jobs on account of race, versus practices that appeared neutral on their face but had discriminatory effects became a fundamental debate in *Griggs*. The EEOC was well aware that companies introduced various racially motivated requirements when they could no longer explicitly restrict employment opportunities for blacks. Among the most popular of these new requirements were employment tests. The EEOC, with added pressure from the civil rights bar, "therefore sought to negotiate a solution that would induce industry to either stop using these tests, or at least, to modify their use so that they did not have a discriminatory effect."[62]

During Title 7's firs five years, the LDF brought forward the cases that clarified and removed the procedural obstacles to using the employment act. These cases and those that followed gave Title 7 much of its force. Procedural obstacles included, but were not limited to, how to timely and accurately process and file complaints with the EEOC, the time frame allowed from filing the initial complaint to bringing suit in federal court, and determining what discriminatory practices were actually under the purview of Title 7, such as whether discrimination occurring prior to the law was permissible as evidence for a complaint of discrimination. Because LDF scholars, economists, and labor experts targeted industries in which lawsuits would have the most immediate impact, blacks, other ethnic minorities, and women won a dramatic increase in jobs as well as higher wages. Jack Greenberg concluded that the impact of the change wrought from the campaign "was almost on a par with the campaign won in *Brown*."[63] That Title 7 became an effective equal employment law and that the EEOC became a potent federal agency is owed in large part to the efforts of the NAACP, LDF, other public interest law centers and their client-activists.

The victories earned by the civil rights bar did not occur due to luck, waning resistance by opponents, or because all judges welcomed their arguments with favorable interpretations. The civil rights bar refined their legal strategies and approaches during yearly workshops coordinated by the LDF. Annual civil rights training institutes held at Airlie Farms in Warrenton, Virginia, were important assemblages of practitioners and strategists designed to achieve at least two important goals. First, the civil rights legal brain trust could physically come together, discuss, and hopefully agree on specific focuses that would encourage courtroom success. Put simply, these meetings worked to get the growing body of civil rights and public interests lawyers waging legal battles on the same accord. The community of practitioners and strategist could interrogate the particulars of the law and pending cases and develop a prospective docket to drive the campaign.

Second, the Airlie meetings were an important support network for the growing body of civil rights attorneys spread across the nation. With its gorgeous, undulating topography in northwestern Virginia, reminiscent of romantic depictions of the plantation South, Airlie Farms was to the civil rights bar what the Highlander School was to marchers and sit-inners. Attorneys from distant and discrete locales could count on the Airlie workshops to provide continued education, direction, and training on the new laws and to rejuvenate and energize them to continue their work locally. As Title 7 cases emerged and progressed, the civil rights community's case law was focused due to Airlie's annual direction-shaping strategy sessions. Whereas NAACP members and black workers in targeted institutions learned how to challenge job discrimination through the Title 7 campaign, Airlie workshops instructed the growing body of civil rights lawyers how to navigate cases through the courts.[64]

Airlie also attracted lawyers working in the government-assigned the task of litigating civil rights cases on behalf of the United States or researching ongoing legal battles. James Jones, one of the first black attorneys hired by the Department of Labor, attended the retreats during his thirteen years (1956–1969) with the government. In his role as a federal legislative attorney, he helped draft rules for Executive Orders 11246 and 10925 and in 1969 helped craft the Philadelphia Plan, which was the federal government's first efforts to establish goals and timetables for minority employment in industries under contractual agreement with the government. Much to the surprise and comfort to LDF attorneys in the immediate aftermath of *Brown* and during the turbulent 1960s, there sat an influential and like-minded African American in the Labor Department who, while not working solely on civil rights issues, certainly understood the realities of employment prejudice and could impact discussions within more discrete federal circles and offer much needed insight on federal bureaucracy. In fact, James Jones and Robert Belton became good friends and regularly roomed together at Airlie. Jones would get little sleep while at the retreat, however. His roommate, either fatigued from the long days of training and strategizing or possibly worn out from the poker games lasting into the early mornings, "snored all night long."[65]

Clearly Title 7 made disparate treatment, or racially motivated employment and promotion practices, illegal. Given that act's language regarding tests, civil rights attorneys faced obvious challenges in eliminating professionally developed employment tests that served to foreclose employment and promotion opportunities to blacks—tests like the Wonderlic, which blocked Willie Boyd's promotion to coal handler. Still, *Griggs* presented as easy a case as possible to redirect a legal environment that adhered to the neutrality of employment practices, not their effects.[66] If during the 1950s the time was ripe to attack blatant Jim Crow on legal grounds, as was done in *Brown*, over a decade later there was a simmering legal environment ripe for an attack on the institutional residue left over by the *Brown* case. *Griggs* and *Brown* may therefore stand as unofficial bookends to the civil rights era of legal activism. The tireless efforts of the civil rights bar are best honored by these words from Martin Luther King: "You should be aware, as indeed I am, that the road to freedom is now a highway because lawyers throughout the land, yesterday, and today have helped clear the obstructions, have helped eliminate roadblocks, by their selfless, courageous espousal of difficult and unpopular causes."[67]

Jay Griggs's and Willie Boyd's efforts with the Reidsville NAACP chapter and the North Carolina NAACP provided the two men with critical knowledge and expertise. They knew the purposes of the civil rights acts and the rights of blacks under them. They also had at their disposal well-trained civil rights lawyers who were part of a long lineage of LDF attorneys challenging racially discriminatory laws and using antidiscrimination legislation to usher in equality.

At the Dan River Station in Draper, North Carolina, Boyd and his fellow workers had long been victims of disparate treatment. They were relegated to one segregated department, received inferior pay, and were denied full access to promotions and other benefits, solely on account of their race. They faced this discrimination with jobs they all could do, and probably had done, at the plant. Once this outright discrimination was banned, black workers were still denied opportunities to advance through the use of ostensibly race neutral employment and promotion barriers: high school diploma requirements and mental and aptitude tests that supposedly measured their ability to perform tasks. Yet all the white men who worked in higher-paying jobs and continued to get promoted to even higher-paying positions had education achievements equal to or lower than the black workers. As Willie Boyd put it rather candidly, "Funny thing how Duke Power worked. A White man with no education—here you got a little bit, six or seventh grade education—yet he knows something. He hadn't even been to school. A white person knows if he has no education. They tell you you're overqualified (if you have more education). They'll find some way to keep you out. If you hadn't been to school at all, you're under qualified."[68]

Legal theorists admit that the issue of disparate impact, opposed to outright disparate treatment, is a more complicated problem to attack, especially since every worker is treated neutrally in the administration of employment practices. The lay public too would have a problem grasping a concept that seemed too dense in legal jargon and expertise.[69] But the black men at the Dan River plant understood the application of this concept even if they had never heard the phrase "disparate impact." They knew they had been overtly discriminated against in past years and they knew the company began to use knew devices to maintain their subordination when Title 7 banned blatant practices. What was less obvious under legal determinations was all too clear to them and countless other black workers during their day-to-day work lives, especially on payday.

Robert Jumper, Herman Martin, and his brother Jesse Martin were the only three black workers at Dan River who had high school diplomas at the time the case began in the fall of 1966.[70] Of the fourteen original laborers who signed the letter voicing their grievances with the company on March 1, 1966, Jesse Martin was not included in the suit. He was the senior laborer with a high school diploma and was promoted to learner in the Coal Handling Department on August 8, 1966, only two months prior to the initiation of the suit but during the EEOC's conciliatory efforts.[71] Jesse Martin's promotion was the extent of "voluntary compliance" under pressure from the EEOC that Duke Power was willing to concede.[72]

From July 2, 1965, the day after Title 7 took effect, and ironically the day Duke Power began using its tests, to the time Chambers and staff completed their "finding of facts" for the district court in April 1968, five white workers without high school diplomas or equivalent educational letters were promoted and were not required to take tests. Again, of the eighty-six white workers at the plant, only sixteen had diplomas, and some had received virtually no schooling. On August 23, 1965, James L. Williams was promoted from helper to coal handling operator with only a sixth grade education. When Williams received his promotion, as many as nine black workers were better educated. Three black workers were high school graduates, Junior Blackstock and Clarence Jackson had seventh grade educations, Willie Griggs and Clarence Purcell had tenth grade educations, and Willie Boyd had an eleventh grade education.[73]

Boyd was enrolled at Rockingham Community College in an adult education program before the case began and earned his high school diploma on May 25, 1969. A few weeks later his son Wesley graduated from Howard University in Washington, D.C. Boyd still proudly wears his class ring and admits, "I will wear it 'til I die."[74] Trial records indicate that Boyd was the only worker in the entire plant taking advantage of the tuition reimbursement program offered by the company.[75] Apparently, white workers felt no compelling pressure to earn diplomas, despite Duke Power having upgraded its employment and promotion requirements.

On April 2, 1966, Otis Shelton, a white worker with a tenth grade education, was promoted from pump operator to control operator without taking a test. J. G. Joyce had an eleventh grade education and was promoted from mechanic B to mechanic A on April 18, 1966, with no test required. C. H. Parker, with only an eighth grade education, was promoted test-free to welder on April 18, 1966, as well. At the time of Parker's promotion at least seven black laborers had earned more education.[76] All of these positions were in departments ranked above the Labor Department and were intradepartmental moves. So although Duke was not in violation of its own testing and promotion policy, which would have amounted to an overt case of disparate treatment, these promotions illustrate that the level of education was not a direct predictor of job success. It also shows that the policy, though applied neutrally, still maintained a racially stratified workplace.[77]

Throughout the trial Duke Power contended that its practices were administered fairly and neutrally, but these promotions alone highlight the gross inequities at Dan River. Similarly, when black workers were promoted, which did not occur for the first time until the EEOC forced the company's hand, they appeared to be token promotions. Boyd described Duke Power's tactics candidly. "What they were doing," he explained, "as one would come capable or qualified, they would pick some kind of a job to give him that was out of where you were, but wasn't going any where. So you still couldn't get no where. They offered me Watchman [after receiving his diploma]. We had studied that Watchman position. . . . They put you in the Watchman and you didn't go no further, you'd die right there. No more promotions, no more money, nothing."[78] Nonetheless, Robert Jumper, a black laborer, was promoted to watchman in January 1968, only one month before the trial hearing.[79] Jumper's new position was not a dead-end job, though. He was later promoted to trainee in the Test and Laboratory Department.

In March 1968, one month after the trial hearing, Herman Martin was promoted out of the Labor Department to watchman. He too was able to advance out of that position to the position of learner in the Coal Handling Department.[80] Neither of these promotions would have occurred, however, had no legal action been taken. And the black workers may truly have been stuck in the watchman position if there had been no appeal. These actions "must have been taken on advice of counsel who knew what was needed to protect the interests of the company in the litigation. After all, the only explanation for these men being in the black department after July 2, 1965, once vacancies had arisen, was their race. Refusal to transfer or promote them would have perpetuated the deliberate racial assignment."[81] All three of the black workers with high school diplomas were promoted to "white jobs" after the lawsuit was filed but before the case was decided by the district court. Duke Power lawyers probably wanted to avoid having the district court find the same racially designated employment patterns that had existed prior to the employment law.[82]

On September 9, 1966, after its efforts at conciliation were rejected by Duke Power, the EEOC sent a letter to the plaintiffs stating, "Under the provisions of Section 706(e) of Title VII of the Civil Rights Act of 1964, the Commission must notify you of your right to bring an action in Federal District Court."[83] On October 20, 1966, Willie Boyd and his fellow workers, with the aid of his fellow grassroots activist Jay Griggs, filed a suit against the Duke Power Company with attorneys Julius Chambers and Robert Belton at the district court in Greensboro. Duke Power failed to voluntarily comply with the conciliatory efforts of the EEOC, thus the *Griggs* party was free to bring suit in federal court. They argued for class action status "on their own behalf and own behalf of all other persons similarly situated who are employed by defendant Duke Power at its Draper, North Carolina, plant."[84] Duke Power fought the class action plea, but it was ultimately accepted on June 12, 1967, and extended to employees hired subsequently once racial discrimination was proven in court.[85]

Even though one black worker had been promoted in August 1966 (Jesse Martin to Learner in the Coal Handling Department), the rest of the black workers were still stuck in the Labor Department at the time the suit was filed. Class-action status became crucial to *Griggs* and other Title 7 cases because class-action suits exposed employers to far-reaching restructuring and back-pay awards to hundreds and sometimes thousands of workers.[86] To change an institutional climate predicated on biased practices, far-reaching restructuring and significantly expensive economic penalties were necessary and most effective in efforts to eradicate deeply rooted patterns and practices.

Directly under question in the case were issues of testing, high school diplomas, and overtime. The plaintiffs alleged in their original claim that "the company was pursuing a policy and practice of limiting the employment opportunities of Negro employees because of race in promotions and transfers, wages, overtime and use of facilities."[87] The workers were limited largely due to the company's use of employment and promotion tests, blatant segregation in facilities, and unfair wage distribution and overtime opportunities. By the time *Griggs* was argued before the district court in February 1968, the Dan River Station had desegregated its facilities. The complaint filed in the district court in Greensboro asserted, "This is a proceeding for injunctive relief, restraining defendant from maintaining any policy, practice, custom or usage of: discriminating against plaintiffs and others of their class because of race with respect to compensations, terms, conditions and privileges of employment and limiting, segregating and classifying employees of defendant in ways which deprive plaintiffs and other Negro persons similarly situated of employment opportunities and otherwise adversely affect their status as employees because of race and color."[88]

The complaint argued that the defendant had followed and continued to follow policies and practices that forced black workers into menial and low-paying jobs. Black workers were not allowed to bid on job openings or advance to positions that included better conditions, privileges, or pay. The *Griggs* party further claimed that the defendant also refused them opportunities for overtime on the same merits and basis that overtime was provided for white employees. What would ultimately be most important in the case was made clear in the initial complaint. Chambers, Belton, and staff brought under question Duke Power's use of test requirements for promotions. The "plaintiffs believe and allege that the test is not professionally developed as required [under Title 7] and that the test, the administration and action upon the results are intended to discriminate against Negro employees because of race." The policies and practices of the company, the *Griggs* legal team asserted, "were intended to and have and will have the effect of discrimination against plaintiffs and others of their class . . . solely because of their race and color in violation of their rights to equal employment opportunities secured to them by Title VII of the Civil Rights Act of 1964."[89]

Duke Power was indeed guilty of discriminating against its black workers prior to the enactment of Title 7. But a crucial question the case would later answer was whether the company violated Title 7 after its effective date. The courts would also need to answer if the tests were professionally developed, with seemingly limited congressional direction. If so, and the company applied them neutrally, as the defendant would argue it had, were black workers still the victims of discrimination? Title 7 did allow certain employment tests. In fact, the very tests under question were widely used by employers across the nation. But were these tests legal if they served to perpetuate the discrimination that had begun under Jim Crow? And were they administered neutrally if whites did not have to take them to gain promotions?

In litigating *Griggs*, LDF attorneys Chambers and Belton knew that Title 7 and the issue of testing had to be dealt with carefully and strategically. Blatant discrimination was easily exposed in court, but these new obstacles to black employment opportunities made for a more ambiguous foe, at least on paper. The effects of the tests were obvious. But how would the legal team show that, administered neutrally and having received some congressional stamping, they were discriminatory mechanisms?

The team would have to demonstrate that the tests had a disparate impact on the black workers. They would have to build a case that brought under question certain employment practices that Title 7 appeared to protect. They would have to show that Duke Power's use of the tests helped maintain discriminatory practices from the past and perpetuated them in the present and future. This would be no easy task because Title 7 was a new, largely ignored provision that had yet to receive full examination from the courts. This task was made all the more difficult given there existed no formal adoption of the "disparate impact" doctrine and thus no direct precedent upon which to base such claims. Effect standards were crucial to civil rights litigation but not readily accepted by the courts or opponents to such legal constructions. Legal arguments such as these would be even harder to sell to judges in North Carolina, particularly wagering them against the stalwart Duke Power.

V

SUBTLETIES OF CONDUCT...
PLAY NO SMALL PART

Griggs at the District Court

As late as 1968, when *Griggs* began its legal journey at the Greensboro district court, the occupational status of African Americans in southern industry had not improved much, if at all. Most employment institutions experienced little legal compulsion to alter their practices despite the legislative demands of Title 7. The Dan River Station made small, token steps to treat its black workers more equitably, but Duke Power as a company seemed more committed to preserving the status quo. The endurance of such employment practices reflects the durability of prevailing attitudes and assumptions regarding race and race relations within southern industries. In many respects, the courtroom provides one space where, through the arguments of lawyers and the proclamations of southern judges, racially chauvinistic attitudes might emerge unfiltered as legal practitioners explain away discriminatory employment practices with some modicum of necessitated candor.

The district court record highlights Duke Power's resistance to entertaining any notions of their practices being discriminatory. Although the white men at the plant wanted to uphold their superior positions relative to black workers, company leadership could not perceive the world through any lenses other than those they had previously worn. To them, discrimination was not inherently wrong or illegal, but was the necessary and correct order of southern society. This was especially true in the workplace, where economic supremacy was secured.

The court transcript underscores the difficulties the LDF and black plaintiffs faced convincing southern judges they were indeed the victims of ongoing workplace prejudice. Presiding district court judge Eugene Gordon was "civil" in the North Carolina tradition, but he too lived in a world that endorsed and promoted segregation. And unless compelled to do so by higher courts, Gordon appeared unwilling to tender rulings contrary to the social order of his day.

Because many aspects of Title 7 remained unclear even three years after its enactment, LDF lawyers Julius Chambers and Robert Belton were cultivating as broad an interpretation of the law as possible. For example, much of what remained unclear was whether judges would only allow a prospective reading of Title 7. Or would the courts examine pre-act discriminatory practices that created post-act employment conditions? Title 7 made no mention of correcting problems associated with past discrimination. Most companies attempted to outmaneuver the provision by providing cosmetic changes to their institutions or creating less flagrant measures that still maintained segregated workforces. If the courts refused to address pre-act practices and instead questioned only post-act practices that appeared racially neutral, then Title 7 would be rendered less effective.

Although *Griggs* ultimately provided the employment arena with the disparate impact theory, this and other detailed points of law were not of central focus until the appeals courts. The phrase "disparate impact" is therefore noticeably absent from district court records and does not surface until the case progressed to the Fourth Circuit Court in Richmond, Virginia. However, Chambers and Belton injected the legal particulars of the concept before Judge Gordon to ensure its ongoing review, beginning the doctrine's formal cultivation and pending adoption. The district court also offers more insight into each party's arguments and therefore provides a deeper look into the issues that brought the parties to trial. The genuineness, then, of the racial disparities Boyd and his fellow workers experienced is authenticated in the district court records.

Eugene A. Gordon was born and raised near Greensboro, North Carolina. He was the eighth of the ten children born to tobacco farmers Charles R. and Carrie Scott Gordon. Gordon recalls "those Saturdays when his sister would pick him up in her 'Model T' Ford and bring him into town to see a movie," driving along Highway 29, then a dirt road passing through Greensboro. He began his undergraduate studies at nearby Elon College and eventually transferred to Duke University, where he went on to complete a law degree in 1941. "Gene" had planned to enter into a career in business after completing his bar examination in August 1941 but found a draft notice awaiting him at home. The next four years saw the young man fighting on battlefields in Europe in the Seventy-eighth Infantry Division. Gordon's exemplary service earned him the Purple Heart and Bronze Star.[1]

Gordon is described as a man who was "both gentle and strong, flexible and resolute, sensitive yet decisive, humble yet quietly confident. He [was] reputed for his patience, his even temper, his quiet easygoing manner, and the careful and deliberate attention he has given to every case he has decided." This may have been most evident in Gordon's handling of the heated school desegregation cases of the early seventies. He was appointed to the federal bench in 1964 at age forty-six by President Lyndon Johnson upon the recommendation of Senators Sam J. Ervin and B. Everett Jordan. Ervin and Jordan were openly opposed to civil rights and uninterested in nominating a racial progressive to the bench. In *Scott v. Winston-Salem/Forsyth County Board of Education*, Gordon was criticized and threatened by community members because of his ruling, which culminated in the transfer of two thousand teachers in the middle of the school year as a result of the Fourth Circuit's desegregation orders. The changing tide of desegregation law dictated Judge Gordon's decision, and he was "painfully aware of the impact that his decision would have on the children." A rather astute and surprisingly legally conscious third grader wrote to Gordon, "Please don't take my teacher away. I cried a lot. You have hurt people and children. Can't you do better?" Judge Gordon replied to the student,

> Often I have to make decisions which are not liked and hurt people. Sometimes my duty requires me to make decisions that I do not like myself. You will understand this someday. It is impossible for me to explain it to you in this letter. I am not so far removed from your age that I cannot remember how I loved my third grade teacher. It would have probably caused me to cry if she had been transferred, and the decision by me that the teachers be transferred was difficult because I knew you and many, as you, would be upset. . . . One explanation for the decision . . . is that the Appellate Court feels that the good should be shared. In other words, Mrs. Keyes, who is good, kind, and imparts knowledge should be shared by you with other children who are not fortunate enough to have Mrs. Keyes. . . . As you request, I will try to do better, and hopefully what I do will meet with your approval. It is not my wish to hurt people.[2]

Chambers admitted that Gordon was a nice man, though he and his team did not expect a favorable ruling from the district court. So as the trial proceedings began, the cooperating attorneys were preparing for appeal.[3] And although Gordon was a "nice man," he was a true southerner. He was a white North Carolinian who had grown up in the Jim Crow South. His parents owned tobacco farms and probably rented to and hired black sharecroppers. Although Gordon and his family were not in direct competition with blacks for labor opportunities, they were nonetheless products of a system that pitted poor whites and blacks against one another for labor opportunities and they were groomed under the constant rhetoric and legal aura that stamped blacks as social inferiors. Duke Power no doubt provided energy to the Gordon household and to their farms. Gordon graduated from Duke University Law School, the school the Duke family singlehandedly financed into being "the Harvard of the South." He was nominated to the bench by staunch opponents to civil rights legislation who sought judges with similar political values. Segregation was as much a part of Gordon's life as it was of any white man born and raised in the Carolinas.

But there is also little question but that he was "civil" in the tradition of race relations in North Carolina. He probably, therefore, was not a hardcore racist. Though he offered a desegregation order as mandated by the appeals court in *Scott v. Winston-Salem* in the early seventies, he heard arguments for *Griggs* in February 1968. There had been no Supreme Court ruling on Title 7, and therefore few changes had occurred to what might have been considered illegal practices in southern industry. The Title 7 cases having received judicial review were district court cases that, though providing direction, offered little authority regarding the employment law or the EEOC. Title 7 had yet to fully evolve into mandating equality and desegregation across American employment institutions. If Gordon followed the law in the desegregation cases of the 1970s, he surely followed the law in the early employment discrimination cases of the late 1960s. Chambers and staff were absolutely correct in preparing for appeal, well before *Griggs* was decided by the district court.

Three fundamental employment practices at the Dan River plant dominated the trial record. Attorneys from both sides jostled back and forth over the following items: the plant's promotion process, the consideration of pre-act violations to inform assessments of post-act practices, and the authority granted to the EEOC over testing mechanisms.

At the trial on February 6 and 9, 1968, Duke Power attorney George Ferguson called Austin C. Thies to the stand as one of the company's primary witnesses. Thies had earned a bachelor of science degree in mechanical engineering from the Georgia Institute of Technology and was the vice president of production and operation for Duke Power, which meant he was responsible for the operations at the Dan River Station. Thies began by detailing the purposes of and the work performed in the various departments at the plant. Then, in an effort to refute the claim of discrimination in promotional practices, Ferguson prompted Thies to highlight the development of vacancies and promotions since the effective date of Title 7, July 2, 1965. Vacancies and promotions had occurred, Thies explained, but not all promotions led to future vacancies, and those promoted were in departments where black workers could not enter. Thies went on to state that Jesse Martin and Robert Jumper had been promoted out of the Labor Department into the watchman classification. Martin was promoted out of watchman to the Coal Handling Department, creating the vacancy to which Jumper could then move. Thies admitted that black and white workers did sometimes perform the same jobs, but his understanding of this arrangement was that higher positions assisted the janitors with their work more often than vice versa.[4]

Ferguson allowed Thies to share for the court the company's promotion policy. Thies stated that as of July 2, 1965, in order for Labor and Coal Handling Department workers to qualify "for a promotion to the higher skilled jobs within the Power Station [employees] must have a High School education or we would accept a GED equivalent to a High School education." As of September 22, 1965, the company began allowing "two tests . . . which are the Wonderlic and Mechanical AA . . . in lieu of a High School education." Thies offered clarity on this change: "The employees in Coal Handling had for some years approached me as I made visits around, and asked me if there wasn't some way they couldn't get into Maintenance." Any new hires would of course have to have a high school education and achieve acceptable scores on the two tests. "For over ten years, we have required a High School education for Watchman, Coal Handling, Maintenance, Operating, Lab and Test jobs," Thies stated. These tests, he added, were not forced on workers. Instead, they were simply accepted in lieu of a high school education. Labor Department hires, however, needed only to pass the Revised Beta Test and need not have earned a high school diploma for initial hire.[5]

Thies argued that the nature of the company's business was becoming more complex as it moved toward nuclear power and into the computer age. The company found that some workers were not astute enough to progress in jobs as needed, which led it to embrace the high school requirement. Thies then stated, "There is nothing magic about it, and it doesn't work all the time because you can have a man who graduated from High School, who is certainly incompetent and go on up." But, he continued, the company believed the education requirement was a reasonable expectation that would yield the type of people capable of grasping the more complex components of the work performed at the plant.[6]

Robert Belton cross-examined Thies and immediately inquired if the company had written job descriptions, to which Thies responded, "We do not." This line of questioning was designed to highlight the company's lack of formalized policies. If these policies were not formalized and not adhered to strictly, Duke Power officials could more easily manipulate the work environment to maintain segregated departments. Belton later asked Thies questions regarding the creation of the auxiliary serviceman position, seeking to show its inutility and its relationship to the continued segregation of the black workers. Thies said the position was created around the middle of 1966 in an effort to offer promotions to a more skilled laborer. In reality, this position was much like the watchman classification, a dead-end job that would not lead to any true upward movement beyond that position. The auxiliary service man, as Thies described the position, "might have as his normal duties, doing janitorial work . . . but he had special skills that on occasion we called on him to exercise." Belton questioned if any white employees were in the Labor Department and inquired as to the race of the labor foreman. Thies admitted there were no white workers in the Labor Department and that the foreman was white and did not have a high school education.[7]

Belton later questioned why many white workers did not have high school degrees yet were promoted to higher positions. Thies again stated that there was nothing magical about the high school education requirement, but that it was a means of hopefully hiring and promoting more qualified people. Belton also asked if there were assessments made to determine the ability of laborers in an effort to promote them out of the Labor Department. Thies denied this as allowable since it would violate the existing policy. Belton persisted in this line of questioning, seeking to show that the Dan River plant was a work environment where black employees could have learned to do various jobs strictly from experience while assisting in various departments outside of Labor.[8]

While being questioned by George Ferguson, Duke Power's attorney, Thies unintentionally opened a key issue in the case: the relevance of pre–Title 7 violations. Ferguson and Thies entered into a discussion of black workers complaining about doing a task that should have been reserved for white coal handlers. Black workers convinced Dan River supervisors to free them from "knocking doors," which meant literally knocking doors off of train cars that carried coal. Thies commented, "Knocking the dog loose to drop a door down is Labor work as far as we can see, and still feel that way, but at the time, the decision was made that . . . if it was making the employees in the Labor Group unhappy, we would just provide that the Coal Handling Operators would do this job."[9] Thies thus suggested that Duke Power was committed to responding to the needs of black workers. Plaintiff attorney Belton objected to the discussion regarding knocking doors on the grounds that throughout the deposition process Duke Power attorneys had instructed their witnesses not to answer any questions regarding company practices prior to July 2, 1965. Ferguson withdrew the question after Judge Gordon gave his ruling on the admission of practices prior to July 2, 1965: "I would rather think that what transpired before would have little bearing on the issue of what happened after the effective date of the [Civil Rights] Act [of 1964], unless we can pose the old rule, 'Something that is established is presumed to continue,' or something like that, but I hate to do that in view of the Law. Well, let's keep it after July 2nd."[10] In other words, Gordon refused to recognize any pre–Title 7 discriminatory tactics and only planned to consider post–Title 7 discrimination.

Belton tried to convince Gordon that "some information as to what transpired before July 2nd, '65, is relevant." Though the judge saw no merit in pre–Title 7 activity since the plaintiff's claim rested on a violation of the law, Gordon agreed to allow the evidence on record to protect the plaintiff attorneys in the event of appeal.[11] Belton relied on the LDF cases *Quarles v. Phillip Morris* and *Bowe v. Colgate* to support allowing pre-Act evidence in Title 7 cases.[12] But Gordon stood steadfast against lending attention to any pre-1965 employment practices.[13] This question over the admissibility of pre-1965 employment activity on the part of Duke Power was regularly revisited throughout the hearing.

For example, Belton attempted to develop the status of the Labor Department prior to July 2, 1965, to which Ferguson objected and Gordon sustained.[14] Referring again to *Quarles*, Belton stated, "Your Honor, let me refer to the language at least in the *Quarles* opinion, which suggests that it's necessary to go back beyond the date—the question that is posed . . . is 'are present consequences of past discrimination covered by the act.'" The court ruled in *Quarles*, Belton continued, that even though Phillip-Morris had halted discriminatory practices, a segment of the black workers were locked into unfavorable job classifications as a result of prior discrimination. Belton stated that "in this case we have the same situation here, because no Negroes have been employed with the Company since the effective date of the Act, and that you have had Negro employees with the company extending back fifteen and twenty years, and they've always been in the category of Laborer, and that this is what we're trying to bring out and develop—this line." Dismissing Belton's argument, Judge Gordon politely responded,

> Well, I will have to disagree with you with much respect, Mr. Belton, for your contention about it. I just simply cannot see how what transpired back of this time will help me decide whether after July 2nd, 1965, this Defendant discriminated or not. This suit was brought in October of '66, some more than a year after this Act went into effect. Now, what transpired back there until July of '65, is certainly, you know, important and pertinent, and if I start back of the effective date of the Act, there is no guide line as to how far you would go back. It just seems to me that it is like any other action, that what happened on a different and separate time from the time that liability is talked about or responsibility is talked about—and I could be wrong about it—I want the record to show the exception of Counsel for the Plaintiffs, so that they can be protected in the event that I am in error, but this isn't a suit that started three days after the Act went into effect. This is a suit that started more than a year after the Act was effective. All right, you may proceed.[15]

To compound matters for the plaintiffs, Gordon, as did many legalists of the time, distinguished discrimination as based purely on subjective intent. An employer would therefore have to admit to intentionally treating employees differently for a showing of discrimination, especially in a case where the practices appeared neutral. In *Griggs*, Gordon was particularly concerned with only recognizing "post-act subjective intent" to discriminate.[16] Or he was only willing to acknowledge whether Duke Power purposefully treated black workers differently on account of their race after Title 7 became effective, which would have blatantly violated the law. Later in the hearing, Gordon and Chambers engaged in the most interesting exchange of the trial. Regarding pre–Title 7 discriminatory practices on the part of the company, Chambers and Gordon had this verbal spar:

> *Mr. Chambers:* Your Honor, might I make one inquiry about the Court's ruling? Is it the Court's ruling that no act of a Company occurring prior to the effective date of the Civil Rights Act of '64, is competent for any purpose?

The Court: I have ruled that it is not competent for what you are talking about in this complaint. You complained that they're in violation of Title 7, specifically, Section so and so of the Act that we referred to as the Civil Rights Act. That's what you said. You referred, Mr. Chambers, to a Section— that Section became effective in July of 1965. Now how could something without the issue as to whether they are in violation of that Act—how would something that happened prior to its effective date—tell me—

Mr. Chambers: Even what transpired prior to the effective date of the Act might still presently affect rights of the employees today, subsequent to the effective date of the Act?

The Court: Yes.

Mr. Chambers: If for instance, a Company discriminated in its initial hiring practice, prior to the effective date of the Act, which admittedly was not prohibited by Federal Statute, and put all Negro employees as Janitors and now it poses a criteria for Negro employees to become employed in positions that were formerly excluded.

The Court: Let's lift it out of the context of Civil Rights for a moment, and say you have an Act that is passed or a law that is passed, and then a person is accused of violating that law. It is just inconceivable to me that it would have value in deciding the issue of whether he was violating the Act, after its effective date that you go back and show what he was doing prior to that date.

Mr. Chambers: Suppose we consider the school cases, where prior to 1954, it was not unconstitutional to discriminate and subsequent to 1954, it became unconstitutional to discriminate, and the Court then talked about the necessity for taking certain corrective steps to eliminate the discriminatory practices that the School Board followed prior to 1954. Now, wouldn't practices that occurred prior to 1954 be competent evidence in pointing out what the Boards needed to do in order to disestablish –

The Court: I don't think that is analogous to the situation that we have here. As I mentioned, this action is pin-pointed and in a different aspect from that. I don't think that would be a comparable situation.[17]

Chambers and Belton knew the importance of convincing Judge Gordon to consider pre-act discrimination, especially when the present policies and practices did little to actually eradicate the effects of discrimination. They also knew the importance of introducing and thus preserving such arguments on the record in the event of an appeal. The LDF lawyers, as the district court transcript shows, were carefully plotting future legal strategies. Similarly, southern officials understood the severity if Title 7 was construed to include discrimination prior to the law's effective date.

By limiting the purview of the case to post–Title 7 practices, Gordon undercut the LDF's efforts to develop an effect standard of discrimination. If pre-act practices were ruled inadmissible, the case would hinge on the legality of the promotion and testing practices, which since their institution appeared to be carried out in a neutral manner. The company had clearly discriminated against black workers prior to July 2, 1965, but after that time black workers with high school educations had been promoted out of the Labor Department. Those without diplomas could take race-neutral exams to progress along with white workers of lower educational achievement. Ultimately, the disparate impact theory would depend on the courts agreeing the tests violated Title 7 because they helped maintain the system created under past discrimination even though they were applied without regard to race. Judge Gordon knew that wholesale changes in southern industry would be required if Title 7 extended to cover the persistence of pre-act discrimination.[18]

The role of the EEOC and its authority over industrial testing mechanisms were of seminal importance. The district court record captured this debate between the federal judiciary and the civil rights bar over the level influence afforded federal policy and governmental oversight of industry. Duke Power's attorney introduced the EEOC's charge of discrimination in order to give Austin Thies a chance to present the company's response since it had ignored the commission's conciliatory recommendations. However, Judge Gordon interjected without prompting, "It's up to you as to whether you want to introduce it or not. I'm not insisting that you do. Whatever the Commission has said about it is not going to have any bearing on me one way or the other, you know. Really, what they put in there I will have to look at it from the evidence that's before me, to determine whether there is or is not." Ferguson promptly replied, "All right, sir. That completes my examination of this witness."[19]

Gordon's decision to not grant the EEOC's charge of discrimination any weight was clear evidence of what some southern justices thought about the federal agency. However, Gordon was completely in bounds with this approach since judges reserved the authority to rule on workplace practices based on the factual evidence presented at trial. The EEOC's findings were suggestions, not binding interpretations. Similarly, the EEOC's *Guidelines on Employment Testing Procedures*, serving as the interpretative instrument of the agency on appropriate testing procedures, would experience a similar fate as the trial progressed.

Gordon's handling of the EEOC dealt a severe blow to Belton and Chambers because the grounds upon which they questioned the exams rested on the EEOC's interpretation of the battery. Belton sought to highlight that the tests were not valid for determining a worker's ability to do jobs throughout the plant based on the EEOC's construction of appropriate testing mechanisms stemming from the *Guidelines*. Duke Power's position on the test's validity, however, focused on the notion that the battery was used simply in lieu of the high school diploma. Austin Thies suggested that requiring a high school diploma helped guarantee the company hired more effective employees, and in the absence of a diploma, passing the tests ensured employees possessed the abilities of high school graduates. The tests amounted to a proxy for the diploma. The testing issue was explored further when each party called their respective expert witnesses.[20]

Richard S. Barrett, then a consultant with Case and Company, a firm that provided management consultation to companies in the fields of psychology, sociology, engineering, management, and finance, was the LDF testing expert. He received his doctoral training as an industrial psychologist from Western Reserve University in 1956. An expert in "Tests and other Selection Procedures for Employment or for Promotion and Upgrading," Barrett's research efforts and work experience fit LDF's agenda well. In an article titled "Differential Selection Among Applicants from Different Socioeconomic or Ethnic Backgrounds," Barrett argued that test scores from tests similar to the Wonderlic and Bennett, "do not predict in the same way for members of these different groups, and that therefore, in order to develop a procedure which will assist in selecting qualified and satisfactory employees, it is desirable to consider major sub-groups independently, where possible to do so."[21] In other words, such tests do not properly predict how well ethnic minorities or those from lower socioeconomic backgrounds will perform on particular jobs. Although members of these groups may score very low on the tests, job performance did not correlate directly. Therefore, Barrett argued that the tests were not valid because they did not properly predict job performance, especially for African Americans. Of the white and black men from the Dan River plant who took the battery, all were from rural North Carolina and few were hardly academically prepared to pass such tests though many of the workers could learn the power plant's required skill sets on the job.

Belton and Barrett moved directly to the validity of the testing battery. Barrett stated that a selection "procedure is valid to the extent to which people who score high, perform well, and people who score low, perform poorly." Similarly, the plaintiff's witness urged that test validation called for a high number of subjects to take the test and help strengthen the validation score. Belton and Barrett contended that Duke Power had not properly validated its testing and promotion procedures because the company implemented the tests without doing the research necessary for proper validation. Though the Wonderlic and Bennett were widely used instruments, plaintiff attorneys suggested they were not automatically valid instruments to predict suitability for employment at the Dan River Station.

During the discussion regarding testing and validation, Belton introduced the EEOC's *Guidelines*, to which Ferguson objected. Ferguson attempted to discredit the writers of the *Guidelines* and the document itself as being "replete with hearsay and opinion evidence." He also declared, "When we adopted this test procedure, this document wasn't even a wink in the eye of the Chairman of the EEOC." Belton promptly responded with statements that urged for deference to be lent to the federal agency charged with patrolling the employment arena for discrimination:

> Title 7 sets up the Equal Employment Opportunity Commission which has the initial responsibility for determining whether an employee is engaged in an act prohibited by the statute. Included in the Statute is a provision that it is not unlawful for an employee to act on a professionally developed test. The agency which has been given the responsibility for administering the Statue in response to questions addressed by a number of employees, has attempted to set up guidelines on testing, to guide employers in the use of tests as a selection process. Again, I might say that Counsel for the Company argues that the guidelines were issued after the Company instituted its battery of tests, but in the same sense where the Legislature said you may, in private discrimination and in private industry, discriminate up to 1965, you can no longer do it; so to the extent that these guidelines have a bearing on the practice of the Company in making a determination as to whether they are acceptable to not acceptable, the fact that they were published after the Company instituted this practice, is not controlling.[22]

In August 1966, the EEOC published its *Guidelines on Employment Testing Procedures* to provide guidance to employers to administer "sound testing procedures." With the assistance of psychologists in the field of testing, the EEOC "sought to provide employers with a scientifically sound, industrially proven, and equitable basis for matching manpower requirements with human aptitudes and abilities." The guidelines considered tests "professionally developed" when they fairly measured the knowledge or skills required to perform a particular job or class of jobs or when they allowed employers to fairly predict an applicant's ability to perform a particular job or class of jobs. Qualified minority applicants, the EEOC determined, may be inadvertently excluded due to inappropriate testing procedures. Tests administered in this manner had the potential to discriminate in employment and promotion just as blatantly as other discrimination during Jim Crow's fiercest years. The commission concluded, "If the facts indicate that an employer has discriminated in the past on the basis of race . . . the use of tests in such circumstances will be scrutinized carefully by the Commission." The EEOC looked to influence both judicial interpretations and industry's use of employment tests in administering the *Guidelines*. By publishing the *Guidelines*, the EEOC could provide a sweeping notice to the regulated community instead of laboring through a case by case process of regulatory policy shaping.[23]

Judge Gordon accepted admission of the *Guidelines* and overruled Ferguson's objection.[24] Gordon had already stated that his decision would not be affected by the EEOC in any way and that the *Guidelines* were no exception. Although the *Guidelines* and other EEOC constructions of the employment law were entitled to judicial deference, they served as nonbinding aids to the courts, with the lower courts vacillating between the levels of deference lent them. It is valuable to note that EEOC interpretations and interpretative documents were clearly not intended to be elevated to the status of law, though EEOC officials sought to offer the courts guidance and direction. To give the *Guidelines* such an elevated position would have denied the courts their interpretive authority. In fact, if the *Guidelines* served as final say without room for judicial clarification, they too could run the risk of aiding in workplace injustices in some cases.[25] However, if Gordon had accepted the *Guidelines* as the authority on testing, he may have been forced to find Duke Power's tests in violation of Title 7 based on the commission's interpretations.

Ferguson's cross-examination of Barrett was designed to show the testing battery was valid insofar as it served as a replacement for a high school degree and nothing more. Duke Power never intended for the tests to be a valid predictor of job performance. The company only used the tests to measure if an employee had the knowledge of a high school graduate. Duke Power was unconcerned with whether its black workers were capable of doing jobs in higher-paying departments. Ferguson stuck to this issue to force Barrett to admit that the tests were valid for the company's purposes. Ferguson also discredited Barrett by highlighting that Barrett had never visited the facilities at Dan River and was unaware of how the tests were administered or how they were scored or acted upon in reference to the company's needs.

Ferguson then asked, referring to Barrett's research, if the industrial psychologist suggested "that there should be some sort of separate treatment for Negroes or minority groups and whites, as far as testing is concerned." Barrett responded that he believed it should be considered and that "special treatment may simply be the appropriate training . . . different job duties—different job classifications" and he was aware that some companies accepted poor test performance from some people due to their racial background. Ferguson immediately pounced on Barrett's admission, charging him with supporting discrimination in reverse if white workers scored higher on tests but a different set of norms were installed to assist various ethnic minorities. "The intent of the test is not to have them exist," Barrett responded. "The intent of the test is to select people who will perform adequately on the job. The issue is not whether they score high or low on the test; the issue is whether they perform satisfactorily on the job."[26]

Daniel Moffie, a graduate of Pennsylvania State University and professor of psychology at UNC–Chapel Hill, served as the company's expert psychologist in the field of industrial and personnel testing. Moffie legitimized the Wonderlic and Bennett tests, the base level scores acceptable for passing, and the company's testing procedures at Dan River. He stated that Richard Lemons, a mechanical engineer from North Carolina State University, had been properly trained to administer the tests in a sound testing environment. Regarding the test, Moffie concluded, "My opinion is, as a substitute for or in lieu of a High School Education, that this is a reasonable request and frankly, as a Psychologist and working in Industry, I think the Company has leaned over backwards, really." In Moffie's opinion, the janitors were lucky to only have to take twelve-minute and thirty-minute exams instead of taking classes to earn a high school diploma or GED. He also testified that the EEOC's *Guidelines* were too narrow because the commission's report demanded that the tests be job related. In fact, Moffie admitted to the test's non-job relatedness indirectly. Under cross-examination from Belton, he disclosed that the tests were not designed to predict performance, nor were they used with any predictive validity in mind. "At Dan River," Moffie stated, "the tests are really not used for Predictive Validity. They are used as a substitute or in lieu of High School education."[27] Clearly Duke Power had violated the EEOC's standards for testing. The EEOC, however, was years away from garnering any clout in employment circles. However, the company had admitted, on record, that the tests were not related to job performance. On appeal, this fact would prove crucial as the EEOC would eventually earn final say.

At the end of the trial the district court deferred making a ruling "until after proposed finding of facts and conclusions of law have been presented in brief to the Court."[28] The brief gave Chambers and Belton the opportunity to develop points of law they were unable to expand upon during the trial and allowed Duke Power to respond to the charges of discrimination and to explain why their practices were within the bounds of Title 7.

As Chambers and Belton prepared their brief, they focused on four sections of Title 7: 703(a), 703(d), 703(h), and 706(g).[29] The plaintiff's brief detailed five points that illuminated the discrimination black workers faced at the Dan River plant. However, the legal team did not question whether the diploma and test requirements alone were discriminatory. The diploma and the testing instruments were administered fairly and were standards many companies had begun to require. Instead, the LDF attorneys focused specifically on the outcomes of these requirements to determine whether the diploma and tests were job related and if they were used to or resulted in discrimination—in other words, if they indeed caused a disparate impact.

It is difficult to prove that superficially neutral devices are intended to discriminate. This calls for an employer to admit to such under oath, which no employer would ever do willfully. The Duke Power legal team knew this, as did Chambers and Belton. Therefore, what had to develop in order for the plaintiffs to prevail was an argument that ignored intent and dealt more directly with the impacts and outcomes of seemingly neutral employment practices.

The first argument the plaintiffs leveled attacked the promotion and transfer policies in general and foreshadowed what would become the disparate impact doctrine. The plaintiffs argued that the high school requirement and passing a battery of tests "have as their purpose the effect of perpetuating the inferior opportunities of Negro employees at Dan River to obtain more attractive and better paying jobs which had previously been reserved for white employees exclusively whether or not these white employees had a high school education."[30]

In providing support to this claim, the plaintiffs detailed the history of discrimination at Duke Power, showing how the practices continued after the institution of tests and high school requirements. They argued that despite the promotions of Jesse Martin in August 1966, during EEOC investigations, and Robert Jumper on January 1, 1968, one month before the case went to trial, the company's policies maintained the segregation of black men into the Labor Department. Herman Martin, the other black worker with a high school diploma, was still classified as a laborer at the time of the trial, although he was soon promoted. The plaintiffs also showed that several whites had been promoted, intradepartmentally, without high school diplomas after the initiation of the new policies.[31]

The lawyers claimed the company introduced a policy in September 1965 that mandated workers without high school diplomas in the coal handling, labor, or watchman classifications pass the battery of tests before receiving a promotion. White workers in other departments, however, were not required to do so. Company records indicated that white employees without high school educations had clearly been promoted to better-paying jobs from various classifications without taking the tests. Chambers and staff thus attempted to prove that the administration and impact of the tests, not the tests themselves, were suspect. The attorneys argued, "There are undoubtedly employers with no past history of discrimination who have and are now using such a requirement for perfectly legitimate reasons. The issue in this case, however, is whether such restrictions are legitimate when it is perfectly obvious that they serve to keep the overwhelming majority of senior Negro employees at Dan River from ever having the opportunity to advance themselves, whereas white employees similarly situated are not so limited."[32]

The LDF argued that Duke Power's practices violated Sections 703(a) (d) and (h) of Title 7 because the black workers were discriminated against in the "terms, conditions, and privileges of employment" due to their race. However, the *Griggs* party did not push for the retroactive application of Title 7. Duke Power showed the tests were not accurate predictors of job performance when the company promoted non–high school educated whites into higher paying positions after the law was effective. The tests and the diploma requirement therefore helped to maintain the current system of racial stratification. What was obvious is that Duke Power's past employment practices carried forward into the post–Title 7 era. And although the plaintiffs did not argue for retroactive redress, the perpetuation of past practices created present unfair conditions. "All that plaintiffs seek," the attorneys wrote, "is that as future opportunities for transfer or promotion arise, Negro employees already working for Dan River not be subjected to further, additional, future disadvantage because of discrimination in the past."[33]

The second argument leveled against the Duke Power Company questioned the lawfulness of the employment testing administered at Dan River. The plaintiffs rested their argument on Section 703(a), the cornerstone of the statute, which stipulates that the basic purpose of the law is the elimination of employment discrimination. However, in *Griggs* the issue of utmost importance was that of testing and testing mechanisms, which have their declarative statements in section 703(h), which states that it shall not be "an unlawful employment practice for an employer to give and to act upon the results of any professionally developed ability test provided that such tests, its administration or action upon the results is not designed, intended or used to discriminate because of race, color, religion, sex or national origin."[34]

Because *Griggs* was one of the early Title 7 cases receiving court interpretation, with particular attention paid to Section 703(h), the LDF was therefore instrumental in the legal cultivation of the law alongside the EEOC. The *Griggs* legal team would have to provide convincing arguments that Duke Power violated Section 703(h), the section of the act that originated from the Tower amendment, which sought to protect companies from an open season on bona fide hiring and promotion tests while showing that the practices at the plant violated the basic nondiscrimination requirements of Section 703(a). In other words, they had to show that "the testing program [did] not measure the skills of employees needed to perform the jobs at Dan River" and therefore had the effect of limiting promotion opportunities for black workers.[35] In attacking the testing practices of Duke Power under section 703(h), the LDF team questioned whether the measurement devices were job related and had any valid business purposes. For support they turned to the administrative authority held by the EEOC and its role of clarifying and interpreting Title 7. Specifically, they leaned heavily on the commission's *Guidelines* and the recent district court case law that served as companion Title 7 cases initiated by other client-activists and LDF cooperating attorneys.

With the weight of the EEOC's determinations regarding testing behind them, the plaintiffs argued that Duke Power's testing procedures were not properly validated and not related to the jobs in question. The commission's *Guidelines* barred measurement instruments that failed to demonstrate a business necessity and that in turn resulted in the perpetuation of discrimination. Rampant discrimination might have gone unchecked had employers been allowed to continue administering tests that failed to accurately and specifically measure job performance. To deal with these very types of employment practices and to give Title 7 teeth, the EEOC provided a firm statement concerning such practices in their *Guidelines*. The LDF attorneys were therefore able to effectively argue with legislative and federal backing that the "totally unvalidated Company's testing program is a blatant example of a highly discriminatory criterion which mocks Title 7 and should be struck down as it applies to incumbent Negro employees."[36]

To further solidify their argument, the plaintiffs used the legislative history of Section 703(h) and the Tower amendment to highlight the intent and purpose of the testing provision, which were clarified during congressional debates over the passage of the 1964 act. Senator Tower's amendment was not introduced, the attorneys argued, to "legalize discriminatory tests." Instead, they argued, it was designed to protect an employer's ability to thoroughly assess job capabilities. The amendment emerged after the *Motorola* decision and amid serious concerns surrounding the potential impact of the case on the future of employment law and practices. In sum, Chambers and staff argued the legislative history of Section 703(h) shows that "the purpose of the Tower Amendment was not to exempt ability tests from the Act's broad prohibition of discriminatory practices, but rather only as insurance that the extreme implications of the *Motorola* decision did not creep into interpretation of Title 7."[37]

If the tests Duke Power forced black workers to take were not job related and properly validated, Chambers and staff questioned whether the battery was professionally developed and in bounds with Section 703(h). The attorneys reasoned that professionally developed tests could not mean any random test developed by professionals that did not pertain to particular job applications. "This reading," they noted, "would permit . . . the use of a typing test to select ditch diggers or the use of the College Boards to select janitors." Duke Power's testing battery was not far from the latter of these two examples. Again relying on the EEOC's *Guidelines*, the plaintiffs quoted the commission: "The fact that a test was prepared by an individual or organization claiming expertise in test preparation does not, without more, justify its use within the meaning of Title VII." Duke Power's testing battery met the muster of the law, but, the LDF concluded, the application and impact of the policy failed to meet the purpose and intent of the testing requirements under Title 7.[38] Even though Chambers and staff were not arguing disparate impact discrimination this early in the case, they were laying the foundation for the maturation of this very real obstacle to fair employment.

The testing requirements were only imposed on workers in the labor, coal handling, and watchman positions and departments. White workers in all other classes were exempt from the policy and continued upward moves without having to take the battery of tests. Because white workers in the Coal Handling Department had ample opportunity to progress out of the department prior to institution of the testing policy and earned a decent wage already, the plaintiff's attorneys argued they chose to stay in the department. Also, white workers hired after the policy became active would have to pass the tests upon employment and thus never have to repeat the battery. This left only black workers in the labor department as victims of the policy, thus locking them into what was still a Jim Crow unit. On this matter Title 7 was clear: Restricting black workers to racially divided departments was illegal.

The third point made in the plaintiffs' brief argued that coal handlers dominated the allocation of overtime and blacks were denied equal access to extra work and extra pay. The Dan River plant used coal to power much of its operation, and periodically unloading and moving coal required extra work hours. Black workers rarely benefited from overtime opportunities, even though they could easily perform the jobs and had done so from time to time during normal working hours. Because overtime was allotted based on plant hierarchy, lower-ranking positions were last to be considered for the extra time and pay. Thus black laborers rarely qualified for overtime because the Labor Department was ranked below the Coal Handling Department. But all other departments, all of them higher than the Coal Handling Department, were allowed ample overtime, even though these white workers were no more qualified to shovel coal for extended hours than were black workers. Most of the time white workers would leave the dirtier, more arduous tasks to black laborers, but overtime coal handling was different. Overtime of course paid more per hour and was nice supplemental income, attracting more workers from various departments. Relying on a January 1968 decision in *Farmer's Cooperative Compress v. NLRB,*[39] plaintiff attorneys argued that Duke Power discriminated in the allocation of overtime.[40]

Fourth, and maybe the most difficult legal argument to shape, the plaintiffs argued there need not be proof of specific intent to discriminate for a violation of Title 7 to be present, further moving their argument toward a disparate impact standard. The racial designations of the Dan River departments were still in effect after Title 7 became law because the transfer and promotion battery helped maintain the system by "inhibiting the opportunities of Negro employees to obtain more desirable, better paying jobs while not similarly affecting the opportunities of white employees." Referring to administrative and judicial interpretations of the National Labor Relations Act, as well as cases from the New York Fair Employment Practices Commission, the plaintiffs argued against the mandate of proof of intent to discriminate. The legal team quoted a 1954 New York FEPC case, *Holland v. Edward,* in which it was determined that "one intent on violating law against discrimination cannot be expected to declare or announce his purpose. Far more likely is that he will pursue his discriminatory practices in ways that are devious, by methods subtle and elusive—for we deal with an area in which 'subtleties of conduct . . . play no small part.'"[41]

Finally, the plaintiffs encouraged the district court to strike down the racially discriminatory policies and practices of the Duke Power Company by relying on related cases and the expertise of the National Labor Relations Board (NLRB). In the 1967 decision *Vogler v. McCarty, Inc.,* Judge Christianberry of the Eastern District of Louisiana found a union had discriminated against black and Mexican workers by using "invidious criteria for membership." The court ordered immediate union admittance to "certain individuals" and ordered the union to cease the practice of requiring prior membership or recommendations from a relative or union member for membership. The January 1968 court order in *Quarles v. Phillip Morris* that required the tobacco company to modify its transfer and promotion policy gave "meaningful and immediate promotional opportunities" to black employees based on their length of service within the company. In related fashion, a district court struck down a racially discriminatory promotion system in *United States v. United Papermakers and Paperworkers, Local 189,* which followed *Vogler* and *Quarles* in 1968.

In two cases, *Hughes Tool Co.* (1964) and *Local 1367, International Longshoremen's Association* 1964), the NLRB used its cease-and-desist powers to eradicate racial groupings and racially segregated work forces. The *Griggs* team used these precedent-setting cases to emphasize the authority and breadth the court could take in remedying violations of Title 7, a statute that further "amplified the duty of employers to refrain from employment discrimination on racial grounds."[42]

Duke Power executed an expected approach to Chambers's and Belton's legal arguments. The four points the Duke Power legal staff submitted to the district court hinged on a reading of Title 7 that required proof of discriminatory intent to sustain a violation of the provision. The company emphasized that its policies applied to all workers, irrespective of race, and there was no evidence of intent to disadvantage blacks. Such arguments established a solid defense. If accepted, they would protect the structural and residual exclusionary practices that survived the end of outright race-based assignments and procedures.

The company argued it had not engaged in any discrimination against the plaintiffs since the effective date of Title 7. It also stated that its "Negro employees" at the Dan River Station, like whites, were no longer forced to work in low-paying, menial jobs and were eligible for progression out of the Labor Department. Evidence to these facts rested in the promotion of black workers with high school educations.[43] Duke Power attorneys neglected the fact that none of these men were promoted until after legal steps had been taken to begin forcing the eradication of the employment culture at Dan River. The attorneys also neglected the reality that white workers were promoted without high school diplomas or having to pass tests in various positions throughout the plant after the effective date of Title 7. Many of the black workers had been at Dan River since the plant opened in 1950 and from indirect and direct experience could perform jobs in other departments.

Duke Power attorneys also argued that "Negro employees . . . do not perform the same or similar work as white employees and receive less wages for such work." Using the depositions of the *Griggs* party, the lawyers showed that the men admitted to not performing jobs of higher classifications and therefore could not claim that the lower wages they received were the result of racial discrimination. Duke Power's argument ignored the black worker's ability to perform the jobs or the lack of opportunities granted them to do so. The lawyers also showed that no discrimination in overtime had taken place since the black workers received "scheduled overtime" and "emergency overtime" was based on job classification.

The defendant's second point, which focused on the testing battery, would become the heart of the case by the time *Griggs* reached the Supreme Court. The defendant argued the tests in use were professionally developed "within the meaning of Title VII and not administered, scored, designed, intended, or used to discriminate because of race or color." Both the Wonderlic and Bennett, Duke Power argued, were widely used across industry, met the necessary standards of reliability and validity for professionally developed instruments, and were deemed the lowest level of testing the company could administer. In short, they were fair and nondiscriminatory employment and promotion mechanisms. The Dan River test proctor, Richard Lemons, examined the facilities at the plant to make sure the lighting, ventilation, seating arrangements, and other environmental factors would have no impact on test performance.[44]

The defendant's attorneys discredited plaintiff expert witness Richard Barrett's testimony by pointing out that he was unaware of what "professionally developed" meant in relation to the statute in question. In addition, Barrett admitted to having little knowledge of the jobs performed at the Dan River Station. Duke Power instituted the tests prior to the EEOC producing its *Guidelines*, which the attorneys argued was proof of no discriminatory intent. In their final statement on whether the tests were professionally developed, the attorneys relied on the Clark-Case memorandum from the legislative history of Title 7 to show the tests did not have to be specifically validated for minority groups. In other words, if blacks fared less well on the exams, Title 7 did not mandate that the tests receive increased scrutiny. The Clark-Case memo stated, "There is no requirement under Title VII that employers abandon bona fide qualification tests where, because of differences in background and education, members of some groups are able to perform better on these tests than members of other groups. An employer may set his qualifications as high as he likes, he may test to determine which applicants have these qualifications and, and he may test to determine which applicants have these qualifications, and he may hire, assign, and promote on the basis of test performance."[45] Duke Power's attorneys thus found no harm arising from the plant's testing procedures.

By accepting minimum test scores as the equivalent of a high school diploma, the company felt it had "leaned over backwards" to provide black workers with an opportunity to move up to higher positions. But in its brief, the company all but ignored the fact that white workers in higher-paying positions and departments had moved upward using skills they had learned on the job even though they had never earned a high school diploma or its equivalent. Vice President of Production and Operations Austin Thies's statement during the trial rang loudly when he stated that "there is nothing magic about a high school education because it does not work all the time."[46]

Finally, Duke Power argued that the high school requirement was applied equally to all workers, did not discriminate against the black employees, and therefore did not violate Title 7. To strengthen the company's position in favor of the high school requirements, the defendant returned to Thies's testimony, during which he stated that Duke Power's operations were becoming more complex as it anticipated using computer and nuclear technology. However, he subsequently admitted that relying on a high school education was not totally reliable. And the company suggested it had experienced poor performances from workers without the high school requirement, thus amplifying the need for better-educated employees and legitimizing the business necessity of the high school requirement.

White employees were hired into higher classifications without high school educations prior the company instituting its high school policy to in 1955. Workers in the Labor, Watchman, and Coal Handling Departments continued to be hired without the high school requirement, but only white workers were promoted prior to the testing requirements. Therefore, the company argued for a prospective reading of Title 7 since only white workers received promotions before the act. Using the Clark-Case memorandum and various cases, the attorneys built an argument grounded in the notions that black workers would compete for future vacancies and that black workers should not be given preferential treatment due to alleged past discrimination.[47] The company had ceased its discriminatory practices, they argued, since two black workers had been promoted and all requirements applied equally to all workers irrespective of race.

Despite the company's arguments, an unavoidable reality was that rigid classifications had developed as a result of prior discrimination. If the court did not question the past discrimination committed against black workers, Duke Power's work force would have a showing of token integration amid the rigid, racially divided departments created years before. If Title 7 was read only as prospective law, and if it also permitted tests that were facially neutral but perpetuated past discrimination, the very statute designed to be an instrument of change could potentially assist in thwarting equal employment opportunity on a mass scale.

To further buttress their argument on the business necessity of their promotional procedures, Duke Power's attorneys reached to a 1959 decision referred to in Judge Butzner's opinion in *Quarles*. Instead of using *Quarles* as precedent, which would injure their case, the company used *Whitfield v. United Steelwork-*

ers of America for support. In *Whitfield*, the employer had racially divided lines of progression similar to those at the Dan River Station. Similarly, once blacks were able to bid for positions, they were forced to take tests assessing their ability to perform the jobs. However, white incumbent employees did not have to take the exams. The court ruled that these practices were not a violation of the union's duty to represent all its members fairly and equally. In *Quarles*, Butzner stated that the decision in *Whitfield* was not comparable to the work situation at Phillip-Morris because

> Present discrimination was allowed in *Whitfield* only because it was rooted in the Negro employees' lack of ability and training to take skilled jobs on the same basis as white employees. The fact that white employees received their skill and training in a discriminatory progression line denied to Negroes did not outweigh the fact that the Negroes were unskilled and untrained. Business necessity, not racial discrimination, dictated the limited transfer privileges under the contract.[48]

Duke Power concluded that its high school requirement had a business purpose because it would produce higher-caliber employees. Its tests were "professionally developed" tools to give black and white workers opportunities to advance, and all forms of discrimination had halted at the Dan River Station. In closing, the attorneys wrote,

> Defendant now finds itself embroiled in an expensive and time-consuming lawsuit because it sought to help the minority group for whose primary benefit Title VII was enacted. . . . Defendant has done its level best to comply with the provisions of Title VII. The plaintiffs choose to ignore the legitimate business purpose of the high school requirement and the legislative history of the Act which unmistakably shows to be prospective in effect. They seek instead to turn back the clock because of alleged past discrimination which they are unable to prove.[49]

Chambers and Belton challenged Duke Power's claim that it had adhered to the requirements of Title 7. In their brief, the LDF attorneys concluded, "Only by closing our eyes to the history of past restrictions on the opportunities for Negroes at Dan River to move out of the laborers classification could we find some plausibility in the claim that a high school education requirement imposed on incumbent Negro employees is a legitimate promotional requirement and does not constitute racial discrimination against Negro employees."[50] District Court Judge Eugene A. Gordon did exactly that in rendering his opinion of the court on September 30, 1968, nearly nine months after the hearing.

Gordon began with a short history of the development of the testing procedures at Dan River, and then discussed sections 703(a), 703(h), and 703(j) of Title 7. "Congress intended the Act to be given prospective application only," Gordon asserted. "Any discriminatory employment practices occurring before the effective date of the Act, July 2, 1965, are not remedial under the Act."[51] The disparate impact of prior inequities was, therefore, beyond the reach of corrective action authorized by the Title 7.[52] The court found that Duke Power followed a policy of overt racial discrimination in the period before the employment law that relegated blacks to the Labor Department, but this conduct had ceased since the black high school graduates were promoted.[53] The high school diploma requirement, Gordon argued, had a legitimate business purpose and was applied evenly. Gordon ignored the odd timing of the promotions occurring after the EEOC complaint was filed, arguing that the only black workers adversely affected by the promotion policy were those without high school diplomas. Thus Gordon implied that the laborers need only earn high school educations to advance because Duke Power had halted restricting black workers to the Labor Department.

In arguing that discrimination had been arrested since those black workers with high school educations were subsequently promoted, Gordon conveniently sidestepped the heart of the case. In a strange twist of logic, he supported his claim that discrimination had halted by detailing the number of white employees in higher classification whose education levels were far below high school level.[54] Clearly, Gordon argued, if these white men, with equal or less education than the non–high school graduates in the Labor Department, could work successfully in higher paying jobs, then the black men without high school degrees would be able to as well. Gordon ignored that the high school diploma requirement and testing battery continued to severely injure incumbent black employees though both appeared to be applied evenly throughout the plant without regard to race.

But Gordon was not completely blind to the reality of workplace discrimination at Dan River. He simply chose to apply a literal interpretation of Title 7. Gordon wrote,

> In providing for prospective application only, Congress faced the cold hard fact of past discrimination and the resulting inequities. Congress also real-

ized the practical impossibility of eradicating all the consequences of past discrimination. The 1964 Act has as its purpose the abolition of the policies of discrimination which produce the inequities. . . . It is obvious that where discrimination existed in the past, the effects of it will be carried over into the present. But, it is also clear that policies of discrimination which existed in the past cannot be continued into the present under the Act. Plaintiffs do labor under the inequities resulting from discriminatory promotional policies of the defendant, but the defendant discontinued those discriminatory practices. . . . The past discrimination was in restricting Negroes to the menial and low paying jobs in the labor department. Had Negroes not been restricted in this fashion prior to the institution of the high school education requirement, there would be no question of the present legality of defendant's policies.[55]

While ruling in favor of the company's use of high school educational requirements Gordon argued that if the plaintiffs were granted relief, Duke Power would not have the right to improve its work force. Or the company might be forced to abandon its current departmental classifications and promotion policy, therefore freezing all workers without a high school education in their current position without opportunity for advancement.[56]

Gordon went on to differentiate the legal issues present in *Quarles* from those in *Griggs*. In *Quarles*, a precedent-setting district court decision, Gordon argued that Phillip Morris merely relaxed its race-based employment restrictions and did so without any business necessity. In *Griggs* however, Gordon determined the transfer requirements were based purely on educational requirements and were void of any racial motive. More frankly, Gordon wrote, "If the decision in *Quarles* may be interpreted to hold that present consequences of past discrimination are covered by the Act, this Court holds otherwise. The text of the legislation redounds with the term 'unlawful employment practice.' There is no reference in the Act to 'present consequences.' Moreover, under no definition of the words therein can the terms 'present consequences of past discrimination' and 'unlawful employment practice' be given synonymous meanings."[57]

Next Gordon declared that Duke Power's testing procedures did not violate Section 703(h) of Title 7, which grants the use of any professionally developed ability tests that do not discriminate on account of race. Gordon interpreted the Tower amendment to mean that it "insure[d] the employer's right to utilize ability tests in hiring and promoting employees." He disagreed with the plaintiff's assertion that the tests should measure job ability and performance and openly disagreed with the EEOC *Guidelines*. Although Gordon agreed that tests used with intent to discriminate violated Title 7, he stated, "Nowhere does the Act require that employers may utilize only those tests which accurately measure the ability and skills required of a particular job or group of jobs. A test which measures the level of general intelligence," he continued, "but is unrelated to the job to be performed is just as reasonably a prerequisite to hiring or promotion as is a high school diploma." Finally, Gordon determined the differences in overtime allocation were not the result of discrimination but more a matter of safety. Laborers were not granted overtime as were coal handlers "because of the danger involved in doing their work at night while the coal handling operations are going on."[58]

In sum, "Duke Power's counsel had correctly anticipated the view of the district court. The district court applied the evil-motive concept of discrimination to the entire case." The court looked for company practices motivated by racial animus such as those that occurred before July 2, 1965, which locked black workers inside the Labor Department. Because black high school graduates had been promoted, the court found no discrimination based on the high school requirement. The high school requirement and the testing procedures were found to be rational management techniques for determining the most qualified applicants. Duke Power, therefore, had not engaged in the promotion practices with any "bad intent" or "evil motive." In fact, the court argued the company had done just the opposite. The tests and high school requirements, Gordon suggested, displayed a "good intent" to develop mechanisms that had a legitimate business necessity. More so, all employees, regardless of race or educational level, had a genuine chance at future promotions. And Duke Power would have an overall sharper work force. Gordon dismissed the plaintiffs' claim that the tests needed to be job-related and ignored the EEOC's determinations. Although the plaintiffs argued that EEOC's *Guidelines* required employment tests to be job-related, Judge Gordon viewed this as "simply an abstract recommendation of a federal agency" and felt free to ignore the agency's construction of the testing battery.[59]

Willie Boyd and his fellow workers would have to endure an appeal for relief. Despite the promotions of all the laborers with high school educations, the *Griggs* party was unwilling to drop the matter. Chambers and Belton appealed

Gordon's decision, and two months later, in January 1970, the Fourth Circuit Court of Appeals in Richmond rendered its opinion in the case. In the meantime, Boyd kept working and going to school on the company's bill, graduating in 1969 with his high school diploma. He and his peers were once told by Assistant Plant Manager Dan Rhyne, described as a hard redneck, that "this [Labor Department position] was all the jobs you gone get." In November 1969, Rhyne would have to give Boyd his first promotion ever—to foreman in the Labor Department.[60]

VI

FAITHFUL TO CONGRESSIONAL INTENT
Griggs on Appeal

By the time the Judge Gordon had handed down his opinion, Robert Jumper, Jesse Martin, and Herman Martin, all high school graduates, had been promoted. Boyd, meanwhile, continued taking classes at Rockingham County Community College, and upon earning his high school equivalent he too was promoted. As official notice that he was qualified for a promotion, Boyd rather sarcastically sent Assistant Plant Manager Dan Rhyne an invitation to his graduation. Rhyne attended, surprising Boyd, and soon after offered Boyd the watchman position. Boyd recounts, "I asked him how much did it pay? A thirty-six cent difference from what I was getting, and I had to drive to work everyday. That was going to eat that up."[1]

Boyd wisely declined Rhyne's offer. "I told him that [the small amount of the raise] wouldn't do me no good," he recalled. "I had been through all this with my son in school, and he was out now, just me and my wife. I told him I could make it until something better came up. That sort of upset him, but it didn't matter to me."[2] Boyd knew the pitfalls of the watchman position. He also knew that after graduating with his high school equivalency, he was, by company policy, properly educated and qualified for a position that paid more money and that led to even higher positions. Plus, Boyd no longer had to take any tests to prove he had the knowledge of a high school graduate.

Willie Boyd was one of the first black men hired at the plant (in November 1948), along with Junior Blackstock and James Tucker. It had taken Boyd nearly twenty years to get promoted out of the Labor Department, a clear example of a pre–Civil Rights Act policy impacting post-act promotion opportunities. Boyd, still sporting his class ring, remembers, "I graduated in May; May the 25 of 1969. My son graduated from Howard [Howard University in Washington

D.C.] on June 6. November come along and he [Rhyne] called me in the office and give me the job being manager over the janitor work, about 12 men. Considerable nice raise. I told him I can get along with this"—probably smiling his infectious smile or even laughing a bit, but definitely feeling more confident about his employment options—"until something better come along."[3]

Boyd knew when the case began with the filing of the EEOC complaint that he was "ahead of the game." He understood that Duke Power's education requirements would continue to stymie his advancement opportunities if he failed to earn his high school equivalency and was fully aware that in order to avoid being a victim of Duke Power's policies he had to make sure his qualifications met those set by the company. More important, he knew that an education opened doors and led to opportunities that could only be denied by discriminatory practices.

Despite the promotion of Boyd and the other high school graduates, the plaintiffs pressed the matter. Under the direction of Chambers and Belton, the party appealed to the Fourth Circuit Court in Richmond, Virginia. The opinion rendered by the Fourth Circuit Court further traces the evolution of the disparate impact doctrine, and developments arising from Richmond suggest the civil rights community and its legal practitioners could rely on fellow legal activists sitting in significant positions within the federal judiciary. Throughout the appeals, Duke Power maintained staunch support of its employment practices. Even though some of the "janitors" were promoted, the company's failure to elevate other blacks underscores its efforts to preserve the racial hierarchy that had crystallized since the plant began operation. The circuit court opinion secured raises for a few more "janitors" but did not include relief for all of the black workers, prompting the LDF to appeal to Washington. When the Supreme Court heard *Griggs*, it was beginning a measured ideological shift, earmarked by the retirement of Earl Warren and the elevation of Warren Burger to chief justice. However, the emergence of newer associate justices and the persistent legal activism of the civil rights community helped maintain the energy of the more liberal decisions stemming from *Brown* and the Warren court.

A three-judge panel reviewed *Griggs* on appeal to the Fourth Circuit Court: Herbert Stephenson Borema, appointed to the bench by President Eisenhower in June 1954; Albert Vickers Bryan, a Kennedy appointment in August 1961; and Simon E. Sobeloff, an Eisenhower appointment in January 1956.[4] The Fourth Circuit reversed the district court's ruling, in part, and Judge Simon

Sobeloff rendered a historic dissent, giving the Supreme Court the support to adopt the disparate impact doctrine of discrimination.

The Fourth Circuit handed down its opinion on January 9, 1970, just two months after Boyd received his promotion. The "janitors" were separated into three groups in the appellate court's opinion based on their employment status relative to the company's high school requirement. The first group included Boyd and the three other black workers who had earned high school degrees. The second group consisted of the six black workers without high school educations who were hired before Duke Power began requiring a high school diploma. This group included Junior Blackstock, the first black worker, who was hired by the company in June 1948; James Tucker, hired in December 1948; William Purcell, who started in September 1950; and Clarence Jackson, Lewis Hairston, and Eddie Galloway, who started in January, June, and October 1951, respectively. The last group included the four black workers who had been hired after Duke Power instituted its high school requirement: David Hatchett, hired in June 1957; Eddie Broadnax, hired in February 1961; Willie Griggs, hired in March 1963; and Clarence E. Purcell, hired in June 1963.[5]

The appeals court offered a split decision, with Boreman and Bryan in the majority and Boreman writing the opinion. After detailing the organizational makeup of the Dan River Station and providing a chronology of the high school and testing requirements, Boreman entered into the heart of the appeals court's ruling. For the four high school educated workers—Jesse and Herman Martin, Robert Jumper, and Boyd—Boreman wrote that "it does appear that the company is not now discriminating in its promotion and transfer policies against Negro employees who have a high school education or its equivalent." The case was therefore moot regarding these four because they each had been promoted and were in jobs leading to further advancement. Boreman wrote that even the "plaintiff Negro employees admit that at the present time Duke has apparently abandoned its policy of restricting all Negroes to the Labor Department."[6]

But the plaintiffs did still complain that the effects of the company's testing and education requirements preserved and continued Duke Power's past racial discrimination and were therefore in violation of Title 7. In a victory for the plaintiffs, Boreman rejected the district court's ruling that Title 7 did not encompass present and continuing effects of past discrimination, writing, "This holding is in conflict with other persuasive authority and is disapproved." The persuasive authority to which Boreman referred was grounded in three very important early Title 7 cases: *Quarles v. Phillip Morris* (1968), *United States v.*

United Papermakers and Paperworkers, Local 189 (1968), and *Local 53 v. Vogler* (1969).[7] Chambers and Belton relied on these decisions to argue their case before the district court and in their briefs to the Fourth Circuit. Each decision supported broadened reach of the employment law.[8]

In *Quarles*, an LDF case argued by attorneys Henry Marsh, Gabrielle Kirk, and Albert Rosenthal, respected appeals court Judge John Butzner rendered a decision that "became the prevailing law, resulting in improved employment opportunities for thousands of blacks and women before it was overturned by the Burger Court ten years later."[9] Butzner declared that present and continuing consequences of past discrimination were indeed covered by Title 7. His decision allowed black workers to transfer to better departments, if qualified, without losing employment date seniority. Butzner also provided the Title 7 campaign with a historic employment critique, stating, "It is also apparent that Congress did not intend to freeze an entire generation of Negro employees into discriminatory patterns that existed before the Act."[10] The *Quarles* decision helped clear the path for the LDF's high success rate in subsequent Title 7 cases over the next decade.[11] As the appeals court decided *Griggs*, Judge Butzner sent a note to his fellow Fourth Circuit judges urging the adoption of the job-related standard for employment tests. "Although a non-panel member," Butzner wrote, "I have been very much interested in your views about this case, particularly about the problem of whether tests should be job related. . . . I hope that when the panel finally agrees upon an opinion it will adopt the requirement that tests must be job related."[12]

While Quarles was under review in March 1968, *United States v. United Papermakers and Paperworkers, Local 189* was making its way out of Bogalusa, Louisiana. In July 1969, the Fifth Circuit, relying on *Quarles*, struck down a seniority system that had the effect of perpetuating past discrimination.[13] The Fifth Circuit in *Local 189* also relied on an earlier 1969 opinion from its bench in *Local 53 v. Vogler*. In *Vogler*, the court of appeals decided that courts were permitted and empowered, if not required, to order such affirmative action as may be appropriate to eliminate the present effects of past discrimination. According to Robert Belton, "These cases, collectively, introduced a new equation for the requisite finding of intentional discrimination: present (post-Act) effects of prior (pre-Act) subjective intent to discriminate on the basis of race is 'intentional' discrimination within the meaning of the Act, even if the challenged practice is facially neutral, and even though the application of Title 7 is intended to be prospective. They were the progenitors of the concept of 'discrimination' ultimately adopted by the Supreme Court in *Griggs v. Duke Power.*"[14]

Having disposed of the plaintiffs with high school diplomas, Justice Boreman shifted the court's attention to the six black workers without high school educations hired prior to Duke Power implementing its high school requirement in 1955. For these six black workers, Boreman ruled the high school requirement and testing battery were discriminatory based on the precedence set in *Quarles, Vogler,* and *Local 189.* Boreman determined these workers were locked into the Labor Department as a result of the adoption of the high school and testing requirements. "Yet on the other hand," Boreman continued, "many white employees who likewise did not have a high school education or its equivalent had already been hired into the better departments and were free to remain there and be promoted or transferred into better, higher paying positions." The same was true, he argued, regarding the testing battery therefore the battery was discriminatory when directed at this group. These six black workers were entitled to relief and for them the high school and testing requirement were ordered waived. The court also required that the seniority of these black workers be measured on a plant-wide rather than departmental basis. To do otherwise, Boreman concluded, "would result in the continuation of present effects of past discrimination."[15]

The four remaining black workers hired after the high school requirement went into effect, however, were not entitled to relief. The Fourth Circuit held that the high school requirement found discriminatory for those workers hired prior to adoption of the policy was not used to discriminate against those hired after the policy was in place:

> Although earlier in this opinion we upheld the district court's finding that the company had engaged in discriminatory hiring practices prior to the Act and we concluded also that the educational and testing requirements adopted by the company continued the effects of this prior discrimination as to employees who had been hired prior to the adoption of the educational requirement, it seems reasonably clear that this requirement did have a genuine business purpose and that the company initiated the policy with no intention to discriminate against Negro employees who might be hired after the adoption of the educational requirement.[16]

The court arrived to this conclusion based on six "compelling" facts. First, Duke Power trained its own employees for supervisory positions instead of hiring new personnel. Second, the high school requirement was implemented in 1955, prior to the passage of the Civil Rights Act of 1964 and before "the civil rights movement had gathered enough momentum to indicate the inevitability of the passage of such an act." Third, the plaintiffs admitted the company had discontinued overtly discriminatory employment, promotion, and transfer practices. Fourth, Duke Power's expert witness had properly validated the tests to insure they could effectively replace a high school education and his research showed that higher positions necessitated a high school education. Fifth, white workers in the watchman and coal handling positions were adversely affected by the educational requirement as well, meaning that not only blacks were impacted by the policy damaging an argument hinging on race. And, finally, Duke's tuition reimbursement program could be used, and was done so by Boyd at least, to assist employees in obtaining the high school equivalency.[17]

The Fourth Circuit ruled the tests were valid under Section 703(h), and the court found no evidence supporting any discrimination in their administration or scoring. The tests were "professionally developed" and the minimal acceptable scores worked as fair, substitute knowledge equal to that of a high school education. The court also rejected the plaintiffs' claim that the tests should be "job-related." In doing so, the Fourth Circuit, parroting the district court decision, agreed the tests were not "job-related" and did not lend deference to the EEOC's employment theory or the agency's *Guidelines on Employment Testing Procedures*.[18] The Fourth Circuit ignored the agency and its interpretative authority over Title 7 and the testing issue despite several opinions lending the EEOC deference. Two federal district courts in *United States v. H. K. Porter* (1969) and *Dobbins v. Local 212* (1968) had already deferred to the EEOC's position regarding the job-relatedness of testing. The Supreme Court would therefore have to settle this dispute in the lower courts.

The plaintiffs introduced other cases to encourage the court of appeals to agree "that an agency established to administer a statute is entitled to great weight." These cases included *Weeks v. Southern Bell* (1969), *Cox v. United States Gypsum Co.* (1968) and *International Chemical Workers Union v. Planters Manufacturing Co.* (1966). Boreman wrote, "Plaintiffs cite these cases . . . to support their argument that this court should adopt the EEOC ruling that tests must be job-related in order to be valid. However, none of these cases stands for the proposition that an EEOC interpretation is binding upon the courts."[19]

The appeals court ignored an important Title 7 case in *Dobbins v. Local 212, IBEW* (1968).[20] The district court in *Dobbins* ruled that a test given for union membership was invalid because it lacked a clear business necessity and therefore blocked black workers from joining the local. In *Dobbins*, Boreman argued that "the reasons for adopting such a requirement compellingly indicated that the purpose of such requirement was discrimination, which is not true in the present case."[21] Relying on the Tower amendment and the Clark-Case memorandum, Boreman wrote,

> At no place in the Act or in its legislative history does there appear a requirement that employers may utilize only those tests which measure the ability and skill required by a specific job or group of jobs. In fact, the legislative history would seem to indicate clearly that Congress was actually trying to guard against such a result. An amendment requiring a "direct relation" between the test and a "particular position" was proposed in May 1968, but was defeated. We agree with the district court that a test does not have to be job-related in order to be valid under §703(h).[22]

The plaintiffs tried to strengthen their case against the tests by relying on the EEOC's testing guidelines, which required a job-related standard. The appeals court, however, rejected this argument because no discrimination in the administration and scoring of the tests was found. The court regarded this requirement as being aimed not at discrimination but at a concern by the commission that the tests be fair: "To the majority, the EEOC's position seemed too close to one . . . that had been rejected by Congress. Thus the Court concluded that the job-related requirement was beyond the power of the EEOC."[23]

In sum, the Fourth Circuit Court of Appeals in Richmond reversed the district court in part. The appeals court agreed that there was no showing of discriminatory purpose by Duke Power in the adoption of the diploma and test requirements. Because the new standard was applied evenly to blacks and whites alike, there was no violation of Title 7. Blacks hired after the adoption of the high school requirement were treated the same as whites hired after its installation. However, the Fourth Circuit did reject the district court's ruling that residual discrimination arising from employment practices prior to Title 7 was insulated from remedial action. In other words, the appeals court held that only those blacks who lacked high school diplomas and had been hired before 1955 were victims of discrimination. Blacks employed in the Labor Department when no high school or test requirements existed could not be held subject to them because whites hired contemporaneously were never subjected to the standards.[24]

The entire appeals court, however, was not in agreement. Judge Simon Soboloff concurred with the court's decision to grant relief to the six black workers hired prior to adoption of the high school requirement, agreeing that "Title VII prohibitions encompass the present and continuing effects of past discrimination." But, he stated, "I dissent from the majority opinion insofar as it upholds the Company's educational and testing requirements and denies relief to the four Negro employees on that basis." Soboloff argued that the Fourth Circuit's ruling put the court in direct conflict with the Fifth Circuit's ruling in *Local 189.*[25] Relying on *Quarles* and the celebrated words of Judge Butzner quoted above, Soboloff found *Griggs* to be an analogous employment scenario. Rendering his own powerful commentary on the residual effects of white employment supremacy, Soboloff questioned "whether [Title 7] shall remain a potent tool for equalization of employment opportunity or shall be reduced to mellifluous but hollow rhetoric." He suggested that Duke Power's tests and educational requirements led to discrimination in their effect, as did the seniority system built upon a pattern of discrimination in *Quarles.* "The pattern of racial discrimination in employment parallels that which we have witnessed in other areas," Soboloff wrote. "Overt bias, when prohibited, has ofttimes been supplanted by more cunning devices designed to impart the appearance of neutrality, but to operate with the same invidious effect as before."[26]

Judge Soboloff linked employment discrimination directly to other civil rights legal battles. In many respects, he trumpeted the legal theories that had guided LDF litigation for decades. Illustrative of the clever devices used to maintain discrimination, Soboloff argued, was the use of grandfather clauses struck down in *Guinn v. United States* (1915)[27] and attempts to avoid desegregating public schools by using pupil transfer plans repudiated in *Goss v. Board of Education* (1963).[28] Soboloff concluded, "It is long recognized constitutional doctrine that 'sophisticated as well as simple-minded modes of discrimination' are prohibited. . . . We should approach enforcement of the Civil Rights Act in the same spirit." Judge Soboloff's dissent demanded an expanded interpretation of Title 7 and the statute's reach. Title 7 was unambiguous Soboloff determined: "Overt racial discrimination in hiring and promotion is banned." Supporting the claim that Title 7 also found disparate impact discrimination illegal, Soboloff continued, "so too, the statute interdicts practices that are fair in form but discriminatory in substance. Thus it has become well settled that 'objective or neutral' standards are indubitably unlawful employment practices." If an employment practice that excludes blacks cannot be shown to have a business necessity and does not stem from legitimate needs, Sobeloff concluded, "the practice must end."[29]

Sobeloff discounted the majority's arguments that the EEOC and the *Griggs* plaintiffs were asking for blacks to be afforded favored treatment to remedy past discrimination. He also discounted the notion that Title 7 sought to provide preferential treatment to blacks by mandating employment opportunities that "the long disfavored group"was ill equipped to perform. On the contrary, Sobeloff wrote, the "argument is only that educational and cultural differences caused by that history of deprivation may not be fastened on as a test for employment when they are irrelevant to the issue of whether the job can be adequately performed."[30] Further, Sobeloff argued that the district court and the majority erred in rejecting the EEOC's *Guidelines*. For support, he offered evidence of the Supreme Court giving deference to presidential executive orders,[31] the Fifth Circuit's ruling in *Weeks v. Southern Bell,*[32] and the *Quarles* decision. "Not only is the Commission's interpretation of §703(h) not unreasonable," Sobeloff concluded, "but it makes eminent common sense."[33]

In Sobeloff's assessment, tests and employment practices must be professionally developed and must accurately measure the job under question. Relying on the legislative history of Title 7, the Clark-Case memo and Tower amendment, Sobeloff argued that job-relatedness was in fact entrenched in Section 703(h), though the words never appeared in the final draft of the act. During debates surrounding the adoption of the Tower amendment, the senator's proposal "provided that a test administered without regard to race was permissible 'if in the case of any individual who is an employee of such employer, such test is designed to determine or predict whether such individual is suitable or trainable with respect to his employment [or promotion or transfer] in the particular business or enterprise involved.'" In quoting Senator Tower, Sobeloff explained that the amendment "would not legalize discriminatory tests." Therefore, he continued, the EEOC's construction of Section 703(h) was well supported by the legislative history, and Duke Power's argument regarding the statute must fail because the company's procedures were clearly not job-related.[34] "In short," Sobeloff wrote, "Duke Power has not demonstrated how the exigencies of its business warrant its transfer standards. The realities of the Duke Power experience reveal that what the majority seizes upon as business need is in fact no more than the Company's bald assertion. The majority opinion's measure of 'genuine business purpose' must be very low indeed."[35]

Sobeloff disapproved of his fellow judges' application of the "evil motive" concept of discrimination to *Griggs* and Title 7. Though the majority determined that because the company had no bad motive or did not design the tests with the conscious purpose to discriminate, Sobeloff maintained that Title 7 was not concerned with "the state of mind of an employer whose policy, in practice, effects discrimination." The law, he continued, would not tolerate unfair treatment of black workers even if the employer did not plan the resulting discrimination. Although the current practice did not constitute outright race discrimination, it had a major impact on blacks, an impact made possible, the judge noted, because of the plant's history of overt discrimination. The result was a Dan River plant in 1969, four years after the passage of Title 7, that looked much like it had before 1965: "The Labor Department is all black; the rest is virtually lily-white."[36] In his handwritten notes for the *Griggs* case, Judge Sobeloff wrote in bold print that the appeals court could "decide this case on the basis of disparate treatment."[37]

Duke Power's "non-job-related" promotion requirements had the effect of "freezing"[38] and excluding blacks from higher paying jobs. "This case deals with no mere abstract legal question," Sobeloff noted. "It confronts us with one of the most vexing problems touching racial justice and tests the integrity and credibility of the legislative and judicial process. We should approach our task of enforcing Title VII with full realization of what is at stake." He urged that the district court's ruling be reversed with relief granted to all of the *Griggs* plaintiffs.[39]

Legal activism was not only reserved for those trained at Howard Law School or lawyers working for the NAACP's Legal Defense and Education Fund. The civil rights community indeed had sympathetic allies within various levels of the federal judiciary and looked to this panel of judges to render opinions in opposition to continued race discrimination in various areas.[40] Simon E. Sobeloff was a lifelong champion of civil rights, and because of the essential role he played in *Griggs's* outcome, a more detailed look into the life of this celebrated legal advocate is warranted.

Born on December 3, 1894, in Baltimore, Maryland, Sobeloff began his legal career at age twelve, working in a law office earning $1.50 a week.[41] He graduated from the University of Maryland Law School in Baltimore and was later admitted to the bar in 1914. By the time Sobeloff dissented in *Griggs* in 1970, he had amassed more than fifty-five years of professional legal experience that included U.S. attorney for the District of Maryland, chief judge for the Maryland Court of Appeals, and solicitor general of the United States—the government's chief advocate before the U.S. Supreme Court. Sobeloff, a trim, vigorous, and immaculately groomed man of Russian-Jewish ancestry, "carried his learning lightly" and was an active and outspoken opponent of racial bigotry. Sobeloff was deeply impacted by his childhood of poverty, leading him to champion the causes of oppressed and subjugated peoples. As early as 1933 he testified before the Senate Judiciary Committee in support of a federal antilynching bill. Sobeloff's appointment to solicitor general by President Eisenhower came in 1954, in time for him to argue the government's case regarding the implementation of *Brown* the following year. Although the Court generally followed the government's proposals, it failed to include Sobeloff's suggestion that school districts be given a ninety-day limit to propose acceptable desegregation plans.[42] Given how states craftily dodged and rejected desegregating school districts, Sobeloff's insight into the responsibility of the courts to regulate efforts aimed at removing racial segregation and discrimination with exact instruction was not superfluous.

Sobeloff had developed a strong relationship with the LDF and the burgeoning civil rights legal community. Thurgood Marshall once stated that Sobeloff, referring to the LDF school desegregation campaign, was "one of only three white lawyers who were at all interested. He stuck with me from the beginning to the end." In fact, Sobeloff's efforts to combat race discrimination, specifically his firm stance against segregated education, led southern Democrats to mount an aggressive rejection of his nomination to the Fourth Circuit Court of Appeals in 1955. Southern senators opposed to Sobeloff's opinions on school integration delayed his confirmation for more than a year. Sobeloff finally took his seat in 1956, becoming the Fourth Circuit's chief judge two years later. Under his leadership, the Fourth Circuit earned a reputation of being one of the most liberal appellate courts in the nation. Applying to law his rather simple "t'aint fair" principle, Sobeloff's judicial activism pushed the court toward a more active defense of civil rights for minorities.[43]

Handing down opinions and dissents that, at the end of the day, would allow him to "live with himself," Sobeloff became one of the most highly respected jurists in the nation. His moral aptitude may have cost him a seat on the nation's highest court, however. Chief Justice Earl Warren once said, "I have every reason to believe that Simon Sobeloff was promised an appointment to the Supreme Court but rendered too many decisions for integration."

The seat to which Warren referred went to the more moderate Potter Stewart in 1958. Supreme Court Justice Hugo Black once lamented to Sobeloff, "How very much I have regretted the fact that we have not been colleagues on this Court."[44]

Sobeloff's legal career clearly indicates that he was in tune with decades of efforts to dismantle the legal underpinnings of race discrimination, and it shows he was far more assertive in his civil rights politics than most judges of his era. His early and continued relationship with Marshall and the LDF gave him fundamental insight into the United States' racial problems and the legal adjudication necessary for their abolition. At a March 1954 Urban League annual meeting dinner honoring Thurgood Marshall, Sobeloff introduced the guest of honor, highlighted their professional relationship, and emphasized the admiration he held for the future Supreme Court justice:

> As a lawyer I glory in the fact that my profession plays a useful role, and Thurgood Marshall has added luster to the profession by exemplifying the lawyer at his shining best—when he strives for right, freedom, equality and justice. . . . We honor Thurgood Marshall because, with singular courage, intelligence, imagination and skill he leads in the fight for human decency. The beneficiaries of his devoted efforts are not only those of his race. Whenever any minority is strengthened and made more secure, all minorities take hope and America itself gains, for it thereby approaches in greater measure the ideal of a free society.[45]

In 1955, in his arguments for the government in the second *Brown* decision, Sobeloff pushed for an impact or effect standard absent any racially discriminatory motive when determining a violation of the equal protection clause of the Fourteenth Amendment.[46] Fourteen years before hearing *Griggs,* Sobeloff understood how decades and centuries of racism had blocked black progress. Even absent intent of racial maltreatment, Sobeloff believed the effects of seemingly nondiscriminatory practices were equally as detrimental. Although the new generation of LDF lawyers may not have cultivated the same relationship with Sobeloff that Marshall enjoyed, they certainly knew of his views on civil rights. And Sobeloff, as his dissent shows, remained conscious of the major obstacles facing blacks. When he received LDF's brief in *Griggs,* he undoubtedly understood the importance of the arguments Chambers, Belton, and his fellow legal activists at LDF were advancing and the potential these arguments had for massive, industry-wide changes in employment if accepted by the Supreme Court. The well-respected Fourth Circuit judge probably hoped to influence the Supreme Court by providing a clear, forceful declaration that effect and not discriminatory intent should be the standard applied to particular problems associated with the residue left by Jim Crow.

After reading the opinion of his fellow Fourth Circuit adjudicators, Judge Butzner sent a note of encouragement to Sobeloff. Butzner was optimistic that Sobeloff's dissent would positively impact an appeal to the Supreme Court and thus the employment arena. "Congratulations," Butzner prophetically wrote. "Your views, though in dissent, will command wide respect. The arguments you marshal and your analysis of the legislative history fully demonstrate that the EEOC has correctly ruled that test must be job-related. I am pleased that you spoke out so forcefully, because Title VII of the 1964 Civil Rights Act is one of the most important statutes of recent years. Your interpretations—faithful to Congressional Intent—will help people get jobs commensurate with their ability, and it will strike the mark of race that all too often banishes them from advancement."[47]

Chambers and Belton did an impressive job arguing for the *Griggs* plaintiffs. On appeal to Washington, however, Jack Greenberg would take over due to his experience arguing before the highest court. Greenberg knew that appealing to the Supreme Court was risky. As the case stood, only four men were without relief, but if they earned high school equivalencies, chances were great they, too, would receive promotions. But a negative opinion from the Supreme Court could spell trouble for the men and would definitely spell trouble for the Title 7 campaign. Sobeloff's dissent provided hope and direction for the lawyers, however, and to leave a case unfinished was not something Chambers, Greenberg, and the other attorneys would consider unless absolutely necessary. If the plaintiffs needed to be assertive in bringing civil rights cases forward, then they too needed to be assertive. Lawyers had to be willing to challenge the legal system fully confident their interpretations and skills would prevail in the courtroom. As far as Chambers was concerned regarding the remaining "janitors" stuck in the Labor Department, Boyd remembers, "he told me, 'Mr. Boyd, we gone get 'em all."[48] But the LDF had much trepidation about the case that needed to be cleared before proceeding.

The LDF had to first question whether the *Griggs* case was "intellectually or politically mature" enough to proceed. The legal team had to determine whether or not the Supreme Court was prepared to make a major pronouncement that would have immediate and widespread impact. The appeals court had determined that testing need not be job-related in order to be in line with Section 703(h) and the Supreme Court could do the same.[49]

Next the legal staff had to consider if the record upon which the case was built presented a sympathetic argument for the plaintiffs. There was no evidence showing blacks scored less well on the tests than whites at Dan River. A professional psychologist had selected the tests and Duke Power was planning to install nuclear equipment, which confirmed the company's argument about its work becoming more complex. Plus, the company had a program that subsidized employees seeking their diplomas. The appeals decision only adversely affected four black workers, and other cases in their pretrial proceedings presented equally as attractive records through which to raise the testing issue.[50]

For example, in *Moody v. Albemarle Paper Co.* (1971),[51] a case also from North Carolina argued by Chambers and Belton, black workers experienced a similar work environment to the one at Duke Power. At Albemarle Paper Company, blacks were relegated to the dirtiest, lowest-paying "outside jobs" and were forced to take the same tests for promotion, the Wonderlic and the Bennett, as well as have a high school diploma. Unlike in *Griggs*, a different North Carolina district court ordered the company to abolish its job seniority system because it perpetuated the effects of past discrimination. The court, however, found the tests valid and refused to rule against them. On the eve of the *Moody* trial, which was after the Supreme Court had decided *Griggs*, the paper company hired an expert in industrial psychology to conduct a validation study on its testing procedures. In addition, the court found the high school requirement unlawful, ruling that the tests were sufficient measures of ability.[52] In *Moody*, the LDF had earned an early victory at the district court, which made ensuing victories more likely. And unlike Duke Power's operation, work at the paper company may not have appeared as complex, further highlighting the uselessness of aptitude tests for manual labor positions. In its initial stages, *Moody* may have appeared more promising, but *Griggs* was much further along in the judicial process.

The LDF knew that an affirmation of the Fourth Circuit's ruling by the Supreme Court would affect not only the four black workers without high school educations but also scores of other African American laborers. If affirmed, these types of tests would receive judicial backing, thus sustaining the discrimination the tests attempted to hide. Moreover, the LDF's Title 7 campaign was at stake. A loss at the Supreme Court would severely hinder its success in later years. But a reversal would be a major victory outlawing non-job-related tests and removing major obstacles to black employment progress.[53]

After the Fourth Circuit's opinion, Jack Greenberg received a friendly letter of advice from John Pemberton, deputy general counsel for the EEOC. Pemberton encouraged Greenberg to accept the Fourth Circuit victory despite its limitations. In its language, Title 7 did not expressly state a job-relatedness standard for professionally developed tests. The employment law literally targeted the intentions surrounding the use of such tests. Plus, the EEOC and its published *Guidelines,* which argued for the job-relatedness standard, still carried little clout in the courts. Appealing to the Supreme Court therefore involved considerable risk.[54]

The case did, however, present a powerful, well-argued dissent by Judge Sobeloff, one of the most respected judges in the federal judiciary and certainly one of the most respected civil rights adjudicators. In his *Griggs* dissent, Sobeloff provided support for a theory of discrimination that disregarded intent and emphasized the effects and impacts of employment policies, and he urged the federal courts to give deference to the EEOC. He insisted that the courts deal honestly with the realities of employment discrimination, which moaned for the evolution and legal definition of an employment theory that complimented and combated the lingering residue of segregation. The EEOC issued updated *Guidelines* in August 1970, which assisted the LDF's decision to appeal.[55] These newer guidelines superseded and expanded the 1966 guidelines by raising the standards of the "job-relatedness" of tests and placing stricter requirements on interpretations of "professionally developed."[56]

Greenberg ignored Pemberton's advice and applied to the Supreme Court for a writ of certiorari. He assumed that *Griggs* was as good a case as any for appealing the testing issue. Greenberg writes, "I thought that the discriminatory impact of testing would be better understood in a case where an IQ test was being used to evaluate someone who wanted to be a coal handler than in some other kind of case." Greenberg was also far braver than his colleagues throughout civil rights legal circles and he did not agree, as did his fellow legal activists, that a loss would be overly damaging to the Title 7 campaign. Greenberg's role as lead counsel for the LDF gave him final say. Though EEOC and Justice Department lawyers argued against appeal, Greenberg determined that a victory would be enormous but a loss would leave workers no worse off. Plus, he continued, "a better case was unlikely to arise. I decided to go ahead."[57] At a practical level, Duke Power and many other industrial giants regularly discriminated against black workers to such a degree the true question was whether the Supreme Court was willing to rule opposite a company on the testing issue.

The LDF and the *Griggs* plaintiffs approached the Court with good company. Pemberton produced a strong amicus brief from the EEOC, which was joined by supporting briefs from the United Steelworkers of America, the attorney general of the state of New York, and Solicitor General Erwin Griswold and Assistant Attorney General Jerris Leonard of the Justice Department. These briefs in support of the *Griggs* party helped balance an opposing amicus brief from the U.S. Chamber of Commerce in favor of Duke Power.[58]

The U.S. Chamber of Commerce brief on behalf of Duke Power argued that discriminatory intent was the determining factor of whether a test was permissible.[59] The chamber touted itself as "a federation . . . with an underlying membership of approximately 5,000,000 business firms and individuals and a direct business membership in excess of 38,000." Its brief stated that 55 percent of all companies in the country used the Wonderlic Personnel Test and more than 20 percent used the Bennett Mechanical Aptitude Test. Thus, filing their brief was in the interest of hundreds of companies that knew the potential, far-reaching, industry-wide consequences that could result if the tests were found suspect. The chamber denied that employers would ever use tests and educational requirements, "the only objective means available to employers" to properly hire and promote employees, as vehicles for discrimination. Its brief argued for "independent evidence" demonstrating that Duke Power used the educational requirements to discriminate. Such evidence would have included investigating if the company used an intelligence test for unskilled jobs, investigating the employer's record regarding race relations, determining if proper tests validation had occurred, and examining the timing of the adoption of the tests compared to the effective date of the employment law.[60]

"Although the Chamber of Commerce probably did not mean to do so," notes Paul Moreno, "its list of independent evidence clearly indicated that Duke had intended to discriminate." The company instituted its new educational standards only after Title 7 was passed and made no attempt to consider the incumbent black employees for promotion or departmental transfer until the black workers filed their complaint. Duke Power instituted the tests at the behest of white coal handlers and never made any attempts to validate the job-relatedness of the battery. The first black worker was promoted out of the labor department only after the EEOC brought charges. And, the company even resisted a *Quarles*-type settlement until the Fourth Circuit's orders. As many legal theorists have concluded, Judge Sobeloff included, Duke Power should have lost the case on the disparate treatment standard. Nonetheless, the chamber of commerce argued in its brief that Duke Power's tests and educational requirements were within the scope of Title 7 because they were professionally developed and they served the company's business purposes. The U.S. Chamber of Commerce ignored the EEOC and its *Guidelines*.[61]

The amicus briefs presented by supporters of the *Griggs* party echoed issues the LDF had slowly developed throughout the process of the case and its Title 7 campaign. The United Steelworkers of America (USWA) estimated that approximately one-quarter of its 1,250,00 members were African American and a rather substantial number of its membership consisted of members of other minority groups. The USWA stated it had actively campaigned for the passage of Title 7 and its prohibition of employment discrimination. For decades, the union argued, it had fought to eliminate non-job-related tests and standards as criteria for job advancement through collective bargaining. These devices were irrelevant for employers in determining job competency and were unfairly weighted against those who had received inferior or inadequate educations. The USWA also argued the devices were culturally biased. Though few employers continued openly prohibiting hiring and promoting workers based on race, the USWA argued, "the same result can be achieved—whether or not so intended— by the utilization of factors 'neutral on their face,' which are unfairly slanted against minority groups." As a result, the USWA agreed that the petitioners had set forth solid legal grounds for a reversal of the appeals court decision.[62]

Louis J. Lefkowitz, attorney general of the state of New York, bragged in the state's brief that in 1945 New York became the first state to enact fair employment practices in an effort to eliminate and prevent discrimination based on race or color. In the state's brief, Lefkowitz admitted that "though the era of overt racial discrimination may be near an end, more subtle and sophisticated modes of excluding racial minorities have emerged to threaten progress toward equal opportunity." Non-job-related requirements had the same prejudicial effects as past, overt discriminatory practices. The *Griggs* case, the attorney general continued, was of great significance in its potential to affect the struggle for equality in employment for minority groups. If companies were able to use tests that failed to have a showing of job-relatedness, unions and employers would have an open door to circumvent federal and state antidiscrimination laws by adopting measures that screened out a disproportionate number of persons otherwise qualified to perform the actual job. New York's brief discounted Duke Power's promotion and employment practices, arguing the practices violated Title 7 and the EEOC's *Guidelines* in that they were unrelated to the jobs in question, not professionally developed, and had a racially discriminatory impact.[63]

The Department of Justice's amicus brief highlighted the federal role in the enforcement of Title 7 through the attorney general, who wrote that "the goal of equal employment opportunity remained unrealized" and the underemployment and unemployment of blacks and other minorities was substantially higher than the population at large. In agreement with the EEOC and the commission's construction of Title 7, the attorney general found that Duke's tests and high school requirement violated the statute. More so, the Justice Department ignored the motive of the company in the development and use of the requirements and argued that this focus misled the Fourth Circuit. The Justice Department brief called for the Supreme Court to lend "great deference" to the EEOC's interpretations of Title 7.[64]

The government's position in *Griggs* rested on prior cases in which the United States acted as a litigant. In a series of voting cases, the Justice Department had "developed the important doctrine that facially neutral policies that perpetuate the effects of past discrimination are themselves unlawfully discriminatory."[65] The department began formulating its position regarding disparate impact during the Kennedy and Johnson administrations. Similarly, the Kerner Commission, appointed by President Johnson, found in 1968 that "artificial barriers to employment and promotion must be removed by both public and private employers. . . . Racial discrimination and unrealistic and unnecessarily high minimum qualifications for employment or promotion often have the same prejudicial effect."[66]

In employment discrimination cases, largely informed by its Civil Rights Division, the Justice Department was well aware that "tests were subject to abuse and manipulation and tended to perpetuate past discrimination." This disparate impact focus in employment stemming from the government was also consistent with President Richard Nixon's support for the 1969 Philadelphia Plan, which endorsed affirmative action remedies—the establishment of goals and timetables—in governmental construction contracts. Brian Landsberg, former attorney in the Civil Rights Division, states that the department's position "stemmed from an amalgam of litigation precedent, core values, views of the Labor Department and EEOC, and presidential policy."[67] Landsberg's analysis of the Justice Department suggests the EEOC and the department synchronized their approaches to further eradicate workplace discrimination.

Although the LDF had an impressive array of allies, it was presenting its arguments to a Supreme Court led by Warren Burger, not Earl Warren. The Warren court is often described as having approached law with a sense of moral responsibility, which resulted in an activist agenda seeking to serve the constitutional rights of racial minorities, particularly African Americans.[68] Julius Chambers argues that "in a series of opinions, beginning with *Brown v. Board of Education*, the Warren court paved the way for the application of the ideals of liberty, equality, and justice embodied in the founding documents of our nation, to Americans of African descent." The following quote by Earl Warren, which is also engraved on his tombstone, captures his efforts as chief justice: "Where there is injustice, we should correct it; where there is poverty, we should eliminate it; where there is corruption, we should stamp it out; where there is violence, we should punish it; where there is neglect, we should provide care; where there is war, we should restore peace; and wherever corrections are achieved we should add them permanently to our storehouses of treasure."[69]

Scholars argue the Warren court and its decisions revolutionized society and the Constitution, offering legal confirmation that it was indeed time to uproot the vestiges of slavery and Jim Crow. According to historian Bernard Schwartz, in regard to civil rights, voting rights, first amendment rights, and defining the limits of police authority, the Warren court had no equivalent in the Court's history.[70] Chief Justice Warren's opinion in *Brown,* likewise, helped ignite the civil rights movement.

In many ways, the Warren court laid the legal foundation for continued efforts to topple American racism. By the time Warren stepped down as chief justice in 1969, "America had changed irrevocably."[71] President Richard Nixon appointed the relatively unknown Warren Burger to follow Earl Warren as chief justice, however, not another liberal crusader to the helm of the nation's highest tribunal. Despite attempts to undue the work of the Warren court, some justices from the Warren era remained, and civil rights crusaders were frequently in the courts, making the task a difficult and complicated one.

The Burger court during *Griggs* included two Nixon appointments, two Roosevelt holdovers, three Eisenhower holdovers, one Kennedy appointment, and one Johnson appointment. Hugo Black was appointed in 1937 and William O. Douglas in 1939. John Marshall Harlan, William J. Brennan, and Potter

Stewart were each appointed by Eisenhower in 1955, 1957, and 1958, respectively. Kennedy appointed Byron White in 1962, and Johnson appointed Thurgood Marshall in 1967. Burger was appointed chief justice in 1969, followed by his childhood friend, Harry Blackmun, as the second Nixon appointee in 1970.[72] In the early years of the Burger court, Harlan and Burger made up the conservative bloc of the court, with Douglas leading the liberal bloc, which included Brennan, Black, and Marshall. Blackmun, Stewart, and White were considered the moderates of the bench. However, during his first term, Blackmun regularly landed on the same side of cases as his childhood friend Burger. The two attended grade school together while growing up in Minnesota and remained close friends. Blackmun even stood as best man at Burger's wedding. Because of their close relationship and their similar records on cases, the press referred to the duo as the "Minnesota Twins," after their hometown baseball team.[73]

The Burger court's approach to constitutional constructions of civil rights legislation, scholars have argued, "included some dismantling of the jurisprudential structure erected under his predecessor." Vincent Blasi's work, *The Burger Court: The Counter-Revolution that Wasn't*, embraces a succinct description of the actual operations of the Burger court in its subtitle. President Nixon and the chief justice may have indeed preferred a counterrevolution to the Warren court's liberal crusade, as many liberals feared, but the legal constructions of the Warren court were not easily undone.[74] In fact, the Burger court actually advanced the civil rights agenda in some respects. As legal scholar Ronald Kahn argues, the Burger court looked to end de facto race discrimination even when inequality of outcomes between races could not be linked to specific wrongdoings. It was willing to view race discrimination as a function of structural complexities and attend to issues of race discrimination in terms of group outcomes.[75]

Much of the inability of the Burger court to mount an all out retreat on the developments of the Warren court's civil rights pronouncements, however, must be attributed to the continued vigilance of the civil rights legal community, as the history of *Griggs* shows. The community's legal strategy had evolved to a group-centered approach, which Kahn argues became the unit of analysis for the Burger court. And civil rights lobbyists had become regular faces in Washington by the late 1960s. Thus the energy from the civil rights community persisted, and as more aggressive and militant stances emerged from the black community—particularly more boisterous rhetoric targeting black equality, urban rebellions, and the emergence of black labor and black political radicalism—the Burger court could hardly attempt a counterrevolution. Social forces from the bottom up had not lost their punch during the early years of Burger's tenure. Scholars searching for answers to this quandary with the Burger court might find solace in assessing the continued activism of the civil rights community, the impact of black power rhetoric, spawning political influence from the black community into the 1970s, and pushes from leftist protest communities.

A more extended discussion of related legal outcomes of the Burger court is best reserved for the focused works on that court. Suffice to say here that among the early, more liberal decisions handed down by the Burger court were "the two most far-reaching civil rights cases" of Burger's tenure, *Griggs v. Duke Power* and *Swann v. Charlotte-Mecklenburg*.[76] Both were LDF cases engineered by Julius Chambers and his staff out of Charlotte, North Carolina, both were heard by the Supreme Court in 1971, and both resulted in landmark decisions that worked to dismantle the vestiges of Jim Crow.

The LDF submitted its *Petition for Writ of Certiorari* for *Griggs* on April 9, 1970, followed by Duke Power's respondent's brief on May 7.[77] When Chief Justice Burger received the petition, he placed it on the "dead list," seeing no merit in the appeal since the Fourth Circuit's compromise seemed fair and sensible. Burger, described as a "law and order" conservative, is reported to have disapproved of his predecessor's liberal crusade, but he brooded over and even disagreed with his conservative public image. The press had largely cast him in that role, often juxtaposing him against his predecessor. But apparently, Burger viewed himself as a moderate justice. Indeed, he displayed a moderate record with respect to civil rights rulings. Even Hugo Black, a passionate proponent of school desegregation, found Burger's civil rights record to be "decent." Justice Brennan recused himself from *Griggs* because he had once represented the company, but he persuaded Justice Stewart to request its full discussion during the Court's judicial conference. Brennan was aware of the discrimination in which Duke Power engaged and "hoped the decision would go against his former client."[78]

Burger was determined to combat his conservative image by finding cases in which he could vote with the liberal wing and write more liberal opinions.[79] *Griggs* provided a perfect opportunity. Burger could make a solid imprint on a case springing from the most significant civil rights legislation to hail from Congress since Reconstruction. He could also make a strong statement regarding employment discrimination and directly target the perpetrators, further polishing his desired moderate persona. On June 29, 1970, the conference voted to grant review of *Griggs* and issued the writ. The LDF submitted its brief in August, and Duke Power responded in October. The Court scheduled oral arguments for December 14, 1970.[80]

By the time *Griggs* appeared before the Supreme Court, the case rested squarely on "whether the intentional use of psychological tests and related formal educational requirements as employment criteria violates . . . Title VII."[81] The lower courts had decided all of the other employment issues involved in the initial charge of discrimination.   In its brief, LDF charged that Title 7 required that tests and diploma requirements be related to job performance, especially where such requirements unequally excluded blacks from employment opportunities. The fund also urged that "Title VII, potentially a remedial milestone in civil rights legislation, bars not only outright refusal to hire blacks; but it also makes unlawful subtle or superficially neutral forms of racial discrimination."[82] These newer, more clandestine forms of discrimination continued to perpetuate unfair employment practices and work situations because the older systems of discrimination were never destroyed. To buttress its argument, the LDF suggested that the Wonderlic and the Bennett tests excluded a disproportionate number of blacks because of the subpar education blacks had received in segregated schools. For support, it relied on *Gaston County v. United States* (1969), in which the Supreme Court sustained an interpretation of the Voting Rights Act of 1965 that found literacy tests in violation of the act due to the disparity of education levels resulting from segregation.[83]

Further, the EEOC and the Office of Federal Contract Compliance (OFCC)[84] both agreed that tests and educational requirements must have a showing of job relatedness.[85] For support, the LDF turned to two cases, *Arrington v. Massachusetts Bay Transportation* (1969) and *United States v. H. K. Porter Co.* (1968).[86] In *Arrington*, non-job-related tests were found to "make little business sense," and when the effect was to discriminate against disadvantaged minorities, they became "unconstitutionally unreasonable and arbitrary." In *Porter*, an Alabama court found that the aptitude measured by a test should be relevant to the aptitudes necessary to perform the job.[87] The LDF wrote, "The use of tests and educational requirements is but one example of a new breed of racial discrimination. While outright and open exclusion of Negroes is passé, the use of various forms of neutral, objective criteria which systematically reduce Negro job opportunity are producing the same result."[88]

Next, the fund showed that the "record below offers no basis for finding that the diploma/test requirement meets a job relatedness standard." If the courts below had made any inquiry beyond a mere affirmative showing of racial animus, they continued, then Duke Power's practices would have been found unlawful. The four black workers under question were therefore denied promotions due to suspect policy. In *Hobson v. Hansen* (1967),[89] a district court found that scores on aptitude tests did not measure ability to perform jobs in question but simply how well people from particular backgrounds score on the exams. In other words, middle-class and more educated whites overall performed better on the tests than poorly educated, low-income blacks. As a result, the court found the tests "practically meaningless."[90]

Finally, the petitioners argued the tests were not protected under Section 703(h) of Title 7, as Duke Power declared. The tests were not professionally developed as required by the EEOC, and because "these requirements tend to prefer whites over blacks, by three to one," the LDF contended, "it is discrimination with a vengeance." The company had a history of discriminating against black workers, and the tests were not instituted until the law "required Duke to drop its overt racial discrimination." Instead of altering the plant structure to provide opportunities, "the company seized on the alternative of a test that continues" to discriminate against blacks by using educational achievement as a prerequisite for jobs throughout the plant. The Tower amendment, the LDF argued, sought to protect only tests designed to predict an individual's suitability or trainability for a particular position. Though the final wording did not expressly state a job-related standard in Section 703(h), the fund argued that this was the initial intent of Senator Tower and it should therefore follow that it was inherent in the final accepted version.[91]

The Tower amendment and the senatorial debates surrounding its adoption require one more assessment. On the one hand, opponents to reading a job-related standard into the amendment easily found fuel for their argument since there was no enunciation of it in the final wording of Section 703(h). But the initial amendment, which was rejected, clearly embraced the heightened standard. Proponents of the job-related standard essentially used the same argument to fuel their position but focused on the inherent job-related standard in the second version though the specific language did not exist. Judge Sobeloff's construction of the amendment in his dissent falls into this category and informed the LDF's interpretation of 703(h). Yet more clarity on the Senate debates is needed here.

The initial Tower amendment was rejected by supporters of Title 7, such as Senator Humphrey, because it injected messier, more confusing questions and language into the law. The initial amendment with the heightened job-related standard was not rejected because Congress opposed the standard. Some legal scholars have missed this important detail. Proponents of Title 7 saw Senator Tower's testing amendment as another attempt to muddy the law and weaken its enforceability, which opponents had attempted throughout the cultivation of Title 7 and the 1964 act in general.

The revised version of the amendment was accepted because it included the "professionally developed" requirement, not because it lacked the job-related standard. The modified version also passed because Section 703(h) denied the use of tests designed, used or intended to discriminate. No matter how one interprets the Tower amendment and its associated Senate debates, a test challenged under Title 7 that lacked job-relatedness would still need to meet the nondiscriminatory requirements of 703(h), leading one to question job-relatedness under the "professionally developed" umbrella. The modified Tower amendment was easily construed to protect workers from tests that lacked job-relatedness despite the actual words being absent in that section of the bill.[92] Thus Sobeloff construed the law to embrace a job-related standard, which then informed Burger to consider a similar construction of the testing amendment.

Duke Power's Supreme Court brief echoed the same arguments the company had advanced throughout the legal proceedings. First, the company argued the high school requirement was adopted in good faith and served a legitimate business purpose. The minimum scores accepted on tests constituted reasonable substitutes for determining if an employee has the general intelligence and overall mechanical comprehension level of the average high school graduate. Second, the respondent argued the tests were professionally developed within the meaning of Title 7 and "were not administered, scored, designed, intended or used to discriminate because of race or color." Finally, Duke Power argued that the lower courts had found the tests and education requirement lawful under Title 7 and ruled that the company had a legitimate business purpose.[93]

In what was a seemingly bigoted declaration to offer before the Supreme Court, in a race discrimination case no less, Duke Power stated, "The fact that some few white incumbents without a high school education had the ability to enter and progress in the higher skilled classifications does not necessarily mean that each of the four Negroes involved here has the same ability, and could likewise progress." The company determined that the minimal scores accepted provided an opportunity for black workers to progress so there could not be any intent to discriminate. Since eleven black workers were affected by this policy and nine white workers, the "number of Negroes affected was not disproportionately greater than the number of whites affected." Duke Power ignored that many whites without high school educations worked in higher positions and performed well. The company also failed to admit that eleven of fourteen laborers equaled nearly 80 percent of the black employee population.

The company relied, as it had throughout litigation, on strict, literal interpretations of Title 7 to support their arguments. In doing so, Duke Power worked to debunk many of the LDF's assertions, such as the timing of the creation of the policy being evidence of intent to discriminate. Also, since the tests were applied evenly, "the Company submits that it is factually impossible to 'use' the test to discriminate against the four black workers." In another peculiar argument, Duke Power determined that the four black workers under question would not have been hired into a department other than Labor because they could not qualify for other positions. Therefore, "The tests were adopted to give these incumbent employees a short-cut to promotional consideration."[94] Duke Power ignored that it had previously relegated blacks to the Labor Department purely because of race, and it ignored that the workers' abilities were never assessed or maximized.

Duke Power's interpretation of the Tower amendment and Clark-Case memorandum remained unchanged. "To be sure," Duke Power asserted, "Section 703(h) permits employers to insist on job-related tests, but nowhere in the legislative history does there appear a requirement that employers must use only those tests which are job related. If Congress had so intended, it could have easily inserted language making such intent clear and unmistakable."[95] Duke Power dismissed the petitioner's reliance on *Dobbins* because that case dealt with questions over discrimination in union membership, facts that were not apparent in *Griggs*. In like fashion, the company argued against other cases LDF used for support and precedence, such as the voting case *Gaston County*. In closing, Duke Power exclaimed, "The Company took this action [requiring tests for promotion] to allow Negroes and whites without a high school diploma to lift themselves up by their bootstraps. It backfired. As a result the Company finds itself embroiled in an expensive and time-consuming suit which has now reached the highest court in this nation. . . . They seek to turn back the clock and thereby gain preferential treatment in promotions and interdepartmental transfers without regard to the qualifications the Company has determined necessary to perform the higher skilled jobs."[96]

Duke Power was appealing to burgeoning neoconservative arguments aimed at antidiscrimination programs and policies designed to increase the presence of African Americans, women, and other minorities in employment institutions. Although more aggressive arguments surrounding reverse discrimination and quota programs that arguably placed unqualified blacks in undeserved positions would emerge in future cases, Duke Power's statements represent early expressions of hostility to equal employment opportunities during the era of affirmative action. The company even reached back to the words of Booker T. Washington when it suggested that black workers "lift themselves up by their bootstraps." These sentiments revert to the apex of the Jim Crow era, when blacks suffered extreme economic marginalization and subjugation while whites prospered from exploiting black agricultural and domestic labor. Duke Power's phraseology can be taken as indication that the company, dominated by white men accustomed to their racial superiority, preferred to maintain the social, economic, and political order present during the turn of the century. The company's words also show that it was unwilling to change its employment practices and policies unless forced to do so by the Supreme Court.

During oral arguments on December 14, 1970, the attorneys offered sound bites of the same legal issues developed at greater length in their briefs. The justices questioned George Ferguson of Duke Power and Lawrence Cohen, appearing on behalf of the Chamber of Commerce, for clarity on the issues of business necessity and job relatedness. Jack Greenberg, meanwhile, hammered the idea that tests unrelated to job performance violated Title 7 as clarified by the EEOC and its *Guidelines*. When arguing before the Court, the LDF relied heavily on the dissent of Fourth Circuit Judge Simon Sobeloff.[97]

Burger eventually voted with the majority as his attempts to derail the case or build a coalition to affirm the Fourth Circuit decision had failed. As the new chief justice, he wanted to be the Court's unmistakable leader. Plus, voting with the majority allowed him to assign himself the task of writing the opinion.[98] Though Burger wrote the opinion, his draft did not pass the full Court without revisions from the other justices. Draft copies circulated fairly easily because the chief justice had one year earlier taken the "necessary steps . . . toward acquiring a Xerox machine." (Though these and other technological advancements made the justices', or more precisely, their clerks', jobs much easier, justices from earlier Courts agree that new technology, such as word processors and personal computers, ultimately decreased their more personal interplay.)[99]

Justice Stewart asked for the removal of two paragraphs supporting tests used to measure "long range" ability to do particular jobs. He believed the paragraphs would further allow employers to continue using tests to discriminate. Stewart wrote to the chief justice, "Not everyone can be promoted. If an employer is allowed to refuse to hire a job applicant because the applicant cannot pass a test for a better or higher job, the employer will be able, if he wishes, to discriminate against applicants who are fully qualified for the jobs for which they apply." In Stewart's estimation the paragraphs were "not necessary in reaching our decision in the case before us."[100] Ultimately, this deletion strengthened the Court's stance against non-job-related testing.

Justice Black was not in Washington, D.C., as Burger prepared the opinion but received his drafts by mail and suggested the opinion include the phraseology "vacate and remand," instead of "reversal," because much of the Fourth Circuit opinion was affirmed. Burger agreed to this change, though it never appeared, and wished Mr. and Mrs. Black well, writing, "The weather shows signs of moderating here and we hope you and Elizabeth have 80 degree weather in Florida."[101] John Marshall Harlan agreed with "and was glad to join [Burger's] opinion." Harlan suggested Burger detail the statement of facts to make clear distinctions between the groups of men without high school educations who were hired before and after the initiation of Duke's policy. He also suggested elaborating the legislative history of Title 7 to support the decision to lend deference to EEOC's *Guidelines*. Harlan wrote, "More particularly I have in mind Senator Tower's proposal that the tests should be in effect job-related, and also certain portions of the Clark-Case memorandum. I would think that this legislative history should be faced up to, although I think it is adequately answered by reliance on the EEOC guidelines." Harlan also agreed with Justice Stewart's suggestion of omitting the two paragraphs allowing tests that measured "long range" ability. All of the justices joined the opinion, the last of whom being Thurgood Marshall on February 18.[102]

On March 8, 1971, after their ritual handshake and coffee from a silver urn,[103] the Court offered a unanimous reversal of the Fourth Circuit. In summing up the role of Title 7, Chief Justice Burger determined,

> The objective of Congress in the enactment of Title VII is plain from the language of the statute. It was to achieve equality of employment opportu-

nities and remove barriers that have operated in the past to favor an identifiable group of white employees over other employees. Under the Act, practices, procedures, or tests neutral on their face, and even in terms of intent, cannot be maintained if they operate to "freeze" the status quo of prior discriminatory employment practices. . . . What is required by Congress is the removal of artificial, arbitrary and unnecessary barriers to employment when the barriers operate invidiously to discriminate on the basis of racial or other impermissible classification.

Burger continued, "The Act proscribes not only overt discrimination but also practices that are fair in form, but discriminatory in operation. The touchstone," he added, "is business necessity. If an employment practice which operates to exclude Negroes cannot be shown to be related to job performance, the practice is prohibited."[104] Burger borrowed language and rationale from Sobeloff's dissent and relied on the EEOC and LDF's arguments regarding the role of Title 7, the legislative history of the testing question, the effect tests had to potentially "freeze" black workers into inferior positions, and the impact objective and neutral requirements had on maintaining past discrimination.

Burger found no fault in the district and appeals courts not finding discriminatory intent. But, he explained, "good intent or absence of discriminatory intent does not redeem employment procedures or testing mechanisms that operate as 'built-in headwinds' for minority groups and are unrelated to measuring job capability." He emphasized that Section 703(h) authorized the use of any "professionally developed test" that is not "designed, intended or *used* to discriminate because of race." Congress, Burger concluded, was concerned more with consequences of employment practices and not simply the motivation behind such practices. In this case, the tests resulted in discrimination and therefore violated EEOC guidelines. "More than that," the chief justice continued, "Congress has placed on the employer the burden of showing that any given requirement must have a manifest relationship to the employment in question."

In framing his job-related argument, Chief Justice Burger echoed the points made by Judge Sobeloff. Though the wording of the amendment made no mention of a job-related standard of professionally developed tests, Burger explained that the debates leading up to the adoption of the amendment mandated tests meet the job related requirement: "Senator Tower of Texas introduced an amendment authorizing 'professionally developed tests.' Proponents of Title VII opposed the amendment because, as written, it would permit an employer to give any test, 'whether it was a good test or not, so long as it was professionally designed. Discrimination could actually exist under the guise of compliance with the statute.' The Amendment was defeated and two days later Senator Tower offered a substitute amendment which was adopted verbatim and is now the testing provision of §703(h)." However, in a very detailed footnote, Burger explained that the original Tower amendment provided that a test would be permissible if it was "designed to determine or predict whether such individual is suitable or trainable with respect to his employment in the particular business or enterprise involved."[105] The legislative history of Title 7, Burger suggested, therefore required that tests be job related.[106]

Burger found Duke Power's requirements of a high school diploma and aptitude tests to be inadequate measures of job performance that, as a consequence, offered the potential for discrimination. Burger, himself a graduate of a little-known night law school, St. Paul College of Law in Minnesota, was particularly bothered by the education requirements Duke Power applied to general laborers. He noted, "History is filled with examples of men and women who rendered highly effective performance without the conventional badges of accomplishment in terms of certificates, diplomas, or degrees. Diplomas are useful servants, but Congress has mandated the commonsense proposition that they are not to become masters of reality."[107]

Burger attempted to clear away any concerns over whether Title 7 endorsed preferential treatment. "Nothing in the Act," he stated, "precludes the use of testing or measuring devices; obviously they are useful. Congress has not commanded that the less qualified be preferred over the better qualified simply because of minority origins." But "what Congress has commanded," as he concluded the opinion, "is that any tests used must measure the person for the job and not the person in the abstract."[108]

"*Griggs v. Duke* Power was the first major Title VII case decided by the Supreme Court," notes Robert Belton.[109] Judge Simon Sobeloff understood the significance of the Court's ruling on the legal questions presented in the case. He opened his dissent of the appellate court's ruling by noting that the "decision we make today is likely to be as pervasive in its effect as any we have been called upon to make in recent years."[110] Sobeloff's dissent was so exacting that Chief Justice Burger relied heavily on his construction of the statute and arguments relating to practices fair in form but discriminatory in their impact; what finally became termed disparate impact discrimination.

The Supreme Court's decision in *Griggs* established a new concept of discrimination that ignored intent and equal treatment, which had previously served as the bases for a finding of racial discrimination. According to Belton, "The *Griggs* concept has been described as 'disparate impact,' 'adverse impact,' 'disproportionate impact,' or statistical discrimination.'"[111] The *Griggs* concept, or the disparate impact standard, is a broad concept of discrimination, much to the liking of the LDF and the civil rights community, that questions the outcomes and effects that employment practices have on employment opportunities. Employment practices became suspect under *Griggs* and the disparate impact doctrine if they entailed present and continuing effects of past discrimination, if there were present effects of past discrimination even when no history of past discrimination is demonstrated, and if past and present employment practices had an adverse effect even when administered fairly, neutrally or with "benevolent motives."[112]

Although the issue before the Court rested squarely on the legality of tests, ultimately the disparate impact doctrine was applied to an array of employment practices, including recruitment, seniority, and promotion practices and supervisory selection procedures. *Griggs* was also the foundation upon which future principles of Title 7 law developed in subsequent court decisions. These principles included the order and allocation of the burdens of proof, the standard of job relatedness, and statistical evidence to establish a pima facie case of discrimination. *Griggs* also provided the EEOC and its *Guidelines* with much-needed deference, finally giving the commission credibility as the chief authority on employment discrimination throughout the nation.

The LDF's Title 7 campaign was in full motion after a victory that included a broad, far-reaching statement on Title 7 and employment discrimination. Immediately after the *Griggs* decision, Jack Greenberg stated, "We are now ready to proceed with scores of cases involving many thousands of workers who have been denied jobs or promotions because of non job-related tests which have come into widespread use since the passage of the Fair Employment Act."[113] The strategy of garnering group-centered results now had the legal support it needed to effectively challenge patterns of institutional racism. The residue left from Jim Crow was met with the most powerful legal weapon it would encounter during the post–civil rights era. Seventeen years after *Brown*, the LDF again helped engineer a legal campaign to catapult African Americans further into the mainstream of American society. In *Griggs*, it won yet another case that signaled a new era of increased opportunity for blacks. In 1971, after nearly six years of legal jockeying, the LDF made school desegregation a reality via busing in *Swann v. Charlotte-Mecklenburg*. The same year, it made fairer employment opportunities and promotions a reality in *Griggs v. Duke Power*. Out of his small, Charlotte-based law firm, Julius LaVonne Chambers, representing the future of LDF and civil rights attorneys, had engineered both.

What began as a typical discrimination case in North Carolina turned into the most significant employment discrimination case of the civil rights era. It also gave rise to the most effective theory of discrimination in the battle against subtle, apparently neutral practices that perpetuated racial discrimination. Yet the *Griggs* opinion received little fanfare. Most major newspapers that Monday offered a routine blurb from the journalist on the Supreme Court beat, but few offered detailed analyses. One editorial in the *Charlotte Observer* recognized that the court's ruling "probably set in motion a revolution in the processes for testing and measuring personnel throughout the country. . . . Negroes have long complained that such tests (intelligence tests and mechanical aptitude tests) were discriminatory since they contained a "cultural bias" that favored whites and the middle class. Their complaints had already aroused a reappraisal of tests and testing procedures, and the Supreme Court's decision will only hasten that needed reform."[114]

Although this was an astute and somewhat sympathetic analysis of the *Griggs* decision from the city that was home to Chambers's law firm, the journalist could not completely anticipate the case's significance to Title 7, the EEOC, the LDF, the civil rights community, African Americans, women, minorities in general, and, of course, the four workers at Dan River awaiting relief. The front page of most newspapers that day was dominated by articles about the war in Vietnam, conscientious objectors cases, and, as indirect commentary on both issues, the first Muhammad Ali versus Joe Frazier fight. Ali, seen by some as a black religious extremist and a draft-dodger and by others as a black nationalist and conscientious objector, had been beaten, knocked down even, by the "black Marciano," Joe Frazier.[115] Ali was twenty or more years away from being hailed an American hero recognized by the larger population and world as a crusader for justice.

Issues of testing and a concept of discrimination called disparate impact were and are rather complicated legal questions. In 1971 there was still rampant disparate treatment that blocked African American employment opportunities. The recognition of disparate impact by the federal courts, though crucial to removing racial barriers, was a topic more aptly reserved for advanced legal discussions. Such discrimination was of course a major obstacle, but it would be rare for nonlegal practitioners to sit and discuss the concept, unless of course they were members of a local NAACP chapter or somehow connected to the Title 7 campaign. Although the average black person could not adeptly define the disparate impact doctrine using legal jargon, they, like the black men at the Dan River Station, knew it when they experienced it. Roughly twenty years later this case would resurface and again play a crucial role in the legal and political discourse surrounding employment discrimination legislation.

Griggs began as a case that sought to improve the lot of fourteen men working at the Dan River Station. It was one of the countless cases LDF hoped would breathe life into Title 7. Of the men who made up the *Griggs* party, most got better jobs, except the man after which the case was named. Willie Griggs now has little to say about the case. He worked the night shift for most of his life following the decision and even quit his job at Duke Power. Eight of the men, however, retired from Duke Power, returning for retiree luncheons at the local Golden Corral steak house. Willie Boyd went on to become the plant's first black supervisor and remained active in the Reidsville NAACP chapter. As Boyd puts it, "We got what we originally went for and that was equal opportunities."[116] The case improved the working environment for these men, for blacks in general, and for other minorities, and it protected groups seeking equal employment opportunities under Title 7. It ushered in an employment environment that sought inclusion of those marginalized from the arena for decades. But although Title 7 and *Griggs* temporarily changed things for many, its role as the catalyst to dramatic transformations in employment for blacks and other minorities was, like so many gains from the civil rights era, ultimately stalled.

VII

THIS THING ISN'T ALL THAT REAL

The Legal Defense Fund won the case it needed to transform Title 7 into a potent tool for breaking down white employment supremacy. In subsequent decades, Title 7 case law and Supreme Court interpretations built upon *Griggs* and in doing so expanded the law to provide a glimmer of hope that the employment arena would approach the vision of equality many longed for during the civil rights era. Title 7 cases from the private bar pushed the limits of the disparate impact doctrine, eventually coercing companies to establish affirmative action programs in order to avoid potential lawsuits.

The disparate impact doctrine has received substantial attention from legal scholars. The cases and policy developments stemming from *Griggs* have been examined in countless law review articles and other scholarly works on Title 7 and affirmative action. Many of these works provide a glimpse into the litigation career of Title 7 during the immediate post–civil rights era and detail the Court's construction of the doctrine. Although the federal judiciary's role in subsequent Title 7 decisions is significant, it does not bear repeating. Instead, I wish to point to the relative employment outcomes stemming from *Griggs* and the era of equal employment opportunity ushered in by the case, as well as unforeseen challenges to continued occupational gains by African Americans.

After the Supreme Court's ruling, Willie Boyd and his fellow workers returned to the district court for an exact determination of their relief. The high school graduates were promoted, and the education and testing requirements were waived for the other workers. Duke Power was also required to promote the laborers as vacancies developed. Many of the black men were offered the watchman job first, and most declined the position. A few years after the case, Duke

Power eliminated the watchman classification altogether. When the *Griggs* plaintiffs returned to the courts, under the direction of attorney Robert Belton, the party complained of continued discriminatory practices, such as the funneling of laborers into the dead-end watchman job.

However, the district court, again under Judge Gordon, found this claim too speculative, arguing, "It is impossible to believe that the defendant would be so obtuse as to consider such a blatantly heavy-handed tactic, even assuming, arguendo, that defendant did wish to discriminate against the plaintiffs."[1] Gordon ruled that because most of the black workers were promoted out of the Labor Department and received increases in their wages, proper relief had already been granted. In fact, Lewis Hairston was promoted to test assistant in the Laboratory and Test Department but was demoted back to the Labor Department and managed to maintain his wage increase. Hairston's demotion was also a focal point of the case when the men returned to the district court, but ultimately the court ruled that this employment action also failed to support the allegation of race discrimination. The record showed, Gordon argued, that Hairston was not properly prepared to perform the job of test assistant.

On appeal, the Fourth Circuit determined the district court had not erred in its recent decision and the plaintiffs would need to file a new complaint with the EEOC because the prior discriminatory practices had been eradicated.[2] The *Griggs* case had finally come to an end four years after the Supreme Court ruling, but not without improving the lot for the plaintiffs and ultimately impacting the employment opportunities for countless other blacks and protected groups under Title 7.

The *Griggs* party did not receive the large payouts some workers embroiled in Title 7 cases earned around the same time. Boyd's comrade Jay Griggs was part of a victory against the American Tobacco Company in 1975 that ended with an award of $3.3 million to the aggrieved workers. Similarly, back-pay awards were approved by the Supreme Court the same year in *Albemarle Paper Company v. Moody*. Both *Russell* and *Moody* were argued by Chambers and staff, and both sets of plaintiffs were instrumental in civil rights activism in their respective locales. Although Jay Griggs and Joe Moody were nearing the end to their career as local activists, the legal outcomes of those careers were still earning significant gains as late as 1975.[3]

But Boyd was correct when he stated that the Duke Power laborers were "winners," despite not winning a major back-pay settlement. The men received fairer opportunities and progressed to better jobs at the Dan River Station, options that six years earlier had seemed unlikely. As a measure of his success, Boyd became Dan River's first black supervisor over white men. Yet Boyd's promotion to supervisor over the Coal Handling Department came with some strife, as Dan River desperately clung to the remnants of its old culture. Boyd recalls,

> "The gentleman over the coal handling retired, the supervisor that is, so I applied for that 'cause I liked that position. They didn't want to give it to me. So I talked to Chambers. He told me, "Mr. Boyd, there is nothing we can do . . . until they do something." He sent me the forms I needed, and said "you just hold them until they make a move. If they put a white man in this job, and leave you out, let me know just as quick as you can." This was about '76, on up in there. I moved over there and that's where I retired from.[4]

Boyd was fully qualified for the supervisor position, but the plant managers wanted to place a white worker in the position. "They don't want to let those white guys fail," Boyd noted. "They gave him the job one day I was off. I didn't know what was going on." Later that evening, the plant managers asked Boyd to come over to the plant and discuss the vacancy and promotion. "It was raining that evening," Boyd recalled. "But I made up my mind, we was gone have some trouble"—hinting at another lawsuit—"if I don't get something I think I ought to have. And, you will pay me for my coming over here. I will complain on you about that too." During the meeting the plant managers tried to persuade or possibly trick Boyd into saying that he was unqualified for the position. Willie would have nothing of the sort. And as the labor history of the plant would have it, Boyd already knew the details of the Coal Handling Department. "That was the first job I had when I went over there," he said. "It wasn't my job but I was filling in. I was on construction when I went to work for the Duke Power Company. So they would pull me off construction to unload coal, and I would see how the machines worked, so I knew the job."[5]

Instead of simply promoting Boyd, one of the most senior workers in the entire plant by this time, regardless of race, plant officials tried to convince him to agree that he was unprepared for supervising the Coal Handling Department. When that failed, the plant managers did something that was far from fiscally responsible. In an effort to preserve the superior position of white workers in the plant, they promoted both Boyd and the white worker. As Boyd remembers, "The job was a two-man job, a manager and assistant. So they had three now; three men on that one job."[6]

But the white worker promoted to supervisor was unable to handle the authority of the position despite the overstaffing. As Boyd described him,

> The fella was a nice guy this white guy, didn't worry about him for nothing. He didn't have the ambition though, but he liked to work. He didn't have the nerve to tell you to go out there and dig up that bush, when that was his job to tell you to do it. He'd rather just shovel it up himself before he'd tell you, he didn't have the nerve. . . . So he stayed on that job from the first of January until May and he told them if they didn't move him back to just a regular coal handler he would quit. It got on his nerves trying to tell people to work, then you know a lot of people resent you telling them, start cursing at you. And he just couldn't stand that. So they did. He worried them until they put him back. And he was one of my men then. And you talking about a good worker? He knew what to do and went on and done it. You didn't have to tell him what to do. He did his work. Man, if I had had about half dozen like that I could have sat in the office and slept most of the time.[7]

The Supreme Court victory in 1971 cemented what had already been infused in the minds of Boyd and his fellow workers: the belief that they deserved to be promoted and given a fair chance. Though Hairston and Willie Griggs had tougher times, the other men progressed and made well of their new positions. The case changed the legal environment of the employment arena to one that assured black workers of protection under Title 7 and the EEOC. A brief account from Cannon Mills in nearby Kannapolis, North Carolina, offers another example of the changes associated with *Griggs*, and it offers another example of the efforts of NAACP members, LDF lawyers, and their sustained legal activism.

According to historian Nancy MacLean, "Something happened at a southern textile mill in 1975 that would have been unthinkable twenty years before. Daisy Crawford, a black weaver with ten years' seniority . . . slapped a white loom fixer named Johnny High across the face."[8] Such responses from black workers would have been unthinkable only ten years earlier, twenty to be sure. High was known to be hostile to blacks and he was known for groping female workers. High had made racially disparaging comments to Crawford regarding her daughter's wedding pictures, which she was sharing with two white coworkers. Then he purposely elbowed Crawford in her breasts as he walked by. "That's when she slapped him," MacLean notes. Cannon Mills "fired and blacklisted Crawford without even asking for her version of the events."[9]

But in 1975, Crawford knew her options under the law. She was a long-time NAACP activist and had filed a suit against Cannon in 1969 for what was then a very common practice in southern industry. Crawford sued the mill, undoubtedly with the help of Chambers' firm, for repeatedly refusing to train her to become a weaver while the company trained less senior white women for the more lucrative position. Cannon Mills also rented company housing to white female heads of household but never rented to their black counterparts. Crawford turned to the EEOC for legal redress and sought support from the formerly segregated Textile Workers Union of America, of which Crawford would become an outspoken member. Six years after a successful suit against the company for blatant, racially motivated employment practices, Crawford was working in a skilled position in what was just recently a fiercely segregated employment line. MacLean acutely notes, "Yet Crawford now worked side-by-side with white women and men and—if the post-wedding chat that preceded the incident with High is any indicator—she was friends with some. At the very least, she had earned the respect of several white co-workers, as was shown by their willingness to swear out affidavits in her support." Ultimately, Cannon Mills was found in contempt for failure to obey the terms of an earlier Title 7–based consent decree.[10]

The story of Willie Boyd and the men at Duke Power, as well as other client-activists the likes of Daisy Crawford, highlight "how southern black working people were able to make use of the reforms won by the civil rights movement, a topic that has so far received little attention from historians, who have concentrated more on the struggles than their outcomes."[11] Title 7 opened the door for "new forms of grassroots activism" characterized by increased legal battles designed to give concrete meaning to decades of struggle and the antidiscrimination laws of the 1960s. Black workers reaped the benefits of the legal protection won in *Griggs*, but equally important, they understood as an outgrowth of the legal victory that their talents demanded and were guaranteed a fair chance at increased employment responsibility and therefore increased wages. At the ten-year anniversary celebration of the EEOC, Boyd and Willie Griggs were flown to Atlanta so that the staff of the EEOC could meet the men who had initiated "the case [that] meant so much to so many people."[12]

Griggs banned practices resulting in a disparate impact on minorities, regardless of their intent, and minimized the significance of all non-job-related criteria that restricted the opportunities for disfavored groups.[13] *Griggs*, or what has been termed the "*Griggs* rule," subsequently affected a host of employment practices that stood as major obstacles to employment opportunities for blacks, women, and other minorities. Maybe most important, many all-white, all-male workplaces and departments received a spattering of gender and racial diversity.

Indeed, the disparate impact doctrine paved the way for improvements in the occupational status of minorities and women. The *Griggs* rule demanded that many employers revise their practices to include minorities and women and laid the foundation for ensuing affirmative action programs.[14] To avoid lawsuits as a result of employment practices that in many cases would be found discriminatory under the disparate impact standard, companies looked to take the necessary "affirmative action," which typically included personnel decisions designed to increase the number of black employees. *Griggs*, in effect "redefine[d] discrimination in terms of consequences rather than motive, effect rather than purpose."[15] Employers no longer needed to treat black workers disparately to be found guilty of discrimination. In fact, plaintiffs basically needed to show that discrimination was still present even absent intentional acts of prejudice. In an effort to comply with *Griggs*, employers were faced with the dual burden of showing their employment practices were neutral and the results of these practices were free from perpetuating the effects of past discrimination. Many employers across the nation were vulnerable to lawsuits under *Griggs*, and victims of discrimination had gained a clear window of opportunity to change their circumstances.

The *Griggs* rule also provided support to President Johnson's Executive Order 11246, written in 1965, which prohibited discrimination on the basis of race, religion, or national origin in governmental contracts and in federal employment. The order required government contractors take affirmative action or develop programs to eradicate racial disparities. However, the order was more effectively enforced when coupled with Title 7. The Labor Department, charged with enforcing the executive order, more seriously addressed those contractors in violation of both the order and Title 7. Since *Griggs* gave Title 7 its muscle, an "employer who challenged the applicability of the Executive Order would still face liability under the *Griggs* principle. Under these circumstances, opposing the Order was scarcely worth the effort."[16]

In sum, *Griggs* provided the underlying justification for race-conscious affirmative action programs because the disparate impact theory of discrimination required employers to become race conscious. Once disparate impact was found, voluntary action to ameliorate the discrimination was necessary to avoid liability. It was this affirmative action that accounted for much of the improvement in minority and female employment opportunity. Companies with government contracts, studies suggest, did a much better job than nongovernmental contractors in providing equal employment opportunity.[17]

Griggs, of course, had an impact on judicial interpretations of Title 7 and employment law in general. But the decision also affected congressional debates regarding Title 7 amendments. The Equal Employment Opportunity Act of 1972 strengthened Title 7 and sought to "lock-in" the early, more favorable Title 7 court interpretations. The 1971 Senate Labor Committee report on the bill stated that "the evidence is clear that while some progress has been made toward bettering the economic position of the Nation's black population, the avowed goal of social and economic equality is not yet anywhere near a reality."[18] In fact, during these debates, both chambers of Congress recognized the importance of *Griggs* and the disparate impact doctrine.[19]

The 1972 amendments to Title 7 extended the reach of the act to private employers and unions with fifteen or more employees or members, to public employers in state and local government, and to educational institutions. They also granted the EEOC limited enforcement power as a result of increased pressure from a still-active civil rights legal community. Many argued that the pace toward employment equality was far too slow, and the civil rights leadership again pushed for cease-and-desist powers to be granted to the EEOC, which led to another filibuster in Congress. The result was a compromise through which the EEOC was authorized to bring suit in federal district court instead of continuing to work largely as a mediator.[20] According to Alfred Blumrosen, "The considerable progress between 1965 and 1970 under the original Title 7, in which cases were heard in federal court, may have contributed to the 'surrender' by the civil rights movement on the cease and desist issue."[21] Adding to the private bar winning Title 7 cases, the EEOC now had a fleet of lawyers spread throughout the nation prepared to wage battle in the courts. The EEOC was granted the power to sue unions and private employers in federal court, a power that previously had belonged solely to the Justice Department. The department was granted the power to sue local and state governments.[22]

What rings loudest of the impact of *Griggs* on the development of the 1972 act is found in the transcripts of the congressional debates. The House report on the 1972 bill stated,

Employment discrimination, as we know today, is a far more complex and pervasive phenomenon. Experts familiar with the subject generally describe the problem in terms of "systems" and "effects" rather than simply intentional wrongs, and the literature on the subject is replete with discussions of the . . . perpetuation of the present effects of earlier discriminatory practices through various institutional devices, and testing and validation requirements. The forms and incidents of discrimination which the Commission is required to treat are increasingly complex. Particularly to the untrained observer, their discriminatory nature may not appear obvious at first glance. A recent striking example was provided by the U.S. Supreme Court in its decision in *Griggs v. Duke Power.* . . . It is increasingly obvious that the entire area of employment discrimination is one whose resolution requires not only expert assistance, but also the technical perception that a problem exists in the first place, and that the system complained of is unlawful.[23]

To effectively assess the direct impact of *Griggs* would call for an intensive, quantitative study limited to specific employment sectors informed by intense statistical analyses. I sincerely hope other scholars have provided such detailed, statistic-laden research. What I provide here is a much broader analysis of the changes to general employment patterns as a result of *Griggs*. If the *Griggs* rule shaped decision making in the courts and the policy-making process in Congress, and if the disparate impact doctrine ultimately shaped equal employment patterns in businesses and industry, then a general analysis of employment patterns would render a solid description of the changes influenced by the *Griggs* decision and the expansion of equal employment ideology throughout the nation under the *Griggs* rule. Research supports the claim that much of the improvement in minority and female employment opportunities in employment occurred during the 1970s when affirmative action was institutionalized under Title 7 and Executive Order 11246.[24] Yet this statement deserves a deeper examination.

Between 1962 and 1970, minorities made substantial progress in many employment sectors. Nearly one million minorities progressed into white-collar craft and semiskilled jobs while four million whites entered these positions. For blacks and other minorities, this translates into a 22.5 percent increase, with only a 7.69 percent increase for whites. Similarly, minority to white unemployment slightly decreased, and the income distribution between minorities and whites moved from 54 to 60 percent. African American wages relative to those of whites increased substantially, especially in the South among skilled workers.[25]

In an extensive report prepared for the Department of Labor, James P. Smith and Finis R. Welch detail the economic progress of African Americans from the 1940s to the 1980s. Their analyses shed light on a number of factors influencing the economic position of blacks.[26] First and foremost, Smith and Welch show that during the forty-year period under examination, wages for black males increased 52 percent faster that those of white men. The average black male earned roughly forty-five hundred dollars in 1940, versus nineteen thousand by 1980. Comparatively, black male workers in 1940 earned 43 percent as much as whites, but by 1980 they earned 73 percent as much. "However," Smith and Welch conclude, "one must remember that even in 1980, black male incomes still significantly lagged behind those of whites."[27]

Smith and Welch argue that the most important factor impacting this racial convergence in economics is education level. In 1980, a black male with an education level equal to that of a white male earned between 75 and 82 percent as much as the white male. Though still a glaring gap, this marks a substantial increase from the roughly 55 percent average that long dominated comparative wage disparities under Jim Crow. The legacy of race discrimination maintained this wage differential between comparably educated blacks and whites until cases brought under Title 7 began to help dismantle the disparity. Smith and Welch agree that the antidiscrimination legislation of the 1960s, particularly Title 7 and ultimately affirmative action programs, played a role in elevating the economic position of blacks. Though they insist that affirmative action programs were not solely responsible for the economic progress of blacks, it is clear that the most rapid increase in black economic growth occurred during the 1960s and 1970s.[28] These years represent the most aggressive period in the history of Title 7 and affirmative action programs. In fact, "85 percent of the improvement in relative wages of black workers took place after 1960, during the era of the EEO laws."[29]

Smith and Welch offer several other important facts related to black economic progress. The racial wage gap was 20 percent greater in the South than other regions until 1960, but between 1970 and 1980 the wage gap declined sharply.[30] This, I argue, is related to the Title 7 campaign, which targeted southern industry; the early efforts of a viable EEOC; and black worker agency, which extracted greater protections from the employment law. Though Smith and Welch attribute this decline in the southern wage gap to the first generation of black children who attended fully desegregated schools and then entered the labor market in the 1970s,[31] which is plausible, the eradication of barriers to employment opportunities through antidiscrimination legislation speaks more directly to what may have truly opened the doors of employment to blacks. Black southerners attended segregated institutions until the *Swann* decision in 1971 and for several years after the Supreme Court ruling. Therefore, an immediate impact from school desegregation on employment and economic progress is unlikely.

As many scholars have shown, one major outgrowth of black economic development has been the growth of the black middle class and a small yet burgeoning black upper class. As Smith and Welch show, three-quarters of black men were impoverished in 1940 and had virtually no chance of improving their economic position or that of their children. Similarly, the black middle class was correspondingly small, including one in five black males. At the opposite end of the spectrum was a very small, exclusive community of black economic elites. By the 1980s, however, the black middle class outnumbered the black poor and "for the first time in American history, a sizeable number of black men are economically better off than white middle-class America."[32] Yet the flip side of the economic coin presents a very grim picture.

Between 1970 and 1980, as employment and wage disparities between blacks and whites appeared to diminish, an opposite and unfortunate reality became apparent. According to sociologist William Julius Wilson, poverty in the nation's fifty largest cities increased 12 percent, and the number of people actually living in poverty-stricken areas increased by more than 20 percent, despite a 5 percent reduction of the total urban-based population in these metropolises.[33] In the nation's five largest cities, despite a 9 percent decrease in total population, the poverty population grew by 40 percent overall. Wilson notes that poverty areas include both poor and nonpoor individuals. But, rather frighteningly, increases in the poor population in these cities were far more severe compared to that of the national population. In New York, Chicago, Detroit, Los Angeles, and Philadelphia, those living in poverty increased by 58 percent, by 70 percent in high-poverty areas, and by a disturbing 182 percent in extreme-poverty areas. For a racial comparison, poor white populations increased by 24 percent, whereas the black poor increased by 164 percent. These massive changes occurred in only a ten-year period, during a time when black unemployment remained more than twice that of whites.[34]

This look at urban communities in the North is important because of the vast numbers of blacks who arrived to those cities during the migration decades. But by the 1980s strikingly similar realities with poverty were prevalent across the rural South. While southern cities such as Atlanta, Richmond, and Charlotte witnessed economic growth and stimulation, changes that encouraged a remigration of professional, middle-class African Americans, and while industrial, blue-collar employment opportunities had been won in the courts, the rural poor remained immersed in dire poverty. According to David Goldfield, a leading historian of the American South,

> But it was the rural South that remained the most shocking exemplar of black poverty. . . . Across the South in the 1980s, there was a direct correlation between the proportion of the black population and the relative poverty of a rural county. In 1986, sociologist Kenny Johnson tallied the extent of rural black poverty, whose victims are primarily women and children: more than 58 percent of black rural women are poor; 76 percent of rural black children are poor; and black children under six years of age fared worst of all with nearly 80 percent living in poverty.[35]

Law professor Ronald Turner describes the intricacies of America's social and economic problems. Turner argues that discrimination in housing, education, and employment comprised the sides "of a vicious triangle that imprison the hopes of blacks and other minorities for full, equal participation in the life of the nation." These three components, Turner argues, are inextricably tied and maintain the destitute position of the nation's poor. Relying on Title 7 to somehow transform the American workplace and to achieve society's goal of equal employment opportunities, Turner continues, is "wrought with peril." Thus, while Title 7 was desperately needed to combat workplace discrimination, the intricacies of racism and poverty in America left the legislation inherently limited.[36] As Wilson argues, programs such as affirmative action can be effective in assisting blacks who have access to socially mobile outlets or the more advantaged elements of the population. The truly deprived members, however, may not be helped at all.[37]

"Segregation and hypersegregation are still prevalent in the United States," Turner argues, despite the presence of fair housing laws. African Americans living in poverty are plagued by inferior schools and experience social isolation making it more difficult to be tied into the job network. These structural problems in many respects are so systematically challenging that they rest far beyond the ability of any one person to change.[38] Despite the nation being more than fifty years removed from the *Brown* decision and more than thirty years past *Swann*, Andrew Hacker's words still ring true: The "United States has few genuinely integrated schools." According to Hacker, more than two-thirds of all black children attend schools that are still fiercely segregated. The impact of this unequal system of education retards the academic achievement of many urban and rural students, which hinders their educational opportunities, and as a result, their employment chances.[39]

Compounding matters, since the 1950s the United States economy has undergone steady changes that exacerbated problems associated with poverty and joblessness. For example, between 1953 and 1962, the United States lost 1.6 million industrial jobs.[40] America gradually moved out of the industrial age into a postindustrial economy that depends less and less on unskilled and skilled labor. No region across the country has been exempt from the impact of these gradual yet dramatic transformations, which were spurred by rapid advances in technology and computer automation. As a byproduct, the entire nation has been pelted by the effects of corporate withdrawal to cheaper labor markets across the world. The South provides a very grim example. Since 1980, dozens of mills have closed leading to the loss of roughly half a million jobs in apparel and textile industries. For blacks specifically, these changes present a major socioeconomic quandary for "no sooner had black activism helped to secure a foothold in the (textile) industry than did jobs began to be eliminated on a widespread basis.[41]

Sociologists Henry Louis Taylor and Mark Naison deconstruct the fateful marriage between occupational racism, black employment activism, and the emergence of a postindustrial economy. "When the industrial era started," they write, "a color occupational system kept blacks locked in low-paying jobs at the bottom of the economic ladder concentrated in technologically obsolete jobs. When the period ended, the color occupational system still kept blacks locked in low-paying dead-end jobs at the bottom of the economic ladder concentrated in technologically obsolete jobs."[42] Under previous economic conditions, industrial employment seemed endless; in today's economy, industrial decline makes for tenuous circumstances for blue-collar laborers. Such economic trends leave scholars tagging the poor, unemployed, and underemployed as a permanent underclass. Those who might have been industrial workers are often depicted as an unemployable, irrelevant, surplus population, a major shift in the perceived options available to working-class people in less than a generation.

Willie Boyd made mention of what he saw as growing troubles in society. He acknowledged that although some things have improved in regards to discrimination, it is still a widespread problem. He also sensed a wind of change in America that sought to reestablish a racial order similar to the one he had worked to dismantle. As a final word, Boyd warned, "What I would like people to know is that these things [racial disparities] have existed. And you need to work hard to keep it from existing again. It can come back. I can feel it on its way here again. But I hope it won't ever go back to the way it was." Boyd also recognized that the aura of equality of opportunity is not guaranteed. He cautioned, "I would like people to know that this thing isn't all that real. You need to stay busy and keep working on it. Because they would love to pull you back into slavery or wherever, as far back as they can."[43] Boyd's warning is insightfully targeted at the rise in neoconservative political opposition to antidiscrimination programs aimed at fostering equality, the very programs for which Boyd fought long and hard to see materialize and programs he had an actual hand in establishing.[44]

Indeed, Willie Boyd has had a long history of battling racism and racial privilege. Though his occupation for most of his life was a semiskilled laborer for the Duke Power Company, he made a career out of fighting for equality in his Reidsville community. He was president of the Reidsville NAACP for ten years, from the late 1970s to the late 1980s. Boyd was also president of his masonic lodge for three years, treasurer for twelve, and he stills proudly wears his masonic ring, which he melded together with his high school class ring. At his church, Boyd was president of the Usher's Convention for twenty-two years, giving up this post just recently at the start of the new millennium. He was also a deacon, president of the Deacon Board, a member of the Usher Board, and chairman of the Trustee Board. When asked how he is able to do so much and stay so active at this late juncture in life, he rather humbly admits, "Keeps me going I guess."[45] Private societies, fraternities and sororities, cultural celebrations, and the religious community are social outlets where post–civil rights era activism lingered, providing social phenomena that beg for more scholarly critiques.

   In 1991 Boyd began receiving more notoriety for his contribution to millions of people who had never heard of him. In a short span of time, Boyd gave interviews to *USA Today,* the *Washington Post,* the *Los Angeles Times,* the *Atlanta Journal and Constitution,* and a number of local and state newspapers. A major national television network set up a studio right on his front porch and taped an extended piece on Boyd and the *Griggs* case, but the show never aired.

"It didn't air because it was the same time as the Clarence Thomas hearings," Boyd says. "That took up all of the space on TV. [The network] was going to let people know how the case helped so many people and how Bush wanted to kill affirmative action. [The network] wanted to let people know what affirmative action really meant."[46]

The interest in Boyd and the *Griggs* case was ignited due to the pending passage of the Civil Rights Act of 1991. In the 1991 act, Congress reaffirmed its support of the disparate impact doctrine of discrimination. According to former Department of Justice attorney Brian Landsberg, "Congress explicitly adopted the *Griggs* rule in 1991, in Section 105 of the Civil Rights Act of 1991, which specifically recognizes that practices with a racially disparate impact are unlawful if the employer 'fails to demonstrate that the challenged practice is job related for the position in question and consistent with business necessity.'"[47] Title 7 and the disparate impact doctrine, though reaffirmed on the books and still effective in related employment case law, are both reeling in the aftershock of the powerful backlash to earlier successes.

Julius Chambers, Robert Belton, and most of the attorneys from the Chambers, Ferguson, Stein and Lanning law firm went on to outstanding legal careers of their own. Several members of the firm became judges, and one of its lawyer was elected to the U.S. House of Representatives for North Carolina, further solidifying the firm's position of influence in the post–civil rights era.[48] Chambers ultimately became the director counsel of the NAACP's Legal Defense and Education Fund, and after his tenure with the LDF he became chancellor of his alma mater, the North Carolina Central University. Belton, a professor at Vanderbilt Law School, is one of the leading Title 7 theorists on in the country. His forthcoming work on Title 7, which will undoubtedly focus largely on the role of *Griggs* in the history of contemporary employment law, should stand as a leading assessment of Title 7 and the *Griggs* case.[49]

As Boyd recognized, the "*Griggs* case was so important, yet it never got down to the little man."[50] Boyd, of course, is referring to people actually having some knowledge of the case; *Griggs* reached many "little people" during its reign as the prevailing legal decision on employment discrimination. And therein lays the beauty in the story. As Julius Chamber remembered some thirty years later, "This was a group of poor black people and they were able to turn to an organization like LDF and bring a lawsuit and prevail. The case was very helpful for that group of people . . . because it also convinced others, rich and poor, that the law was there to provide protection."[51] Title 7 and *Griggs* provided expanded employment protection and equal opportunities if but for a brief moment in contemporary, post–civil rights era history.

However, the case's potential for sustaining continued changes in employment institutions was ultimately stalled. Despite the civil rights community's campaigns in the 1970s, the group did not succeed in the ways it had hoped. While the members of the community understood southern race relations and the complex jockeying within the federal government, especially the federal judiciary, they had no way of predicting the formidable morphing, regeneration, and remobilization of oppositional forces at the behest of neoconservative politics. Added to the political minefield of affirmative action was a declining labor market, goaded by rapid technological development, globalization, and international labor competition, all of which were systemic forces the movement had no way of predicting or combating. These forces and others undercut the chances for the awesome potential of Title 7 and *Griggs* to be fully realized.

Notes

INTRODUCTION

1. *Griggs v. Duke Power Co.*, 401 U.S. 424 (1971).

2. Address before the Seventy-fifth annual NAACP convention by Damon J. Keith, "NAACP: Paladin of the People," in *From the Black Bar: Voices for Equal Justice*, ed. Gilbert Ware (New York: G. P. Putnam's Sons, 1976), 321.

3. Disparate impact is the theory of discrimination recognized by the Supreme Court in the *Griggs* case.

4. This book will not debate the merits of race-based affirmative action, as some might suggest it should do, for a number of reasons. First, such a debate would greatly detract from the historical significance of the plaintiffs and lawyers who brought forward and won a bevy of Title 7 cases in the early stages of the Civil Rights Act. This book demands readers view the importance of *Griggs* (and related cases), the efforts of the plaintiffs, and the strategizing of the lawyers as extensions of the legal activism of the civil rights movement. This activism occurred after the direct-action protest phase of the movement and during the black power era. In many ways the historical discourse over equal employment opportunity has downplayed the efforts of civil rights workers and instead jumped into the debate over affirmative action, quotas, preferential treatment, and so on, politicizing an important phase of the black freedom movement. This work calls for an intrusive look into one of the primary cases of the Title 7 campaign, which was intended to continue and in some ways complete African Americans' journey toward full and equal inclusion into the United States' economic mainstream. The early Title 7 cases, as indicated by *Griggs*, of course led to race-based affirmative action programs, but nowhere in my research did I encounter a systematic plan to make race the sine qua non of equal employment opportunity and outcomes. Instead, as has been well documented by legal scholars, many race-based initiatives emerged as quick fixes to institutions riddled with employment biases hampering black workers. Second, because affirmative action is such a politicized discussion, inevitably my personal and research-informed perspective will be decried as advocacy and unreasoned debate. I am a proponent of affirmative action, unapologetically, and any other reasonable antidiscrimination program that targets marginalized populations. Critics of race-based affirmative action almost never give alternate solutions, they practically ignore the successes of gender-based programs, and they do

not admit that the prevalence of discrimination forced the courts into accepting race-based solutions, particularly as companies needed quick answers to biases many refused to address until forced into compliance. Plus, critics and opponents, under the auspices of nonbiased research and color-blind constitutionally based theory, can easily demean antidiscrimination programs with little recognition given to the aforementioned employment realities. So a discussion of race-based affirmative action will ultimately lead us into the same trite debate, with its predictable outcomes. Third, this is a book about the civil rights legal community and the struggles of those who languished under labor apartheid for decades. Ultimately, their activism forced industrial employers to recognize the masses of blacks as workers deserving equal pay and equal treatment. In my opinion, the heart of this story is the willingness with which working-class blacks, not the middle-class guard of the civil rights community, dashed to the courts to make sense out of Title 7 and not the debate over the emergence of race-consciousness, quotas, and accusations of preferential treatment in employment. (Though these debates certainly have their place in the legal discourse over Title 7 and equal employment, no matter how predictable and politicized they have become.)

5. Although this work is a sociolegal case study, it adds to the body of literature detailing the social history of grassroots activists leading indigenous movements during the civil rights era. See George Lipsitz, *A Life in the Struggle: Ivory Perry and the Culture of Opposition* (Philadelphia: Temple University Press, 1988). Literature on grassroots activism out of Mississippi are some of the most important works that help shape the discourse on local civil rights workers. These works include John Dittmer, *Local People: The Struggle for Civil Rights in Mississippi* (Chicago: University of Illinois Press, 1994), Charles M. Payne, *I've Got the Light of Freedom: The Organizing Tradition and the Mississippi Freedom Struggle* (Berkeley and Los Angeles: University of California Press, 1995), Gilbert R. Mason and James Patterson Smith, *Beaches, Blood, and Ballots: A Black Doctor's Struggle* (Jackson: University Press of Mississippi, 2000), and Aaron Henry and Constance Curry, *Aaron Henry: The Fire Ever Burning* (Jackson: University Press of Mississippi, 2000). For North Carolina, however, several works are particularly important to this discussion: William Chafe, *Civilities and Civil Rights: Greensboro, North Carolina, and the Black Struggle for Freedom* (New York: Oxford University Press, 1980), David Cecelski, *Along Freedom Road: Hyde County North Carolina, and the Fate of Black Schools in the South* (Chapel Hill: University of North Carolina Press, 1994), Timothy B. Tyson, *Radio Free Dixie: Robert F. Williams and the Roots of Black Power* (Chapel Hill: University of North Carolina Press, 1999), and Marcellus C. Barksdale, "Robert F. Williams and the Indigenous Civil Rights Movement in Monroe, North Carolina, 1961," *Journal of Negro History* 69 (Spring 1984): 73–89.

6. J. Clay Smith quote regarding the historic case *Dred Scott v. Sandford* from an Internet exchange on H-Law regarding the most significant cases, lawyers, and plaintiffs in American history, September 8, 2000. H-Law forum, http://www.h-net.org/~law.

7. Lipsitz, *Life in the Struggle*, 2.

8. The forthcoming work on the law firm by Richard Rosen will provide the insight emphasizing this fact.

9. Manfred Berg, *"The Ticket to Freedom": The NAACP and the Struggle for Black Political Integration* (Gainesville: University Press of Florida, 2005).

10. See, for example, Davison Douglas, *Reading, Writing, and Race: The Desegregation of the Charlotte Schools* (Chapel Hill: University of North Carolina Press, 1995); Bernard Schwartz,

Swann's Way: The School Busing Case and the Supreme Court (New York: Oxford University Press, 1986).

11. Douglas, *Reading, Writing, and Race.*

12. Lipsitz, *Life in the Struggle,* 4.

13. Ibid., 9–10.

14. Ibid.

15. James Boggs, *The American Revolution: Pages from a Negro Worker's Notebook,* 40th anniversary ed. (Detroit: Leadfoot Press, 2003).

I. RACE, LABOR, AND CIVIL RIGHTS

1. EEOC Report No. 1, Job Patterns for Minorities and Women in Private Industry (1968).

2. Timothy Minchin, *Fighting Against the Odds: A History of Southern Labor Since World War II* (Gainesville: University Press of Florida, 2005), 8.

3. Henry Louis Taylor Jr., Vicky Dula, and Ha Song-Ho, "The Battle against Wage Slavery: The National Urban League, the NAACP, and the Struggle over New Deal Policies," in *Historical Roots of the Urban Crisis: African Americans in the Industrial City, 1900–1950,* ed. Henry Louis Taylor Jr. and Walter Hill (New York: Garland, 2000), 210.

4. Minchin, *Fighting Against the Odds,* 26, 29.

5. Ibid., 74–76.

6. Michael Goldfield, *The Color of Politics: Race and the Mainsprings of American Politics* (New York: New Press, 1997).

7. Ibid., 183. For tobacco worker unionism, see Robert Rogers Korstad, *Civil Rights Unionism: Tobacco Workers and the Struggle for Democracy in the Mid-Twentieth-Century South* (Chapel Hill: University of North Carolina Press, 2003).

8. Herbert Hill, "Black Workers, Organized Labor, and Title VII of the 1964 Civil Rights Act: Legislative History and Litigation Record," in *Race in America: The Struggle for Equality,* ed. Herbert Hill and James E. Jones (Madison: University of Wisconsin Press, 1993); Robin D. G. Kelley, *Hammer and Hoe: Alabama Communists During the Great Depression* (Chapel Hill: University of North Carolina Press, 1990); Timothy J. Minchin, *Hiring the Black Worker: The Racial Integration of the Southern Textile Industry, 1960–1980* (Chapel Hill: University of North Carolina Press, 1999). Minchin's work explores the racial integration of the textile mill industry in the Carolinas. Its significance is best represented by the reality that success in integrating mills came after the passage of Title 7 and Civil Rights Act of 1964. In fact, a major jolt to this development came from the joint efforts of black mill workers and the NAACP. Nancy MacLean, *Freedom Is Not Enough: The Opening of the American Workplace* (New York: Harvard University Press, 2006); Judith Stein, *Running Steel, Running America: Race, Economic Policy, and the Decline of Liberalism* (Chapel Hill: University of North Carolina Press, 1998). Although Stein's work offers a broader discussion about postwar liberalism, it does highlight the efforts of black workers challenging racism in the industry and USWA, in most cases with the help of civil rights organizations. Key movements and legal battles emerge out of New York, Maryland, Virginia, and Alabama. Heather Thompson, *Whose Detroit? Politics, Labor, and Race in a Modern American City* (Princeton: Princeton University Press, 2001). Thompson's *Whose Detroit,* among its many important arguments, explains the growth, success, and decline of black labor radicalism in Detroit. Roger Horowitz, *"Negro and*

White, Unite and Fight!" A Social history of Industrial Unionism in Meatpacking, 1930–1980 (Chicago: University of Illinois Press, 1997). In select caveats, Horowitz highlights the overall significance of blacks to the UPWA and the efforts of black UPWA members in garnering inclusion. Korstad, *Civil Rights Unionism;* Michael Honey, *Southern Labor and Black Civil Rights: Organizing Memphis Workers* (Chicago: University of Illinois Press, 1993); Alan Draper, *Conflict of Interests: Organized Labor and the Civil Rights Movement in the South, 1954–1968* (Ithaca, New York: ILR Press, 1994). Although Draper's work is more generally a discussion about organized labor, its leadership, and its internal challenges to secure labor equality, the undercurrent of black labor radicalism helps sustain this argument throughout the work.

9. For an extended discussion on important alternate modes of resistance, see Robin D. G. Kelley, "'We Are Not What We Seem': Rethinking Black Working-Class Opposition in the Jim Crow South," *Journal of American History* 80, no. 1 (June 1993): 75–112. Also see Kelley's *Race Rebels: Culture, Politics, and the Black Working Class* (New York: Free Press, 1994).

10. Paul Escott, *Many Excellent People: Power and Privilege in North Carolina, 1850–1900* (Chapel Hill: University of North Carolina Press, 1985).

11. Minchin, *History of Southern Labor*, 6.

12. Charles "Joey" Gordon, interview by author, June 2001, Detroit, Mich.

13. For a more detailed examination of shifting patterns of residential segregation, see Thomas Sugrue, *The Origins of the Urban Crisis: Race and Inequality in Postwar Detroit* (Princeton: Princeton University Press, 1996).

14. Gordon interview.

15. Ibid.

16. Ibid.

17. Ibid.

18. Andrew Edmund Kersten, *Race, Jobs, and the War: The FEPC in the Midwest, 1941–1946* (Chicago: University of Illinois Press, 2000), 15–18.

19. Executive Order 8802, Preamble, 3 C.F.R., 1938–1943 Comp., 957.

20. Kersten, *Race, Jobs, and the War*, 17.

21. Darlene Clark Hine, William C. Hine, and Stanley Harold, *African Americans: A Concise History, Volume Two: Since 1865* (New York: Prentice-Hall, 2004), 433–435.

22. James Jones, "The Transformation of Fair Employment Practices Policies," *Industrial Relations Research Institute* 6 (1976): 160.

23. Kersten, *Race, Jobs, and the War*, 18, 19.

24. Executive Order 9346, 8 FR 7183, May 29, 1943.

25. David R. Goldfield, *Black, White, and Southern: Race Relations and Southern Culture, 1940 to the Present* (Baton Rouge: Louisiana State University Press, 1990), 33–35.

26. Kersten, *Race, Jobs, and the War*, 126–127.

27. See ibid., 7. See also Eileen Boris, "Black Workers, Trade Unions, and Labor Standards," in *Historical Roots of the Urban Crisis: African Americans in the Industrial City, 1900–1950*, ed. Henry Louis Taylor Jr. and Walter Hill (New York: Garland, 2000), 264, 254.

28. Minchin, *History of Southern Labor*, 24.

29. Berg, *Ticket to Freedom*, 4; Minchin, *History of Southern Labor*, 17.

30. Herbert Hill, "Twenty Years of State Fair Employment Practice Commissions: A Critical Analysis with Recommendations" *Buffalo Law Review* 14, no. 1 (Fall 1964): 22–69.

31. See Anthony S. Chen, "'The Hitlerian Rule of Quotas': Racial Conservatism and the Politics of Fair Employment Legislation in New York State, 1941–1945," *Journal of American History* (March 2006): 1238–1264. Chen's article is particularly important because it shows that opposition to equal opportunity programs, particularly affirmative action, did not have its genesis in the 1960s and 1970s. As Chen writes, "Well before the advent of affirmative action, business groups, Republican legislators, and rural whites in wartime New York State joined forces to oppose a color-blind law, fashioning and disseminating key elements in a powerful new language of resistance." That new language used terms such as "quotas," and "preferential treatment" to attack FEP laws in the 1940s.

32. Hill, "Twenty Years."

33. Herbert Hill, *Black Labor and the American Legal System: Race, Work, and the Law* (Madison: University of Wisconsin Press, 1985), 95.

34. Herbert Hill, interview by author, November 2003, Madison, Wisc.

35. Jones, "Transformation of Fair Employment Practices Policies," 160.

36. Hill, *Black Labor*, 17–19.

37. Minchin, *History of Southern Labor*.

38. Hill, "Black Workers."

39. Hill interview.

40. *Gomillion v. Lightfoot*, 364 U.S. 339 (1960).

41. J. Morgan Kousser, *Colorblind Injustice: Minority Voting Rights and the Undoing of the Second Reconstruction* (Chapel Hill: University of North Carolina Press, 1999).

42. Paul Moreno, *From Direct Action to Affirmative Action: Fair Employment Law and Policy in America 1933–1972* (Baton Rouge: Louisiana State University Press, 1997), 199–200.

43. Barry Bearak and David Lauter, "Affirmative Action: The Paradox of Equality," *Los Angeles Times*, November 3, 1991.

44. William Julius Wilson, *The Truly Disadvantaged: The Inner City, the Underclass, and Public Policy* (Chicago: University of Chicago Press, 1987), 31.

45. James E. Jones Jr., "Equal Employment Opportunities: The Promises of the 60s—The Reality of the 70s," *Black Law Journal*, 1971, 6–8.

46. Ibid.

47. Bearak and Lauter, "Affirmative Action."

48. Edward Maltz, "The Legacy of *Griggs v. Duke Power Co.*: A Case Study in the Impact of a Modernist Statutory Precedent," *Utah Law Review*, 1994, 1353–1372.

49. Bearak and Lauter, "Affirmative Action."

50. Alfred W. Blumrosen, "Strangers in Paradise: *Griggs v. Duke Power Co.* and the Concept of Employment Discrimination," *Michigan Law Review* 71 (1972): 59.

51. Moreno, *From Direct Action to Affirmative Action*, 212.

52. Blumrosen, *Modern Law: The Law Transmission System and Equal Employment Opportunity* (Madison: University of Wisconsin Press, 1993), 112.

53. Moreno, *From Direct Action to Affirmative Action*, 212–214; Blumrosen, *Modern Law*, 45, 110; Hugh Davis Graham, *Civil Rights and the Presidency: Race and Gender in American Politics, 1960–1972* (New York: Oxford University Press, 1992), 75.

54. Moreno, *From Direct Action to Affirmative Action*, 214.

55. Roger L. Goldman, "The Next Ten Years: Title VII Confronts the Constitution," *Saint Louis Law Review Journal* 20 (1976): 312.

56. EEOC, *Legislative History of Titles VII and XI of Civil Rights Act of 1964* (Washington, D.C.: U.S. Government Printing Office, 1968).

57. Ibid., 111; MacLean, *Freedom Is Not Enough.*

58. *Myart v. Motorola,* 9 Race Relations L. Rep. 1911 (FEPC Ill. 1964).

59. Graham, *Civil Rights and the Presidency,* 83–84.

60. EEOC, *Legislative History,* 3130–3135. Myart had been arrested for sodomy, which opens a range of questions about Motorola's interpretation of such behaviors.

61. Hugh Steven Wilson, "A Second Look at *Griggs v. Duke Power Company*: Ruminations on Job Testing, Discrimination, and the Role of the Federal Courts," *Virginia Law Review* 58, no. 5. (May 1972): 853.

62. Moreno, *From Direct Action to Affirmative Action,* 217.

63. Graham, *Civil Rights and the Presidency,* 85; EEOC, *Legislative History,* 3130–3135.

64. Moreno, *From Direct Action to Affirmative Action,* 220; EEOC, *Legislative History,* 3130–3135.

65. Graham, *Civil Rights and the Presidency,* 85; EEOC, *Legislative History,* 3130–3135.

66. Moreno, *From Direct Action to Affirmative Action,* 223–225.

67. EEOC, *Legislative History,* 3160.

68. Ibid.

69. Blumrosen, "Strangers in Paradise," 64.

70. Graham, *Civil Rights and the Presidency,* 103.

71. Ibid.; Records of the Equal Employment Opportunity Commission Files, Compliance Division, Box 1, National Archives and Records Administration.

72. Moreno, *From Direct Action to Affirmative Action,* 225.

73. Ibid.

74. Blumrosen, *Modern Law,* 48.

75. George Cooper and Richard Sobol, "Seniority and Testing Under Fair Employment Laws: A General Approach to Objective Criteria of Hiring and Promotion," *Harvard Law Review* 82 (1969): 1614.

76. Robert Belton, "Title VII of the Civil Rights Act of 1964: A Decade of Private Enforcements and Judicial Developments," *St. Louis University Law Journal* 20 (1976): 229.

77. Hugh Davis Graham, *The Civil Rights Era: Origins and Development of National Policy* (New York: Oxford University Press, 1990), 237.

78. Bearak and Lauter, "Affirmative Action."

79. Honey, *Southern Labor and Black Civil Rights.*

II. The Only Thing You Had Was the Labor: A Sharecropper's Journey through Rural North Carolina

1. Willie Boyd, interview by author, July 2001, Reidsville, N.C.

2. Ibid.

3. Ibid.

4. Jeffrey J. Crow, Paul D. Escott, and Flora J. Hatley, *The History of African Americans in North Carolina* (Raleigh: North Carolina Department of Cultural Resources, Division of Archives and History, 1992), 130.

5. Boyd interview, July 2001.

6. Douglas C. Abrams, "Irony of Reform: North Carolina Blacks and the New Deal," *North Carolina Historical Review* 66, no. 2 (April 1989): 150.

7. David L. Carlton and Peter A. Coclanis, *Confronting Southern Poverty in the Great Depression: The Report on Economic Conditions of the South* (New York: Bedford Books of St. Martin's Press, 1996).

8. Crow, Escott, and Hatley, *History of African Americans in North Carolina*, 140–141.

9. Abrams, "Irony of Reform," 159.

10. Crow, Escott, and Hatley, *History of African Americans in North Carolina*, 141, 144.

11. Taylor, Dula, and Song-Ho, "Battle against Wage Slavery," 211.

12. Boyd interview, July 2001.

13. Minchin, *Fighting Against the Odds*, 81.

14. Ibid., 35.

15. Abrams, "Irony of Reform," 152.

16. Crow, Escott, and Hatley, *History of African Americans in North Carolina*, 13s.

17. Boyd interview, July 2001.

18. See Chafe, *Civilities and Civil Rights*; Crow, Escott, and Hatley, *History of African Americans in North Carolina*.

19. Crow, Escott, and Hatley, *History of African Americans in North Carolina*, 119.

20. Douglas, *Reading, Writing, and Race*, 14; Crow, Escott, and Hatley, *History of African Americans in North Carolina*, 123, 155.

21. This concept is borrowed from John H. Haley, *Charles N. Hunter and Race Relations in North Carolina* (Chapel Hill: University of North Carolina Press, 1987), 217. Although Haley was specifically referring to a few religious-based organizations to which Hunter belonged, which were biracial in definition, this idea can be attributed to the entire scope of coalitions and commissions that discussed problems facing blacks but danced around the real issues of political and social marginalization and economic deprivation.

22. Crow, Escott, and Hatley, *History of African Americans in North Carolina*, 119.

23. Jeffrey J. Crow, "An Apartheid for the South: Clarence Poe's Crusade for Rural Segregation," in *Race, Class, and Politics in Southern History: Essays in Honor of Robert F. Durden*, ed. Jeffrey J. Crow, Paul D. Escott, and Charles L. Flynn Jr. (Baton Rouge: Louisiana State University Press, 1989), 227.

24. Raymond Gavins, "The NAACP in North Carolina During the Age of Segregation," in *New Directions in Civil Rights Studies*, ed. Armstead Robinson and Patricia Sullivan (Charlottesville: University Press of Virginia, 1991), 105–126.

25. Ibid.,107.

26. Emancipation Day observances celebrated the end of slavery, as did other celebrations of this nature in black southern culture.

27. Crow, Escott, and Hatley, *History of African Americans in North Carolina*, 126.

28. Ibid.

29. Ibid.

30. Walter B. Weare, *Black Business in the New South: A Social History of the North Carolina Mutual Life Insurance Company* (Durham, N.C.: Duke University Press, 1993). This text is an outstanding and wonderfully written discussion of North Carolina Mutual Life Insurance Company. Weare unbraids the complexities of the issues presented in this work in much more detail.

31. Ibid., 3–28.

32. Ibid., 21.

33. Ibid., 29–31.

34. Ibid.

35. Ibid., 33–34.

36. Ibid., 48–50.

37. Boyd interview, July 2001.

38. "Reidsville, NC Commandos Correspondence," 1963, Floyd B. McKissick Papers, Southern Oral History Project, Wilson Library, University of North Carolina, Chapel Hill.

39. Boyd interview, July 2001.

40. Ibid.

41. Bearak and Lauter, "Affirmative Action"; Drew Jubera, "How Willie Griggs Changed the Workplace," *Atlanta Constitution and Journal,* July 1, 1991.

42. Minchin, *Fighting Against the Odds,* 10–11.

43. Boyd interview, July 2001.

44. Bearak and Lauter, "Affirmative Action."

45. *The National Cyclopedia of American Biography* (New York: James T. White, 1927), 382–383, and Diane Pascal, ed., *International Directory of Company Histories* (Detroit: St. James Press, 1992), 600–602.

46. Robert F. Durden, *The Dukes of Durham, 1865–1929* (Durham, N.C.: Duke University Press, 1975), 8–9.

47. Ibid., 10–13.

48. Ibid., 13–19.

49. Escott, *Many Excellent People,* 178–179.

50. Durden, *Dukes of Durham,* 17–35.

51. *National Cyclopedia of American Biography,* 382–383; Pascal, *International Directory of Company Histories,* 600–602.

52. Joe Maynor, *Duke Power: The First Seventy-Five Years* (Albany, N.Y.: Delmar Press, 1980), 2.

53. Ibid., 8; Durden, *Dukes of Durham.*

54. John K. Winkler, *Tobacco Tycoon: The Story of James Buchanan Duke* (New York: Random House, 1942), 61.

55. Maynor, *Duke Power,* 9.

56. Ibid., 10.

57. Ibid., 10.

58. Ibid., 23, 25.

59. Winkler, *Tobacco Tycoon,* 214.

60. *National Cyclopedia of American Biography,* 382–383; Pascal, *International Directory of Company Histories,* 600–602.

61. Weare, *Black Business in the South,* 26.

62. Durden, *Dukes of Durham,* 177–191.

63. Jacquelyn Dowd Hall, James Leloudis, Robert Korstad, Mary Murphy, Lu Ann Jones, and Christopher Daly, *Like a Family: The Making of a Southern Cotton Mill World* (Chapel Hill: University of North Carolina Press, 1987), 29.

64. Escott, *Many Excellent People,* 217.

65. Hall et al., *Like a Family*, 48.

66. Maynor, *Duke Power*, 34.

67. Carl Horn, *The Duke Power Story, 1904–1973* (New York: Newcomen Society in North America, 1973), 10.

68. Robert Durden, *Electrifying the Piedmont Carolina: The Duke Power Company, 1904–1997* (Durham, N.C.: Carolina Academic Press, 2001), 32.

69. For a detailed examination, see Durden's *Electrifying the Piedmont Carolina*.

70. The Dan River Station is now located in Eden, North Carolina, in the city formerly known as Draper.

71. "Answer to Interrogatories," Exhibit Volume, *Griggs v. Duke Power Co.*, United States Supreme Court Case File, 24b.

72. "Opinion of the U.S. Court of Appeals for the Fourth Circuit," *Petition for Writ of Certiorari to the United States Court of Appeals, Griggs v. Duke Power Co.*, United States Supreme Court Case File, 19a–20a.

73. Ibid.

74. *Griggs et al. v. Duke Power Co.*, 401 U.S. 424.

75. "Opinion of the U.S. Court of Appeals for the Fourth Circuit," 19a–20a.

76. Boyd interview, July 2001.

77. Graham, *Civil Rights Era*, 383.

78. Bearak and Lauter, "Affirmative Action."

79. Graham, *Civil Rights Era*, 383.

80. Brief for Petitioner, *On Writ of Certiorari to the United States Court of Appeals for the Fourth Circuit, Griggs v. Duke Power Co.*, United States Supreme Court Case File, 5.

81. Minchin, *Fighting Against the Odds*, 97. See also Minchin's *Hiring the Black Worker*.

82. Boyd interview, July 2001.

83. Ibid.; Bearak and Lauter, "Affirmative Action."

84. Bearak and Lauter, "Affirmative Action."

85. "Brief for Respondent in Opposition," *On Petition for Writ of Certiorari to the United States Court of Appeals for the Fourth Circuit, Griggs v. Duke Power Co.*, United States Supreme Court Case File, 3.

86. The watchman position was not a job in the Labor Department or Coal Handling. It was an entrance classification into any of the higher plant classifications. The watchman received visitors and provided security. However, the position was often considered a dead-in job because it was outside of other departments.

87. "Opinion of the U.S. Court of Appeals for the Fourth Circuit," 21a.

88. "Opinion of the District Court, Middle District of North Carolina," *On Petition for Writ of Certiorari to the United States Court of Appeals for the Fourth Circuit, Griggs v. Duke Power*, United States Supreme Court Case File, 4a.

89. Ibid.; Graham, *Civil Rights Era*, 383–384; *Griggs v. Duke Power Co.*, 401 U.S. 424.

90. *Griggs v. Duke Power Co.*, 401 U.S. 424.

91. "Opinion of the District Court, Middle District," 4a.

92. Those who took the Wonderlic Test needed to achieve a minimal acceptable score of 20 and on the Bennett a 39. Both scores could be altered slightly by making up the difference on the other (e.g., Wonderlic 19, Bennett 40).

93. "Opinion of the District Court, Middle District," 4a.

94. Cooper and Sobol, "Seniority and Testing," 1642–1643. George Cooper and Richard Sobol, experts on the matter of discriminatory testing practices, provided this commentary regarding the employment exams: "It is sometimes argued that standardized intelligence tests are inherently related to business needs on the ground that every employer is entitled to prefer more intelligent employees. Similarly, mechanical comprehension tests are sometimes thought of as related to business needs in any industrial situation where machinery is used. This notion misconceives the function of tests. Industrial employers need people who can do industrial jobs better; to the extent that requires a certain mental capacity, the employer can be said to need a more intelligent employee or one with certain kinds of comprehension. But a paper and pencil test asking general questions does not necessarily measure the relevant mental capacity. It measures the capacity to answer the questions on the test. This may or may not be related to the capacity to perform well on particular jobs. . . . Contrary to popular belief, the likelihood that scores on any particular aptitude test will correlate significantly with performance on any particular job is very slim indeed."

95. *Petition for Writ of Certiorari to the United States Court of Appeals for the Fourth Circuit,* United States Supreme Court Case File, 9.

96. Moreno, *From Direct Action to Affirmative Action,* 269.

97. Graham, *Civil Rights Era,* 383; *Griggs v. Duke Power Co.,* 401 US 424; Jack Greenberg, *Crusaders in the Courts: How a Dedicated Band of Lawyers Fought for the Civil Rights Revolution* (New York: Basic Books, 1994), 418.

III. So We Just Started Pushing: Civil Rights in North Carolina

1. Douglas, *Reading, Writing, and Race,* 17–18.

2. Gavins, "NAACP in North Carolina," 116.

3. Richard Kluger, *Simple Justice: The History of Brown v. Board of Education and Black America's Struggle for Equality* (New York: Vintage Books, 1975), 155.

4. Conrad O. Pearson, interview by Walter Weare, April 18, 1979, transcript, Southern Oral History Project, Wilson Library, University of North Carolina, Chapel Hill.

5. Ibid.

6. See Kluger, *Simple Justice;* Douglas *Reading Writing and Race;* Mark Tushnet, *The NAACP's Legal Strategy Against Segregated Education, 1935–1950* (Chapel Hill: University of North Carolina Press, 1987).

7. Gilbert Ware, *William Hastie: Grace Under Pressure* (New York: Oxford University Press, 1984), 48.

8. Ibid.

9. Kluger, *Simple Justice,* 155.

10. Gilbert Ware, "Hocutt: Genesis of Brown," *Journal of Negro Education* 52, no. 3 (1983): 227.

11. Pearson interview; Ware, "Hocutt," 228.

12. Ware, "Hocutt," 228.

13. Pearson interview.

14. Kluger, *Simple Justice,* 157; Douglas, *Reading, Writing, and Race,* 18.

15. Pearson interview.

16. Ibid.

17. Ibid.

18. Kluger, *Simple Justice*, 157: Douglas, *Reading, Writing, and Race*, 18.

19. Pearson interview.

20. Kluger, *Simple Justice*, 158.

21. Ibid., 49.

22. Kluger, *Simple Justice;* Douglas, *Reading, Writing, and Race;* Ware, "Hocutt."

23. Pearson interview.

24. Ibid.

25. Kluger, *Simple Justice*, 52.

26. Douglas, *Reading, Writing, and Race;* 18.

27. Pearson interview.

28. Ware, "Hocutt," 233.

29. Juanita Jackson, "Young Colored American Awakes," *Crisis* 43 (September 1938): 289.

30. Pearson interview.

31. Ibid.

32. Gavins, "NAACP in North Carolina,"108.

33. Douglas, *Reading, Writing, and Race*, 19.

34. John Egerton, *Speak Now Against the Day: The Generation Before the Civil Rights Movement in the South* (Chapel Hill: University of North Carolina Press, 1994), 131–132.

35. Ibid.

36. Ibid., 232.

37. See *Missouri ex. rel. Gaines v. Canada*, 305 U.S. 337 (1938).

38. Pauli Murray, *Song in a Weary Throat: An American Pilgrimage* (New York: Harper & Row, 1987), 109.

39. *Missouri ex. rel. Gaines v. Canada*, 305 U.S. 337 (1938).

40. Murray, *Song in a Weary Throat*.

41. Egerton, *Speak Now Against the Day*, 233; see also Murray, *Song in a Weary Throat*, 113.

42. Murray, *Song in a Weary Throat*, 116.

43. Douglas, *Reading, Writing, and Race*, 23.

44. Egerton, *Speak Now Against the Day*, 306.

45. Crow, Escott, and Hatley, *History of African Americans in North Carolina*, 150, and Gavins, "NAACP in North Carolina," 109.

46. Ibid.

47. Egerton, *Speak Now Against the Day*, 305.

48. Gavins, "NAACP in North Carolina," 109.

49. Crow, Escott, and Hatley, *History of African Americans in North Carolina*, 150.

50. Gavins, "NAACP in North Carolina," 109.

51. Ibid., 110.

52. Ibid.

53. Ibid., 119.

54. Douglas, *Reading, Writing, and Race*, 62.

55. Ibid., 23.

56. Gavins, "NAACP in North Carolina," 117.

57. Douglas, 21.

58. Crow, Escott, and Hatley, *History of African Americans in North Carolina*, 165, 167.

202 Notes to Pages 75–84

59. Boyd interview, July 2001.

60. Douglas, *Reading, Writing, and Race*, 28–29.

61. Ibid., 30.

62. Ibid., 29–34; Crow, Escott, and Hatley, *History of African Americans in North Carolina*, 167–171.

63. Crow, Escott, and Hatley, *History of African Americans in North Carolina*, 167–171.

64. Ibid.

65. Ibid.

66. Douglas, *Reading, Writing, and Race*, 32.

67. Ibid., 34.

68. Chafe, *Civilities and Civil Rights*; *Swann v. Charlotte-Mecklenburg*, 402 U.S. 1.

69. Crow, Escott, and Hatley, *History of African Americans in North Carolina*, 165.

70. Johnathan Birnbaum and Clarence Taylor, *Civil Rights since 1787: A Reader on the Black Struggle* (New York: New York University Press, 2000), 721.

71. Donald Nieman, *Promises to Keep: African Americans and the Constitutional Order, 1776–Present* (New York: Oxford University Press), 154–155.

72. Ibid., 161.

73. Robert Weisbrot, *Freedom Bound: A History of America's Civil Rights Movement* (New York: Plume, 1990), 1.

74. Ibid.

75. Weisbrot, *Freedom Bound*. For an interesting reinterpretation of prisons as spaces of transformations during the protest era, see Seneca Vaught, "Narrow Cells and Lost Keys: The Impact of Jails and Prisons on Black Protest, 1940–1972" (Ph.D. diss., Bowling Green State University, 2006).

76. Robert F. Williams, *Negroes with Guns* (New York: Marzani and Munsell, 1962).

77. Ibid.; Tyson, *Radio Free Dixie*.

78. *Kissing Case*—a young white girl recognized a childhood friend or played a game and kissed the young boy on the cheek. When she went home to tell her mother of the news of seeing her old friend, the mother charged the young boy with raping her daughter. Yet in Monroe there were several cases of black women being beaten and raped but the offenders were never indicted.

79. For a detailed history of the Monroe NAACP chapter's efforts at armed resistance, see Williams, *Negroes with Guns* (quote on 62) and Tyson, *Radio Free Dixie*.

80. "Reidsville, NC Commandos Correspondence," Commandos Correspondence, 1963, Floyd B. McKissick Papers, 4930, Box 3.3.1, Folder 7141g, Wilson Library, University of North Carolina, Chapel Hill.

81. Boyd interview, July 2001.

82. Ibid.

83. Ibid. These demands, emerging as part of Reidsville and other local movements, suggest some relationship to the black power ideologies encapsulated in Carmichael' quote, borrowed from Hine, Hine, and Harrold, *African Americans*, 435. Such statements suggest a far closer relationship between the practices of local civil rights movements and the rhetoric of black power advocates than previously explored.

84. Korstad, *Civil Rights Unionism*.

85. Rochelle Tucker, "Reidsville, North Carolina—A Struggle for Progress," unpublished paper; "Griggs Honored," *Reidsville Review*, August 23, 1973, 8.

86. Ibid.

87. Ibid.; Bearak and Lauter, "Affirmative Action."

88. Kelly Alexander Papers, J. Murrey Atkins Library, University of North Carolina, Charlotte (hereafter cited as Alexander Papers).

89. Bearak and Lauter, "Affirmative Action"; Boyd interview, July 2001.

90. Boyd interview, July 2001.

91. Bearak and Lauter, "Affirmative Action."

92. Boyd interview, July 2001.

93. Bearak and Lauter, "Affirmative Action."

94. Ibid.

95. Boyd interview, July 2001.

96. Ibid.

97. Ibid.

98. "Plaintiff's Exhibit 9," Exhibit Volume, *Griggs v. Duke Power Co.*, United States Supreme Court Case File, 2b.

99. Ibid.

100. Boyd interview, July 2001.

101. Ibid.

102. Ibid.

103. Ibid.

104. *Files of the EEOC, Compliance Division,* National Archives and Records Administration.

105. Belton, "Title VII," 229. The first actual case was *Brinkley v. The Great Atl. and Pac. Tea Co.*

106. "Plaintiff's Exhibit 10," Exhibit Volume, *Griggs v. Duke Power Co.*, United States Supreme Court Case File, 5b.

107. "Opinion of the U.S. Court of Appeals for the Fourth Circuit," 21a–22a.

108. Boyd interview, July 2001.

109. "Plaintiff's Exhibit 10," 5b.

110. Bearak and Lauter, "Affirmative Action."

111. Blumrosen, *Modern Law,* 58.

IV. Phase Two; Namely, Economic Freedom: The Title 7 Campaign

1. Greenberg, *Crusaders in the Courts,* 14.

2. Ibid., 26.

3. Julius LaVonne Chambers, interview by author, July 5, 2001, Tega Cay, S.C. The Herbert Lehman Fund gave cooperating attorneys a three-year contract, which included upstart money.

4. Willie Boyd, interview by author, May 2005, Reidsville, N.C.

5. James Ferguson, interview by author, September 2005, Charlotte, N.C.

6. Ella Hand, interview by author, September 2005, Charlotte, N.C.

7. Minchin, *Fighting Against the Odds,* 94.

8. "Speech Delivered by Chairman Adam Clayton Powell at Labor banquet of National Convention of the National Association for the Advancement of Colored People," July 14, 1961, Philadelphia, Alexander Papers.

9. "Excerpts of a Speech," by Dr. Eli Ginzberg, Professor of Economics, Columbia University, NAACP 54th Annual Convention Chicago, Alexander Papers.

10. "Some Questions and Answers on the Civil Rights Bill" and "The President's Civil Rights Program: What It Provides, What More It Needs, and How You can Help," Alexander Papers.

11. "Speech by Samuel Jackson," Alexander Papers.

12. Ibid.

13. Maurice Carroll, "Man in the News; Rights Under New Leader," *New York Times,* June 13, 1984, 17.

14. Chambers interview.

15. Ibid.

16. *Swann v. Charlotte-Meckelnburg,* 402 U.S. 1 (1971).

17. *Griggs v. Duke Power Co.,* 401 U.S. 424.

18. Douglas, *Reading, Writing, and Race,* 108–110.

19. Chambers interview.

20. Douglas, *Reading, Writing, and Race,* 109.

21. Ibid.

22. Adam Stein, interview by author, October 2005, Chapel Hill, N.C.

23. Chambers interview.

24. Ibid.

25. Ibid.; Taylor Branch, *Parting the Waters: America in the King Years, 1954–63* (New York: Simon and Schuster, 1989), 525–562.

26. Chambers interview.

27. Douglas, *Reading, Writing, and Race,* 109.

28. Schwartz, *Swann's Way,* 21.

29. James E. Ferguson, interview transcript, Southern Oral History Project, Wilson Library, University of North Carolina, Chapel Hill.

30. Fred Alexander would get elected to state Assembly in 1970s. See Crow, Escott, and Hatley, *History of African Americans in North Carolina,* 202; Douglas, *Reading, Writing, and Race,* 62.

31. Crow, Escott, and Hatley, *History of African Americans in North Carolina,* 199.

32. Ibid.

33. Ferguson interview, September 2005.

34. An example of this relationship between civil rights attorneys and black radicals is evident in *State v. Ben Chavis* (1971), often referred to as the Wilmington 10 case. In 1971, Chambers and the firm also represented the Wilmington 10, nine black and one white protestor, after violent demonstrations erupted in Wilmington, North Carolina, over city officials refusing the activist's requests to hold a memorial service for Martin Luther King. The Wilmington 10 spent nearly a decade in jail after being charged and convicted with firebombing a business and engaging in shootouts with the police. In December 1980, the Fourth Circuit Court of Appeals overturned all of the convictions after finding the state had illegally withheld material evidence and the trial court had denied the defendants their constitutional rights to confront witnesses by restricting the cross examination of the state's main witnesses. All charges were dropped against the Wilmington 10 in 1981. This is but one example. However, such examples encourage more scholarship on the ways in which the black power community and civil rights community shared complimentary goals and worked in concert with each other even if the tactics diverged. The polarized depiction of the two camps is merely one assessment that does not offer a full critique of these protest communities and, thus, the overall movement era.

35. Ferguson interview, September 2005.

36. Stein interview; see also Joseph L. Raugh Jr., "The Role of the Leadership Conference on Civil Rights in the Civil Rights Struggle of 1963–1964," in *The Civil Rights Act of 1964: The Passage of the Law that Ended Racial Segregation,* ed. Robert D. Loevy (Albany: State University of New York, 1997).

37. Stein interview.

38. James Lanning joined the law firm soon after Ferguson and Stein making the firm Chambers, Ferguson, Stein and Lanning. A host of other lawyers passed through the law firm, many on the road to successful legal careers. James Lanning, Karl Adkins, Yvonne Evans-Mimms, and Charles Becton became judges. Mel Watt went on to be elected to Congress as District 8 representative, which was the debated district in *Shaw v. Reno* (1990). Robert Belton joined the professoriate at Vanderbilt University. This is in no way a detailed list, but it does highlight the talent pool of lawyers the law firm attracted and molded.

39. Chambers interview.

40. Ferguson interview, September 2005.

41. Ferguson interview, Southern Oral History Project.

42. Douglas, *Reading, Writing, and Race,* 108.

43. Alfred Blumrosen, interview by author, August 2, 2001, Sussex, N.J.

44. Ferguson interview, September 2005.

45. Robert Belton, "A Comparative Review of Public and Private Enforcement of Title VII of the Civil Rights Act of 1964," *Vanderbilt Law Review* 31 (1978): 934.

46. Greenberg, *Crusaders in the Courts,* 413–414.

47. Belton, "Comparative Review," 926; Greenberg, *Crusaders in the Courts,* 413.

48. Stein interview.

49. Greenberg, *Crusaders in the Courts,* 413–414.

50. Belton, "Comparative Review," 926; Greenberg, *Crusaders in the Courts,* 413.

51. Funded by the NAACP and their organizations, TEAM was a major effort designed to increase African Americans' employment opportunities in the textile industry.

52. Minchin, *Hiring the Black Worker.*

53. Ibid., 81, 39, 6.

54. Frankfurter received widespread notoriety for being one of the most progressive justices to serve on the Supreme Court.

55. Greenberg, *Crusaders in the Courts,* 416.

56. Belton, "Comparative Review," 927.

57. Greenberg, *Crusaders in the Courts,* 418–419.

58. Blumrosen, *Modern Law,* 370.

59. Hill interview.

60. Blumrosen, "Strangers in Paradise," 66.

61. Blumrosen interview.

62. Blumrosen, "Strangers in Paradise," 60.

63. Greenberg., *Crusaders in the Courts,* 412.

64. Ferguson interview, September 2005; Hill interview; Geraldine Sumpter, interview by author, September 15, 2005.

65. James E. Jones Jr., interview by author, November 2003, Madison, Wisc.

66. Vincent Blasi, *The Burger Court: The Counter Revolution that Wasn't* (New Haven: Yale University Press, 1983), 120–121.

67. Genna Rae McNeil, *Groundwork: Charles Hamilton Houston and the Struggle for Civil Rights* (Philadelphia: University of Pennsylvania Press, 1983), 3.

68. Boyd interview, July 2001.

69. Chambers interview.

70. All fourteen men included Willie S. Griggs, James S. Tucker, Jesse Martin, Herman E. Martin, William C. Purcell, Clarence M. Jackson, Robert A. Jumper, Lewis H. Hairston Jr., Willie R. Boyd, Junior Blackstock, John D. Hatchett, Clarence C. Purcell, Eddie Galloway, and Eddie Broadnax. See "Plaintiff's Proposed Findings of Fact and Conclusions of Law," United States District Court–Middle District North Carolina Case File, April 16, 1968, 15, 16.

71. "Opinion of the District Court, Middle District," 6a.

72. Blumrosen, "Strangers in Paradise," 75.

73. "Plaintiff's Proposed Findings of Fact," 15.

74. Boyd interview, July 2001.

75. "Transcript of Hearing," *Petition for Write to United States Court of Appeals, Fourth Circuit, Griggs v. Duke Power Co.*, United States Supreme Court Case File, 91a.

76. "Plaintiff's Proposed Findings of Fact," 15.

77. Exhibit Volume, *Griggs v. Duke Power Co.*, United States Supreme Court Case File, 72b.

78. Boyd interview, July 2001.

79. "Plaintiff's Brief," *Griggs v. Duke Power Co.*, United States District Court–Middle District North Carolina Case File, 10.

80. "Opinion of the U.S. Court of Appeals for the Fourth Circuit," 22a.

81. Blumrosen, "Strangers in Paradise," 75.

82. Ibid.; Blumrosen, *Modern Law,* 59.

83. "Plaintiff's Exhibit 10," 5b.

84. "Plaintiff's Memorandum in Support of the Right to Maintain this Action as a Class Action," United States District Court–Middle District North Carolina Case File, March 5, 1967, 21.

85. "Civil Action No. C-210-G-66 Order," United States District Court–Middle District North Carolina Case File, June 19, 1967, 25.

86. Greenberg, *Crusaders in the Courts*, 415.

87. "Brief for Plaintiffs," April 16, 1968, United States District Court–Middle District North Carolina Case File, 5.

88. "Complaint," *Appendix to Writ of Certiorari to the United States Court of Appeals to the Fourth Circuit, Griggs v. Duke Power Co.*, United States Supreme Court Case File, 3a.

89. Ibid., 6a, 7a.

V. Subtleties of Conduct . . . Play No Small Part: *Griggs* at the District Court

1. Michelle Ripon, "Meet the Federal Judges: The Middle District of North Carolina," *North Carolina State Bar Quarterly* 37, no. 4 (Fall 1990): 32–34.

2. Ibid.

3. Chambers interview.

4. "Transcript of Hearing," 55a–70a.

5. Ibid., 85a–88a.

6. Ibid., 93a.

7. Ibid., 96a.

8. Ibid., 102a–104a.

9. Ibid., 73a.

10. Ibid., 75a.

11. Austin Thies was brought back to the stand at the end of the trial and Robert Belton was able to ask all of the necessary pre–Civil Rights Act questions, under objection by the defendant, to secure the information in the trial record.

12. In *Quarles v. Phillip Morris, Inc.*, the tobacco company had long hired blacks but placed them in the most undesirable, lower paying jobs. Seniority was based on departmental- and job-based service and not on a plant-wide basis, so blacks rarely sought to move out of the department because their seniority would be severely diminished. Judge Butzner ruled that blacks could transfer and maintain seniority level, though they could not "bump" white employees out of jobs; they only need wait for an opening. The court in this case also found that prior discriminatory practices did have present impacts and consequences. *Quarles* was one of the first Title 7 cases, but it was rendered from the district court in Richmond by a respected judge, and neither the company nor union involved appealed; thus it became the prevailing law. (Greenberg, *Crusaders in the Courts*). In *Bowe v. Colgate-Palmolive Co.*, the company and union had continued to maintain seniority and jobs based on gender classifications after Title 7 was in effect. The court allowed both parties to introduce evidence as far back as World War II.

13. "Transcript of Hearing," 75a–79a.

14. Ibid., 96a–98a.

15. Ibid., 100a–101a.

16. For a detailed discussion of the development of discrimination being based on "subjective intent" see Belton, "Title VII."

17. Ibid., 158–159.

18. Blumrosen, *Modern Law*, 97.

19. Ibid., 92a.

20. Ibid., 103–105a.

21. Ibid., 141a.

22. Ibid., 117a–139a.

23. "Guidelines on Employment Testing Procedures, EEOC," Exhibit Volume, *Griggs v. Duke Power Co.*, United States Supreme Court Case File, 130b.; Blumrosen, *Modern Law*, 71.

24. "Transcript of Hearing," 117a–139a.

25. "Employment Testing: The Aftermath of *Griggs v. Duke Power Company*," *Columbia Law Review* 72, no. 5. (May 1972): 920; Blumrosen, *Modern Law*, 71, 238.

26. "Transcript of Hearing," 148a–155a.

27. Ibid., 161a–181a.

28. Ibid., 205a.

29. "Brief for Plaintiffs," 7; Title 7 sections relevant to *Griggs* include the following:

703(a)—It shall be an unlawful employment practice for an employer—1) to fail or refuse to hire or to discharge any individual, or otherwise to discriminate against any individual with respect to his compensation, terms, conditions or privileges of employment, because of such individual's race, color, religion, sex or national origin; or 2) to limit, segregate, or classify his employees in any way which would deprive or tend to deprive any individual of employment opportunities or otherwise adversely affect his status as an employee, because of such individual's race, color, religion, sex or national origin. . . .

703(d)—It shall be an unlawful employment practice for any employer, labor organization, or joint labor-management committee controlling apprenticeship or other training or retraining, including on-the-job training programs to discriminate against any individual because of his race, color, religion, sex, or national origin in admission to, or employment in, any program established to provide apprenticeship or other training. . . .

703(h)—Notwithstanding any other provision of this title, it shall not be an unlawful employment practice for an employer to apply different standards of compensation, or different terms, conditions, or privileges of employment pursuant to a bona fide seniority or merit system, or a system which measures earning by quantity or quality of production or to employees who work in different locations, provided that such differences are not the result of an intention to discriminate because race, color, religion, sex or national origin, nor shall it be an unlawful employment practice for an employer to give and to act upon the results of any professionally developed ability test provided that such tests, its administration or action upon the results is not designed, intended or used to discriminate because of race, color, religion, sex or national origin. . . .

706(g)—If the court finds that the respondent has intentionally engaged in or is intentionally engaging in an unlawful employment practice charged in the complaint, the court may enjoin the respondent from engaging in such unlawful employment practice, and order such affirmative action as may be appropriate, with or without back pay (payable by the employer, employment agency, or labor organization, as the case may be, responsible for the unlawful employment practice). Interim earnings or amounts earnable with reasonable diligence by the person or persons discriminated against shall operate to reduce the back pay otherwise allowable.

30. "Brief for Plaintiffs," 8.

31. Ibid., 10.

32. Ibid., 11–12.

33. Ibid., 13.

34. Civil Rights Act of 1964, Title VII, 42 U.S.C. Section 200e, Section 703(h).

35. "Brief for Plaintiffs," 18.

36. Ibid., 23.

37. Ibid., 25.

38. Ibid., 26.

39. In *Farmers Cooperative Compress v. NLRB*, African American and Mexican American workers challenged the practice of an employer that racially discriminated in the allocation of overtime. The court ruled in favor of the workers and found the respondent guilty of racial discrimination.

40. "Brief for Plaintiffs," 31.

41. Ibid., 34.

42. Ibid., 36–38.

43. "Defendant Brief," United States District Court–Middle District of North Carolina Case File, 6.

44. Ibid., 12.

45. Ibid., 14.

46. "Plaintiff's Proposed Findings of Facts," 16.

47. "Defendant Brief," 23.

48. Ibid., 19.

49. Ibid., 28–29.

50. "Brief for Plaintiffs," 11.

51. "Opinion of the District Court, Middle District," 6a–7a.

52. *Griggs v. Duke Power Co.*, 401 US 42; see also Bearak and Lauter, "Affirmative Action"; Graham, *Civil Rights Era*, 384.

53. Blumrosen, "Strangers in Paradise," 75.

54. "Opinion of the District Court, Middle District," 7a.

55. Ibid., 9a–10a.

56. Ibid., 10a.

57. Ibid., 12a.

58. Ibid., 13a–16a.

59. Blumrosen, "Strangers in Paradise," 75, 76; Blumrosen, *Modern Law*, 113.

60. Boyd, July 2001.

VI. Faithful to Congressional Intent: *Griggs* on Appeal

1. Boyd interview, July 2001.

2. Ibid.

3. Ibid.

4. *Biographical Directory of the Federal Judiciary, 1789–2000* (White Plains, Md.: Bernan, 2001).

5. "Answer to Interrogatories #14—Initial Starting Wages," 74b–82b.

6. "Opinion of the U.S. Court of Appeals for the Fourth Circuit," 22a.

7. *Quarles v. Phillip Morris, Inc.*, 279 F. Supp. 505, 516 (E.D. Va. 1968); *United States v. Papermakers and Paperworkers, Local 189*, 282 F. Supp. 39, 44 (E.D. La. 1968), affirmed, No. 25956-F.2d.-(5 Cir. 1969); *Local 53 v. Vogler*, 407 F.2d. 1047, 1052 (5 Cir. 1969).

8. "Opinion of the U.S. Court of Appeals for the Fourth Circuit," 24a.

9. Greenberg, *Crusaders in the Court*, 416.

10. *Quarles v. Phillip Morris, Inc.*, 279 F. Supp. 505, 516 (E.D. Va. 1968).

11. Greenberg, *Crusaders in the Court*, 418.

12. 4th Circuit Court of Appeals, Container 98 (*Griggs v. Duke Power Co.*), Folder I, Simon Sobeloff Papers, Library of Congress (hereafter cited as Sobeloff Papers).

13. "Opinion of the U.S. Court of Appeals for the Fourth Circuit," 24a.

14. Belton, "Title VII," 243.

15. "Opinion of the U.S. Court of Appeals for the Fourth Circuit," 25a, 37a.

16. Ibid., 28a.

17. Ibid., 28a–30a.

18. EEOC published *Guidelines on Testing* in 1966 and expanded the guidelines in August 1970.

19. "Opinion of the U.S. Court of Appeals for the Fourth Circuit," 31a; *United States v. H. K. Porter*, 59 L.C. 9204 (M.D. Ala. 1969) and *Dobbins v. Local 212, IBEW*, F. Supp 413 (S.D. Ohio 1968);

Weeks v. Southern Bell Telephone and Telegraph Co., 408 F.2d 228, 235 (5 Cir. 1969), *Cox v. United States Gypsum Co.,* 284 F. Supp. 74, 78 (N.D. Ind. 1968), and *International Chemical Workers Union v. Planters Manufacturing Co.,* 259 F. Supp. 365, 366 (N.D. Miss. 1966).

20. *Dobbins v. Local 212, IBEW*—a summary of the *Dobbins* case borrowed from Cooper and Sobol, "Seniority and Testing," 1655. Cooper and Sobol summarize that in *Dobbins* the district court found the test for union membership, illegal though it was, "objectively fair and objectively fairly graded, because it was unnecessarily difficult. The court essentially ruled that "the test must be properly selected and reasonably related to job performance." In the same decision, "the Dobbins court found lawful tests administered by an apprenticeship committee composed of union an employer representatives, on the grounds that these tests 'were reasonably related to the proper attitudes' and 'properly selected by an expert consultant.'"

21. "Opinion of the U.S. Court of Appeals for the Fourth Circuit," 31a–32a.

22. Ibid., 34a–35a.

23. Blumrosen, "Strangers in Paradise," 77.

24. Graham, *Civil Rights Era,* 385; *Griggs v. Duke Power Co.,* 401 US 424.

25. "Opinion of the U.S. Court of Appeals for the Fourth Circuit," 39a.

26. Ibid., 39a–40a.

27. *Guinn v. United States,* 238 U.S. 347 (1915).

28. *Goss v. Board of Education,* 373 U.S. 683 (1963).

29. "Opinion of the U.S. Court of Appeals for the Fourth Circuit," 41a–42a.

30. Ibid., 44a.

31. *Udall v. Tallman,* 380 U.S. 1 16 (1965).

32. *Weeks v. Southern Bell Telephone and Telegraph Co.,* 408 F.2d 228 (5th Cir. 1969). In this Title 7 sex discrimination case, the Fifth Circuit gave "considerable weight" to the EEOC guidelines.

33. "Opinion of the U.S. Court of Appeals for the Fourth Circuit," 47a–53a.

34. Ibid.

35. Ibid., 59a.

36. Ibid., 57a–60a.

37. 4th Circuit Court of Appeals, Container 98 (*Griggs v. Duke Power Co.*).

38. Belton, "Comparative Review," 940–941.

39. "Opinion of the U.S. Court of Appeals for the Fourth Circuit," 62a.

40. See Jack Bass, *Unlikely Heroes* (Tuscaloosa: University of Alabama Press, 1981). This work chronicles the efforts of the 5th Circuit and explores the judicial activism of its bench during the civil rights era.

41. Morton Wallerstein, *The Public Career of Simon Sobeloff* (Richmond: Marlborough House, 1975).

42. *Dictionary of American Biography* (New York: Charles Scribner's Sons, 1994), 743–744; John A. Garraty and Mark C. Carnes, eds., *American National Biography* (New York: Oxford University Press, 1999), 353–354.

43. Ibid.

44. Ibid.

45. Speeches and Writings (1954–55 Brown era), Container 311, Sobeloff Papers.

46. *Dictionary of American Biography,* 743–744; Garraty and Carnes, *American National Biography,* 353–354.

47. 4th Circuit Court of Appeals, Container 98 (*Griggs v. Duke Power Co.*).

48. Boyd interview, July 2001.

49. Belton, "Comparative Review of Public and Private Enforcement," 941.

50. Ibid., 942.

51. *Moody v. Albemarle Paper Co.*, 4 F.E.P. Cas. 561 (E.D.N.C. 1971).

52. Belton, "Enforcement of Title VII," 941–942; Belton, "Title VII of the Civil Rights Act of 1964," 270; Greenberg, *Crusaders in the Courts*, 421.

53. Ibid.

54. Graham, *Civil Rights Era*, 385.

55. Graham, *Civil Rights and the Presidency*, 183.

56. Belton, "Decade of Developments," 268.

57. Greenberg, *Crusaders in the Courts*, 419.

58. Graham, *Civil Rights Era*, 385.

59. Moreno, *From Direct Action to Affirmative Action*, 273.

60. "Brief of Amicus Curiae on Behalf of the Chamber of Commerce of the United States of America," *On Writ of Certiorari to the United States Court of Appeals for the Fourth Circuit, Griggs v. Duke Power Co.*, United States Supreme Court Case File.

61. Moreno, *From Direct Action to Affirmative Action*, 273; "Brief of Amicus Curiae on Behalf of the Chamber of Commerce."

62. "Brief for United Steelworkers of America, AFL-CIO, Amicus Curiae" *On Writ of Certiorari for the United States Court of Appeals for the Fourth Circuit*, United States Supreme Court Case File.

63. "Brief of the Attorney General of the State of New York as Amicus Curiae in Support of Reversal," *On Writ of Certiorari to the United States Court of Appeals for the Fourth Circuit*, United States Supreme Court Case File.

64. *On Writ of Certiorari to the United States Court of Appeals for the Fourth Circuit*, United States Supreme Court Case File.

65. *United States v. Louisiana*, 380 U.S. 145 (1965), *United States v. Duke*, 332 F.2d 759 (5th Cir. 1964); Brian K. Landsberg, *Enforcing Civil Rights: Race Discrimination and the Department of Justice* (Lawrence: University Press of Kansas, 1997), 127–131.

66. *Report on the National Advisory Commission on Civil Disorders* (New York: New York Times, 1968), 416.

67. Landsberg, *Enforcing Civil Rights*, 127–131.

68. Ronald Kahn, *The Supreme Court and Constitutional Theory, 1953–1993* (Lawrence: University of Kansas Press, 1994), 30–31.

69. Julius L. Chambers, "Race and Equality: The Still Unfinished Business of the Warren Court," in *The Warren Court: A Retrospective*, ed. Bernard Schwartz (New York : Oxford University Press, 1996), 21.

70. Schwartz, *Swanns Way*, 25.

71. Ibid., 25.

72. Box 64, Folder 2—Conferences, Memoranda, General, Thurgood Marshall Papers, Library of Congress (hereafter cited as Marshall Papers).

73. Schwartz, *Swann's Way*, 42; Numerous authors have provided in-depth accounts of the Burger Court, this information is borrowed form the work of Bernard Schwartz, *A History of the Supreme Court*, his edited work *The Burger Court*, and Blasi, *Burger Court*.

74. Bernard Schwartz, ed., *The Burger Court: Counter-Revolution or Confirmation* (New York: Oxford University Press, 1998); Blasi, *Burger Court.*

75. Kahn, *Supreme Court and Constitutional Theory,*159.

76. Derrick A. Bell, "Burger Court's Place on the Bell Curve of Racial Jurisprudence," in *The Burger Court: Counter-Revolution or Confirmation,* ed. Bernard Schwartz (New York: Oxford University Press, 1998), 61.

77. *Griggs v. Duke Power Co.*

78. Bob Woodward and Scott Armstrong, *The Brethren: Inside the Supreme Court* (New York: Simon and Schuster, 1979), 122–123.

79. Ibid; Graham, *Civil Rights Era,* 386–387.

80. Box 201, Folder1 and Box 224, Folder 1, William Brennan Papers, Library of Congress.

81. "Brief for Petitioner," 2.

82. Ibid., 10.

83. *Gaston County, North Carolina v. United States,* 395 U.S. 285 (1969).

84. EEOC, *Guidelines on Employment Testing Procedures,* August 24, 1966, Exhibit Volume, Plaintiff's Exhibit 33, 1296–1360. The Office of Federal Contract Compliance is given the task of enforcing Executive Order 11246, which bans discrimination in governmental contracts.

85. "Brief for Petitioner," 10, 11, 19–21.

86. *Arrington v. Massachusetts Bay Transportation Authority,* 306 F. Supp, 1355 (D. Mass. 1969) and *United States v. H. K. Porter Co.,* 296 F. Supp. 40 (M.D. Ala. 1968).

87. "Brief for Petitioner," 24.

88. Ibid., 25.

89. *Hobson v. Hansenm,* 269 F. Supp. 401 (D.D.C. 1967).

90. "Brief for Petitioner," 30, 34.

91. Ibid., 49–50.

92. EEOC, *Legislative History,* 3136–3163.

93. "Brief for Respondent,"1–10.

94. Ibid., 17, 22, 23, 26.

95. Ibid., 38.

96. Ibid., 55–56.

97. "Transcript of Oral Arguments," *Griggs v. Duke Power Co.,* United States Supreme Court Case File.

98. Graham, *Civil Rights Era,* 386–387.

99. Bernard Schwartz, *A History of the Supreme Court* (New York: Oxford University Press, 1993), 311.

100. Box 70, Folder 9, No. 124, *Griggs v. Duke Power,* Marshall Papers.

101. Ibid.

102. Ibid.

103. Nina Totenberg, "Behind the Marble, Beneath the Robes," *New York Times Magazine,* March 16, 1975.

104. *Griggs v. Duke Power Co.,* 401 U.S. 424.

105. Ibid.

106. This is a particularly point in the scholarship. Sobeloff and Burger use the failed Amendment as justification for the job-related standard while the actual language in the statute makes

no mention of the requirement. Some could argue that the Court read more into the legislative history than statute dictates.

107. *Griggs v. Duke Power Co.*, 401 U.S. 424; Bearak and Lauter, "Affirmative Action."

108. Ibid.

109. Belton, "Decade of Developments," 244. The first actual Title 7 case decided by the Supreme Court was *Phillips v. Martin Marietta Corp.*, 400 U.S. 542 (1971), a sex discrimination case.

110. "Opinion of the U.S. Court of Appeals for the Fourth Circuit," 39a.

111. Belton, "Enforcement of Title VII," 906.

112. Belton, "Title VII of the Civil Rights Act of 1964," 245.

113. *Charlotte Observer*, May 9, 1971.

114. *Charlotte Observer*, March 11, 1971.

115. *Raleigh Times*, March 9, 1971.

116. Boyd interview, July 2001.

VII. This Thing Isn't All that Real

1. *Griggs v. Duke Power Co.*, No. C-210-G-66., United States District Court–Middle District of North Carolina, 1974.

2. *Griggs et. al. v. Duke Power Co.*, 515 F.2d 86 (1975).

3. Boyd interview, July 2001; *Russell v. American Tobacco Company*, 528 F.2d 357 (4th Cir. 1975); *Albemarle Paper Co. v. Moody*, 422 U.S. 405 (1975); Hand interview.

4. Boyd interview, July 2001.

5. Ibid.

6. Ibid.

7. Ibid.

8. Nancy MacLean, "Redesigning Dixie with Affirmative Action: Race, Gender and the Desegregation of the Southern Textile Mill World," in *Gender and the Southern Body Politic: Essays and Comments*, by Peter Bardaglio (Jackson: University Press of Mississippi, 2000), 161.

9. Ibid., 161–163.

10. Ibid., 162–163. A consent decree is a voluntary agreement between both parties of a lawsuit then issued by a judge as a court order. A consent decree terminates litigation but binds only the parties involved.

11. Ibid.

12. Boyd interview, July 2001.

13. Alfred Blumrosen, "Legacy of *Griggs*: Social Progress and Subjective Judgments," *Chicago Kent Law Review* 63 (1987): 1–42.

14. Ibid.

15. Blumrosen, "Strangers in Paradise," 62.

16. Blumrosen, "Legacy," 6.

17. Ibid.

18. *The Equal Employment Opportunity Act of 1972* (Washington, D.C.: Bureau of National Affairs, 1973), 230.

19. Ibid.; Blumrosen, *Modern Law*, 147.

20. *The Equal Employment Opportunity Act of 1972*.

21. Blumrosen, *Modern Law,* 149–150.

22. Ibid.

23. Ibid., 148–1499; House Report 238, 92d Congress, 1st session, 1971: 8; *The Equal Employment Opportunity Act of 1972,* 162.

24. Blumrosen, "Legacy."

25. Blumrosen, *Modern Law,* 146.

26. James P. Smith and Finis R. Welch, *Closing the Gap: Forty Years of Economic Progress for Blacks* (Santa Monica, Calif.: Rand, 1986).

27. Ibid., vii.

28. Ibid., ix–xi.

29. Blumrosen, *Modern Law,* 308.

30. Smith and Welch., *Closing the Gap,* xv.

31. Ibid., xvi.

32. Ibid., ix

33. Wilson, *Truly Disadvantaged,* 46.

34. Ibid.

35. Goldfield, *Black, White, and Southern,* 244–248.

36. Ronald Turner, "Thirty Years of Title VII's Regulatory Regime: Rights, Theories and Realities," *Alabama Law Review* 46 (Winter 1995): 6, database on line, Lexis-Nexis Academic Universe, http://www.lexisnexis.com (accessed January 4, 2008).

37. Wilson, *Truly Disadvantaged,* 115.

38. Turner, "Thirty Years," 6–7.

39. Andrew Hacker, *Two Nations: Black and White Separate, Hostile, and Unequal* (New York: Scribner's, 1992), 162, as quoted in Turner's "Thirty Years."

40. Henry Louis Taylor Jr. and Mark Naison, "Epilogue: African Americans and the Dawning of the Postindustrial Era," in *Historical Roots of the Urban Crisis: African Americans in the Industrial City, 1990–1950,* ed. Henry Louis Taylor and Walter Hill (New York: Garland, 2000), 280–282.

41. Minchin, *Hiring the Black Worker,* 270.

42. Taylor and Naison, "Epilogue."

43. Boyd interview, July 2001.

44. See MacLean, *Freedom Is Not Enough,* for a detailed examination of the rise of a neoconservative backlash to equal employment gains.

45. Ibid.

46. Ibid.

47. Brian K. Landsberg, *Enforcing Civil Rights: Race Discrimination and the Department of Justice* (Lawrence: University Press of Kansas, 1997), 130.

48. Mel Watt, who is currently chair of the Congressional Black Caucus, began his legal career with the firm of Chambers, Ferguson, Stein and Lanning.

49. Professor Belton declined an interview, given how close this work is to his own research. Also, Duke Power officials were unable to discuss the case due to legal reasons.

50. Boyd interview, July 2001.

51. Chambers interview.

Selected Bibliography

BOOK AND ARTICLES

Abrams, Douglas C. "Irony of Reform: North Carolina Blacks and the New Deal." *North Carolina Historical Review* 66, no. 2 (April 1989): 149–178.

Alleyne, Reginald H., Jr. "Legal Remedies for Racial Discrimination in Employment: The Evolving Search for Effectiveness." *Black Law Journal* (1972): 282–303.

Anderson, Bernard E. "Affirmative Action Policy Under Executive Order 11246: A Retrospective View." In *Civil Rights and Race Relations in the Post–Reagan-Bush Era*, ed. Samuel L. Myers Jr. Westport, Conn.: Praeger, 1997.

Anderson, Eric. *Race and Politics in North Carolina, 1872–1901: The Black Second*. Baton Rouge: Louisiana State University Press, 1981.

Baker, Lee D. *From Savage to Negro: Anthropology and the Construction of Race, 1896–1954*. Los Angeles: University of California Press, 1998.

Ball, Howard. *The Bakke Case: Race, Education and Affirmative Action*. Lawrence: University Press of Kansas, 2000.

Barksdale, Marcellus C. "Robert F. Williams and the Indigenous Civil Rights Movement in Monroe, North Carolina, 1961." *Journal of Negro History* 69 (Spring 1984): 73–89.

Bell, Derrick A. *Faces at the Bottom of the Well: The Permanence of Racism*. New York: Basic Books, 1992.

———. "Remembrances of Racism Past: Getting Beyond the Civil Rights Decline." In *Race in America: The Struggle for Equality*, ed. Herbert Hill and James E. Jones, 73–82. Madison: University of Wisconsin Press, 1993.

———. "The Burger Court's Place on the Bell Curve of Racial Jurisprudence." In *The Burger Court: Counter-Revolution or Confirmation*, ed. Bernard Schwartz, 57–65. New York: Oxford University Press, 1998.

———, ed. *Civil Rights Leading Cases*. Boston: Little, Brown, 1980.

———. *Race, Racism, and American Law*. Boston: Little, Brown, 1992.

Belton, Robert. "Title VII of the Civil Rights Act of 1964: A Decade of Private Enforcement and Judicial Developments." *Saint Louis University Law Journal* 20 (1976): 225–307.

———. "A Comparative Review of Public and Private Enforcement of Title VII of the Civil Rights Act of 1964." *Vanderbilt Law Review* 31 (1978): 905–961.

———. "Discrimination and Affirmative Action: An Analysis of Competing Theories of Equality and *Weber*." *North Carolina Law Review* 59 (1981): 531–598.

———. "The Dismantling of the Griggs Disparate Impact Theory and the Future of Title VII: The Need for a Third Reconstruction." *Yale Law & Policy Review* 8 (1990): 223–256.

Berg, Manfred. *"The Ticket to Freedom": The NAACP and the Struggle for Black Political Integration*. Gainesville: University Press of Florida, 2005.

Biographical Directory of the Federal Judiciary, 1789–2000. White Plains, Md.: Bernan, 2001.

Birnbaum, Johnathan, and Clarence Taylor. *Civil Rights Since 1787: A Reader on the Black Struggle*. New York: New York University Press, 2000.

Blasi, Vincent ed. *The Burger Court: The Counter-Revolution that Wasn't*. New Haven: Yale University Press, 1983.

Blumrosen, Alfred. *Black Employment and the Law*. New Brunswick, N.J., Rutgers University Press, 1971.

———. "Strangers in Paradise: *Griggs v. Duke Power* and the Concept of Employment Discrimination." *Michigan Law Review* 71 (November 1972): 59–110.

———. "Legacy of *Griggs*: Social Progress and Subjective Judgments." *Chicago Kent Law Review* 63 (1987).

———. *Modern Law: The Law Transmission System and Equal Employment Opportunity*. Madison: University of Wisconsin Press, 1993.

Boggs, James. *The American Revolution: Pages from a Negro Worker's Notebook 40th Anniversary Edition*. Detroit: Leadfoot Press, 2003.

Bowen, William, and Derek Bok. *The Shape of the River: The Long-Term Consequences of Considering Race in College and University Admissions*. Princeton: Princeton University Press, 1998.

Bowling, Michael. "The Case against Employment Tester Standing under Title VII and 42 U.S.C. Section 1981." *Michigan Law Review* 101, no. 1. (October 2002): 235–272.

Branch, Taylor. *Parting the Waters: America in the King Years, 1954–63*. New York: Touchstone, 1989.

Burstein, Paul. *Discrimination, Jobs and Politics: The Struggle for Equal Employment Opportunity in the United States Since the New Deal*. Chicago: University of Chicago Press, 1985.

Cantor, Melvin, ed. *Black Labor in America*. Westport, Conn.: Negro Universities Press, 1969.

Carlton, David L., and Peter A. Coclanis. *Confronting Southern Poverty in the Great Depression: The Report on Economic Conditions of the South.* New York: Bedford Books of St. Martin Press, 1996.

Cecelski, David. *Along Freedom Road: Hyde County North Carolina, and the Fate of Black Schools in the South.* Chapel Hill: University of North Carolina Press, 1994.

Chafe, William H. *Civilities and Civil Rights: Greensboro, North Carolina and the Black Struggle for Freedom.* New York: Oxford University Press, 1980.

Chambers, Julius LaVonne. "The Law and Black Americans: Retreat from Civil Right." In *The State of Black America 1987*, by Julius LaVonne Chambers, 15–30. New York: National Urban League, 1987.

———. "Race and Equality: The Still Unfinished Business of the Warren Court." In *The Warren Court: A Retrospective*, ed. Bernard Schwartz, 21–67. New York: Oxford University Press, 1996.

Cooper, George, and Richard Sobol. "Seniority and Testing Under Fair Employment Laws: A General Approach to Objective Criteria of Hiring and Promotion." *Harvard Law Review* 82 (1969): 1598–1679.

Cooper, Phillip J. *Battles on the Bench: Conflict Inside the Supreme Court.* Lawrence: University of Kansas Press, 1995.

Cox, Reavis. *Competition in the American Tobacco Industry, 1911–1932.* New York: Columbia University Press, 1933.

Crow, Jeffrey J. "An Apartheid for the South: Clarence Poe's Crusade for Rural Segregation." In *Race, Class, and Politics in Southern History: Essays in Honor of Robert F. Durden*, ed. Jeffrey J. Crow, Paul D. Escott, and Charles L. Flynn Jr., 216–259. Baton Rouge: Louisiana State University Press, 1989.

Crow, Jeffrey J., Paul D. Escott, and Flora J. Hatley. *The History of African Americans in North Carolina.* Raleigh: North Carolina Department of Cultural Resources, Division of Archives and History, 1992.

Dee, Christopher. "Disparate Impact and Subjective Employment Criteria under Title VII." *University of Chicago Law Review* 54, no. 3 (Summer 1987): 957–979.

"Developments in the Law: Employment Discrimination and Title VII of the Civil Rights Act of 1964." *Harvard Law Review* 84, no. 5. (March 1971): 1109–1316.

Dewey, Donald. "Negro Employment in Southern Industry." *Journal of Political Economy* 60, no. 4 (August 1952): 279–293.

Dictionary of American Biography. New York: Charles Scribner's Sons, 1994.

Dittmer, John. *Local People: The Struggle for Civil Rights in Mississippi.* Chicago: University of Illinois Press, 1994.

Douglas, Davison M. *Reading Writing and Race: The Desegregation of the Charlotte Schools.* Chapel Hill: University of North Carolina Press, 1995.

Drake, W. Avon, and Robert D. Holsworth. *Affirmative Action and the Stalled Quest for Black Progress.* Chicago: University of Illinois Press, 1996.

Draper, Alan. *Conflict of Interest: Organized Labor and the Civil Rights Movement in the South, 1954–1968.* Ithaca, N.Y.: ILR Press, 1994.

Durden, Robert F. *The Dukes of Durham, 1865–1929.* Durham, N.C.: Duke University Press, 1975.

———. *Electrifying the Piedmont Carolina: The Duke Power Company, 1904–1997.* Durham, N.C.: Carolina Academic Press, 2001.

Egerton, John. *Speak Now Against the Day: The Generation Before the Civil Rights Movement in the South.* Chapel Hill: University of North Carolina Press, 1994.

"Employment Testing: The Aftermath of *Griggs v. Duke Power Company.*" *Columbia Law Review* 72, no. 5 (May 1972): 900–925.

The Equal Employment Opportunity Act of 1972. Washington, D.C.: Bureau of National Affairs, 1973.

Escott, Paul D. *Many Excellent People: Power and Privilege in North Carolina, 1850–1900.* Chapel Hill: University of North Carolina Press, 1985.

Foner, Philip S. *Organized Labor and the Black Worker, 1619–1981.* New York: International Publishers, 1982.

———. *The Black Panthers Speak.* New York: De Capo Press, 1995.

Garfinkel, Herbert. *When Negroes March: The March on Washington Movement in the Organizational Politics for FEPC. With a New Preface by Lewis M. Killian.* New York: Atheneum, 1969.

Garraty, John A., and Mark C. Carnes, eds. *American National Biography.* New York: Oxford University Press, 1999.

Gavins, Raymond. "The Meaning of Freedom: Black Carolina in the Nadir, 1880–1900." In *Race, Class, and Politics in Southern History: Essays in Honor of Robert F. Durden,* ed. Jeffrey Crow, Paul Escott, and Charles Flynn, 175–215. Baton Rouge: Louisiana State University Press, 1989.

———. "North Carolina Black Folklore and Song in the Age of Segregation: Toward Another Meaning of Survival." *North Carolina Historical Review* 66, no. 4 (October 1989): 412–442.

———. "The NAACP in North Carolina During the Age of Segregation." In *New Directions in Civil Rights Studies,* ed. Armstead Robinson and Patricia Sullivan, 105–125. Charlottesville: University Press of Virginia, 1991.

Genovese, Michael A. *The Nixon Presidency: Power and Politics in Turbulent Times.* New York: Greenwood Press, 1990.

Gibbons, Kathryn A. "Testing for Special Skills in Employment: A New Approach to Judicial Review." *Duke Law Journal* 3 (August 1976): 596–622.

Gilmore, Glenda Elizabeth. *Gender and Jim Crow: Women and the Politics of White Supremacy in North Carolina, 1896–1920.* Chapel Hill: University of North Carolina Press, 1996.

Goldberg, David Theo. *Racist Culture: Philosophy and the Politics of Meaning.* Cambridge: Blackwell, 1993.

Goldfield, David. *Black, White, and Southern: Race Relations and Southern Culture, 1940 to the Present.* Baton Rouge: Louisiana State University Press, 1990

Goldfield, Michael. *The Color of Politics: Race and the Mainsprings of American Politics.* New York: New Press, 1997.

Goldman, Roger. "The Next Ten Years: Title VII Confronts the Constitution." *St. Louis University Law Journal* 20 (1976): 308–345.

Graham, Hugh Davis. *The Civil Rights Era: Origins and Development of National Policy.* New York: Oxford University Press, 1990.

———. *Civil Rights and the Presidency: Race and Gender in American Politics, 1960–1972.* New York: Oxford University Press, 1992.

Greenberg, Jack. *Crusaders in the Courts: How a Dedicated Band of Lawyers Fought for the Civil Rights Revolution.* New York: Basic Books, 1994.

Greene, Kathanne. *Affirmative Action and Principles of Justice.* New York: Greenwood Press, 1989.

Greenwood, Janette Thomas. *Bittersweet Legacy: The Black and White "Better Classes" in Charlotte, 1850–1910.* Chapel Hill: University of North Carolina Press, 1994.

Hacker, Andrew. *Two Nations: Black and White Separate, Hostile and Unequal.* New York: Scribner's, 1992.

Haley, John H. *Charles N. Hunter and Race Relations in North Carolina.* Chapel Hill: University of North Carolina Press, 1987.

Hall, Jacquelyn Dowd, James Leloudis, Robert Korstad, Mary Murphy, Lu Ann Jones, and Christopher B. Daly. *Like a Family: The Making of a Southern Cotton Mill World.* Chapel Hill: University of North Carolina Press, 1987.

Hall, Kermit L., ed. *Oxford Companion to the Supreme Court of the United States.* New York: Oxford University Press, 1992.

Henry, Aaron, and Constance Curry. *Aaron Henry: The Fire Ever Burning.* Jackson: University Press of Mississippi, 2000.

Higginbotham, A. Leon. *Shades of Freedom: Racial Politics and Presumptions of the American Legal Process.* New York: Oxford University Press, 1996.

Hill, Herbert. "Black Workers, Organized Labor, and Title VII of the 1964 Civil Rights Act: Legislative History and Litigation Record." In *Race in America: The Struggle for Equality,* ed. Herbert Hill and James E. Jones, 263–341. Madison: University of Wisconsin Press, 1993.

———. "Black Labor and the American Legal System: Race, Work, and the Law." In *Equal Employment Opportunity: Labor Market Discrimination and Public Policy,* ed. Paul Burstein. New York: Aldine de Gruyter, 1994.

Honey, Michael. *Southern Labor and Black Civil Rights: Organizing Memphis Workers* Chicago: University of Illinois Press, 1993.

Horn, Carl, Jr. *The Duke Power Story, 1904–1973.* New York: Newcomen Society in North America, 1973.

Horowitz, Roger. *Negro and White, Unite and Fight: A Social History of Industrial Union-ism in Meatpacking, 1930–90*. Chicago: University of Illinois Press, 1997.

Howard, John R. *The Shifting Wind: The Supreme Court and Civil Rights from Reconstruc-tion to Brown*. New York: State University of New York Press, 1999.

Jackson, Juanita. "Young Colored American Awakes." *Crisis*, September 1938, 43.

Jones, James E., Jr. "Equal Employment Opportunities: The Promises of the 60s—The Reality of the 70s." *Black Law Journal* (1971): 5–20.

———. "The Transformation of Fair Employment Practices Policies." *Industrial Rela-tions Research Institute* 6 (1976): 160.

Kahn, Ronald. *The Supreme Court and Constitutional Theory, 1953–1993*. Lawrence: Uni-versity of Kansas Press, 1994.

Keith, Damon J. "NAACP: Palladin of the People: Address before the Seventy-fifth An-nual NAACP Convention." In *From the Black Bar: Voices for Equal Justice*, ed. Gilbert Ware, 317–325. New York: G. P. Putnam's Sons, 1976.

Kelley, Robin D. G. *Hammer and Hoe: Alabama Communists during the Great Depression*. Chapel Hill: University of North Carolina Press, 1990.

———. "We Are Not What We Seem": Rethinking Black Working-Class Opposition in the Jim Crow South. *Journal of American History* 80, no. 1 (June 1993): 75–112.

Kersten, Andrew Edmund. *Race, Jobs, and the War: The FEPC in the Midwest, 1941–46*. Urbana: University of Illinois Press, 2000.

Kluger, Richard. *Simple Justice: The History of Brown v. Board of Education and Black America's Struggle for Equality*. New York: Vintage Books, 1975.

Korstad, Robert Rogers. *Civil Rights Unionism: Tobacco Workers and the Struggle for De-mocracy in the Mid-Twentieth-Century South*. Chapel Hill: University of North Caro-lina Press, 2003.

Kousser, J. Morgan. *The Shaping of Southern Politics: Suffrage Restriction and the Establish-ment of the One-party South, 1880–1910*. New Haven: Yale University Press, 1974.

———. *Colorblind Injustice: Minority Voting Rights and the Undoing of the Second Recon-struction*. Chapel Hill: University of North Carolina Press, 1999.

Landsberg, Brian K. *Enforcing Civil Rights: Race Discrimination and the Department of Justice*. Lawrence: University Press of Kansas, 1997.

Lee, Williams S. *Duke Power Company: The Roots that Nourish the Future*. New York: Newcomen Society, 1987.

"Legal Implications of the Use of Standardized Ability Tests in Employment and Educa-tion." *Columbia Law Review* 68, no. 4. (April 1968): 691–744.

Leiter, Samuel, and William M. Leiter. *Affirmative Action in Antidiscrimination Law and Policy: An Overview and Synthesis*. New York: SUNY Press, 2002.

Leloudis, James L. *Schooling the New South: Pedagogy, Self, and Society in North Carolina, 1880–1920*. Chapel Hill: University of North Carolina Press, 1996.

Lipsitz, George. *The Possessive Investment in Whiteness: How White People Profit from Identity Politics.* Philadelphia: Temple University Press, 1998.

Loevy, Robert. *The Civil Rights Act of 1964: The Passage of the Law that Ended Racial Segregation.* Albany: State University of New York Press, 1997

Lofgren, Charles A. *The Plessy Case: A Legal-Historical Interpretation.* New York: Oxford University Press, 1987.

Logan, Frenise. *The Negro in North Carolina, 1876–1894.* Chapel Hill: University of North Carolina Press, 1964.

Mabry, William Alexander. *The Negro in North Carolina Politics Since Reconstruction.* New York: AMS Press, 1940.

MacLean, Nancy. "Redesigning Dixie with Affirmative Action: Race, Gender and the Desegregation of the Southern Textile Mill World." In *Gender and the Southern Body Politic: Essays and Comments,* ed. Peter Bardaglio, 161–198. Jackson: University Press of Mississippi, 2000.

———. *"Freedom Is Not Enough:" The Opening of the American Workplace.* Cambridge: Harvard University Press, 2006.

Maltz, Edward M. "The Legacy of *Griggs v. Duke Power Co.*: A Case Study in the Impact of a Modernist Statutory Precedent." *Utah Law Review* (1994). Database on line. Available from Lexis-Nexis Academic Universe.

Marable, Manning. *How Capitalism Underdeveloped Black America: Problems in Race, Political Economy and Society.* Boston: South End Press, 1983.

———. *Race, Reform and Rebellion: The Second Reconstruction in Black America, 1945–1982.* Jackson: University Press of Mississippi, 1984.

Marshall, Ray, Charles B. Knapp, Malcolm H. Liggett, and Robert W. Glover. *Employment Discrimination: The Impact of Legal and Administrative Remedies.* New York: Praeger, 1978.

Mason, Gilbert R., and James Patterson Smith. *Beaches, Blood, and Ballots: A Black Doctor's Struggle.* Jackson: University Press of Mississippi, 2000.

Maynor, Joe. *Duke Power: The First Seventy-Five Years.* Albany, N.Y.: Delmar Press, 1980.

McNeil, Genna Rae. *Groundwork: Charles Hamilton Houston and the Struggle for Civil Rights.* Philadelphia: University of Pennsylvania Press, 1983.

Minchin, Timothy J. *Hiring the Black Worker: The Racial Integration of the Southern Textile Industry, 1960–1980.* Chapel Hill: University of North Carolina Press, 1999.

———. *Fighting Against the Odds: A History of Southern Labor Since World War II.* Gainesville: University Press of Florida, 2005.

Mobley, Joe A. "In the Shadow of White Society: Princeville, a Black town in North Carolina, 1865–1915." *North Carolina Historical Review* 3 (July 1986): 340–384.

Moreno, Paul. *From Direct Action to Affirmative Action: Fair Employment Law and Policy in America 1933–1972.* Baton Rouge: Louisiana State University Press, 1997.

———. *Black Americans and Organized Labor: A New History.* Baton Rouge.: Louisiana State University Press, 2006.

Murray, Charles. *Losing Ground: American Social Policy, 1950–1980.* New York: Basic Books, 1984.

The National Cyclopedia of American Biography. New York: James T. White, 1927.

Nieman, Donald. *Promises to Keep: African Americans and the Constitutional Order, 1776 to the Present.* New York: Oxford University Press, 1991.

———, ed. *African American Life, 1861–1900.* Vol. 11, *African Americans and the Emergence of Segregation, 1865—1900.* New York: Garland, 1994.

———. "After the Movement: African Americans and Education since the *Brown* Decision. In *Upon These Shores: Themes in the African American Experience, 1600 to the Present,* ed. William R. Scott and William G. Shade, 389–403. New York: Routledge, 2000.

Northrup, Herbert R., Richard L. Rowan, Donald T. Barnum, and John C. Howard. *Negro Employment in Southern Industry: A Study of Racial Policies in Five Industries.* Philadelphia: Wharton School of Finance and Commerce, University of Pennsylvania, 1970.

Obadele-Starks, Ernest. *Black Unionism in the Industrial South.* College Station: Texas A&M University Press, 2000.

Pascal, Diane, ed. *International Directory of Company Histories.* Detroit: St. James Press, 1992.

Payne, Charles M. *I've Got the Light of Freedom: The Organizing Tradition and the Mississippi Freedom Struggle.* Berkeley and Los Angeles: University of California Press, 1995.

Pfeffer, Paula F. *A. Phillip Randolph: Pioneer of the Civil Rights Movement.* Baton Rouge: Louisiana State University Press, 1990.

Quadagno, Jill. *The Color of Welfare: How Racism Undermined the War on Poverty.* New York: Oxford University Press, 1994.

Report on the National Advisory Commission on Civil Disorders. New York: New York Times, 1968.

Ripon, Michelle. "Meet the Federal Judges: The Middle District of North Carolina." *North Carolina State Bar Quarterly* 37, no. 4 (Fall 1990): 32–36.

Rose, David Lee. "Twenty Five Years Later: Where Do We Stand on Equal Employment Opportunity Law Enforcement." *Vanderbilt Law Review* 42 (1989): 1121–81.

Rothschild, Michael, and Gregory J. Werden. "Title VII and the Use of Employment Tests: An Illustration of the Limits of the Judicial Process." *Journal of Legal Studies* 11, no. 2 (June 1982): 261–280.

Ruchames, Louis. *Race, Jobs and Politics: The Story of FEPC.* Westport, Conn.: Negro Universities Press, 1971.

Schwartz, Bernard. *Swann's Way: The School Busing Case and the Supreme Court.* New York: Oxford University Press, 1986.

———. *A History of the Supreme Court.* New York: Oxford University Press, 1993.

———, ed. *The Burger Court: Counter-Revolution or Confirmation.* New York: Oxford University Press, 1998.

Small, Melvin. *The Presidency of Richard Nixon.* Lawrence: University Press of Kansas, 1999.

Smith, James P., and Finis Welch. *Closing the Gap: Forty Years of Economic Progress for Blacks.* Santa Monica, Calif.: Rand, 1986.

Smith, J. Clay. *Emancipation: The Making of the Black Lawyer, 1844–1944.* Philadelphia: University of Pennsylvania Press, 1993.

Sovern, Michael I. *Legal Restraints on Racial Discrimination in Employment.* New York: Twentieth-Century Fund, 1966.

Stein, Judith. *Running Steel, Running America: Race, Economic Policy and the Decline of Liberalism.* Chapel Hill: University of North Carolina Press, 1998.

The Story of the EEOC: Ensuring the Promise of Opportunity for 35 Years. Washington, D.C.: Equal Employment Opportunities Commission, 2000.

Sugrue, Thomas J. *The Origins of the Urban Crisis: Race and Inequality in Postwar Detroit.* Princeton: Princeton University Press, 1996.

Taylor, Henry Louis, and Walter Hill, eds. *Historical Roots of the Urban Crisis: African Americans in the Industrial City, 1990–1950.* New York: Garland, 2000.

Thompson, Heather. *Whose Detroit? Politics, Labor, and Race in a Modern American City.* Princeton: Princeton University Press, 2001.

Tucker, Rochelle. "Reidsville, North Carolina—A Struggle for Progress." Unpublished paper, in possession of the author.

Turner, Ronald. "Thirty Years of Title VII's Regulatory Regime: Rights, Theories and Realities." *Alabama Law Review* 46 (Winter 1995): 375.

Tushnet, Mark. *The NAACP's Legal Strategy Against Segregated Education, 1935–1950.* Chapel Hill: University of North Carolina Press, 1987.

Tyson, Timothy B. *Radio Free Dixie: Robert F. Williams and the Roots of Black Power.* Chapel Hill: University of North Carolina Press, 1999.

United States Equal Employment Opportunity Commission (EEOC). *Legislative History of Titles VII and XI of Civil Rights Act of 1964.* Washington, D.C.: U.S. Government Printing Office, 1968.

Urofsky, Melvin I. *Affirmative Action on Trial: Sex Discrimination in Johnson v. Santa Clara.* Lawrence: University Press of Kansas, 1997.

U.S. Commission on Civil Rights. *Employment.* Washington, D.C.: U.S. Government Printing Office, 1961.

———. *The Fifty States Report.* Washington, D.C.: U.S. Government Printing Office, 1961.

Vaught, Seneca. "Narrow Cells and Lost Keys: The Impact of Jails and Prisons on Black Protest, 1940–1972." Ph.D. diss., Bowling Green State University, 2006.

Wallerstein, Morton L. *The Public Career of Simon E. Sobeloff.* Richmond: Marlborough House, 1975.

Ware, Gilbert. "Hocutt: Genesis of Brown." *Journal of Negro Education* 52, no. 3 (1983): 227–233.

———. *William Hastie: Grace Under Pressure.* New York: Oxford University Press, 1984.

Weare, Walter B. *Black Business in the New South: A Social History of the North Carolina Mutual Life Insurance Company.* Durham, N.C.: Duke University Press, 1993.

Welch, III, Kermit Alfonso. "The Conservative Era of the 1980s: The Changing Disparate Impact Theory of Employment Discrimination." *Howard Law Journal* 34 (1991).

Weisbrot, Robert. *Freedom Bound: A History of America's Civil Rights Movement.* New York: Plume, 1990.

Whalen, Charles, and Barbara Whalen. *The Longest Debate: A Legislative History of the 1964 Civil Rights Act.* Washington, D.C.: Seven Locks Press, 1985.

Wilkinson, J. Harvie. *From Brown to Bakke: The Supreme Court and School Integration: 1954–1978.* New York: Oxford University Press, 1979.

Williams, Juan. *Thurgood Marshall: American Revolutionary.* New York: Random House, 1998.

Williams, Robert F. *Negroes with Guns.* New York: Marzani and Munsell, 1962.

Wilson, Hugh Steven. "A Second Look at *Griggs v. Duke Power Company:* Ruminations on Job Testing, Discrimination, and the Role of the Federal Courts." *Virginia Law Review* 58, no. 5. (May 1972): 844–874.

Wilson, William Julius. *The Declining Significance of Race: Blacks and Changing American Institutions.* Chicago: University of Chicago Press, 1980.

———. *The Truly Disadvantaged: The Inner City, the Underclass, and Public Policy.* Chicago: University of Chicago Press, 1987.

Winkler, John K. *Tobacco Tycoon: The Story of James Buchanan Duke.* New York: Random House, 1942.

Wolninson, Benjamin W. *Blacks, Unions, and the EEOC: A Study of Administrative Futility.* Lexington, Mass.: Lexington Books, 1973

Woodward, Bob, and Scott Armstrong. *The Brethren: Inside the Supreme Court.* New York: Simon and Schuster, 1979.

Woodward, C. Vann. *The Strange Career of Jim Crow,* 3d ed. New York: Oxford University Press, 1974.

Wright, Bruce. *Black Robes, White Justice.* New York: Carol Publishing, 1987.

Table of Cases

Albemarle Paper Co. v, Moody, 422 U.S. 405 (1975)

Arrington v. Massachusetts Bay Transportation Authority, 306 F. Supp, 1355 (D. Mass. 1969)

Bowe v. Colgate-Palmolive Co. 67 LRRM 2714 (D.C.S.D. Ind. June 30, 1967)

Brinkley v. The Great Atl. and Pac. Tea Co., No. 65–1107 (E.D.N.C. 1965)

City of Richmond v. J.A. Croson Co., 488 U.S. 469 (1989)

The Civil Rights Cases, 109 U.S. 1 (1883)

Cox v. United States Gypsum Co., 284 F. Supp. 74, 78 (N.D. Ind. 1968)

Cramer v. Virginia Commonwealth University, 415 F. Supp. 673 (E.D. Va. 1976)

Dobbins v. Local 212, IBEW, F. Supp 413 (S.D. Ohio 1968)

Farmers Cooperative Compress v. NLRB, 169 NLRB No. 70, 67 LLRM 1266 (January 23, 1968)

Firefighters Local Union No.1794 v. Stotts, 467 U.S. 561 (1984)

Franks v. Bowman Transportation, 424 U.S. 747 (1976)

Fullilove v. Klutznick, 448 U.S. 448 (1980)

Gaston County, North Carolina v. United States 395 U.S. 285 (1969)

Goss v. Board of Education, 373 U.S. 683 (1963)

Griggs et al. v. Duke Power Co., 515 F.2d. 86 (1975)

Griggs v. Duke Power Co., 401 U.S. 424 (1971)

Griggs v. Duke Power Co., No. C-210-G-66., USDC-MDNC (1974)

Guinn v. United States, 238 U.S. 347 (1915)

Hazelwood v. United States, 433 U.S. 299 (1977)

Hobson v. Hansen, 269 F. Supp. 401 (D.D.C. 1967)

Hocutt v. Wilson, North Carolina Superior Ct., County of Durham, Civil Issue Docket
    #1–188, March 28, 1933

International Chemical Workers Union v. Planters Manufacturing Co., 259 F. Supp. 365,
    366 (N.D. Miss. 1966)

Johnson v. Transportation Agency Santa Clara County, 480 U.S. 616 (1987)

Kaiser Aluminum and Chemical Corp. v. Weber, 443 U.S. 193 (1979)

Local 28 Sheet Metal Workers v. EEOC, 478 U.S. 421 (1986)

Local 53 v. Vogler, 407 F.2d. 1047, 1052 (5 Cir. 1969)

Local Number 93, International Association of Firefighters v. City of Cleveland, 478 U.S. 501
    (1986)

McAleer v. American Telephone and Telegraph, 416 F. Supp. 435 (D.D.C. 1976)

McDonnell Douglas Corp. v. Green, 411 U.S. 792 (1973)

Missouri ex. rel. Gaines v. Canada, 305 U.S. 337 (1938)

Moody v. Albemarle Paper Co, 4 F.E.P. Cas. 561 (E.D.N.C. 1971)

Phillips v. Martin Marietta Corp. 400 U.S. 542 (1971)

Plessy v. Ferguson, 163 U.S. 537 (1896)

Quarles v. Phillip Morris, Inc., 279 F. Supp. 505, 516 (E.D. Va. 1968)

Regents of the University of California v. Bakke, 438 U.S. 265 (1978)

Swann v. Charlotte-Mecklenburg 402 U.S. 1

Teamsters v. United States, 431 U.S. 324

Udall v. Tallman, 380 U.S. 1 16 (1965)

United States v. Duke, 332 F.2d. 759 (5th Cir. 1964)

United States v. H, K. Porter, 59 L.C. 9204 (M.D. Ala. 1969)

United States v. H. K. Porter Co., 296 F. Supp. 40 (M.D. Ala. 1968)

United States v. Louisiana, 380 U.S. 145 (1965)

United States v. United Papermakers and Paperworkers, Local 189, 282 F. Supp. 39, 44 (E.D. La. 1968); *Affirmed,* No. 25956-F.2d. (5 Cir. 1969)

Wards Cove Packing Co. v. Antonio, 490 U.S. 642 (1989)

Watson v. Fort Worth Bank and Trust Co, 487 U.S. 977 (1988)

Weeks v. Southern Bell Telephone and Telegraph Co., 408 F.2d 228, 235 (5 Cir. 1969)

Collections

Alexander, Kelly, Sr. Papers. J. Murrey Atkins Library. University of North Carolina, Charlotte.

Brennan, William. Papers. Library of Congress, Washington, D.C.

Duke University Oral History Project Collection. Duke University, Durham, N.C.

Griggs v. Duke Power Co. United States Supreme Court Case File. U.S. Supreme Court Library, Washington, D.C.

Griggs v. Duke Power. United States District Court for the Middle District of North Carolina Case File. National Archives and Records Administration Regional Branch, Atlanta, Ga.

Marshall, Thurgood. Papers. Library of Congress, Washington, D.C.

McKissick, Floyd B. Papers. Wilson Library. University of North Carolina, Chapel Hill.

National Association for the Advancement of Colored People Papers. Library of Congress, Washington, D.C.

Records of the Equal Employment Opportunity Commission Files. National Archives and Records Administration, College Park, Md.

Sobeloff, Simon. Papers. Library of Congress, Washington, D.C.

Southern Oral History Project. Wilson Library. University of North Carolina, Chapel Hill.

Interviews

Boyd, Willie. Interview by author. July 11, 2001. Reidsville, N.C.

Blumrosen, Alfred. Interview by author. August 2, 2001. Sussex, N.J.

Chambers, Julius LaVonne. Interview by author. July 5, 2001. Tega Cay, S.C.

Ferguson, James E. Interview by author. September 29, 2005. Charlotte, N.C.

Ferguson, James E. Interview J-4. Transcript. Southern Oral History Project. Wilson Library. University of North Carolina, Chapel Hill.

Gordon, Charles "Joey." Interview by author. June 10, 2001. Detroit, Mich.

Hand, Ella. Interview by author. September 8, 2005. Charlotte, N.C.

Hill, Herbert. Interview by author. October 6, 2003. Madison, Wisc.

Jones, James E. Interview by author. October 7, 2003. Madison, Wisc.

Pearson, Conrad O. Interview by Walter Weare. April 18, 1979. Interview H-218. Transcript. Southern Oral History Project. Wilson Library. University of North Carolina, Chapel Hill.

Stein, Adam. Interview by author. October 13, 2005. Charlotte, N.C.

Sumpter, Geraldine. Interview by author. September 15, 2005. Charlotte, N.C.

NEWSPAPERS AND PERIODICALS

Bearak, Barry, and David Lauter. "Affirmative Action: The Paradox of Equality." *Los Angeles Times*, November 3, 1991.

Carroll, Maurice. "Man in the News: Rights Under New Leader." *New York Times*, June 13, 1984.

Charlotte News and Observer, March 9, 1971.

Charlotte Observer, March 8, 11, May 9, 1971.

"Civil Rights and the Warren Court." *Ebony*, February 25, 1970.

"Griggs Honored." *Reidsville Review*, August 23, 1973.

Jubera, Drew. "How Willie Griggs Changed the Workplace." *Atlanta Constitution and Journal*, July 1, 1991.

New York Times, March 9, 1971.

Raleigh Times, March 9, 1971.

Totenberg, Nina. "Behind the Marble, Beneath the Robes." *New York Times Magazine*, March 16, 1975.

Index